BULLYING
in AUSTRALIAN
(and other)
WORKPLACES

Dr John W. Murphy PhD

with Barrie Thomas
and Dr Max Liddell PhD

First published in 2021 by Across the Ditch Publishing, PO Box 406, DROMANA, Victoria 3936, Australia

www.bullyinginaustralianworkplaces.com

ISBN: 978-0-6452237-0-5 (Paperback)

ISBN: 978-0-6452237-1-2 (EPUB)

This book is an independent not-for-profit project funded by the Triple A Foundation.

DISCLAIMER

The information provided in this publication may assist readers in a general way only. Readers should make their own assessment as to its relevance for their purposes and obtain appropriate professional guidance. Advice from books and the Internet on this topic should always be combined with individual guidance from informed people familiar with the reader's circumstances such as a general practitioner, counsellor, trade union representative, workplace health and safety authority or lawyer.

Case studies

The names, places and alleged events have been altered so as not to compromise anyone. Similarities to the circumstances of specific individuals or organisations is coincidental.

Caution

Readers who have been bullied at work should be aware that reading this book may prompt distressing thoughts about their experience. Supports available include Emergency Services 000, Lifeline 13 11 14, Beyond Blue 1300 22 46 36, the emergency department of a hospital, general practitioners, psychologists and qualified counsellors.

A catalogue record for this book is available from the National Library of Australia

CONTENTS

This book is dedicated to my family

Corinne, Kathryn, Joshua, Michael, Amelia, Harry, Ellen, Ritchie, Lena, John, Mietta, Esse, Karen, Stu

and to my dear friend

Joe Cauchi

1948–2019

The end result of kindness is that it draws people to you.

Dame Anita Roddick, The Body Shop Founder

FOREWORD

I am pleased to be involved with this special project which addresses the serious social and economic problem of workplace bullying. Dr John Murphy, my colleague and friend for many years, describes in the Preface how the project came about.

We are not new to pursuing social and organisational changes, which are among the aims of this project. For example, in the first 20 years of the new millennium we contributed chapters on important social issues to several major Australian publications, including *Social Capital and Public Policy in Australia* (2000) and *Mental Health at Work* (2002). We have published three books aiming to empower grass-roots community groups and the people they serve, including one on the benefits of businesses and small not-for-profits working in partnership on community projects. We have presented papers at many local and international conferences about building strong communities and presented workshops and seminars on the topic to government and community groups throughout Australia and New Zealand.

What this project on workplace bullying has in common with our previous efforts is that it addresses a serious social problem which has been largely overlooked by governments and other stakeholders. This is not to say that nothing has been done by them, but with bullying rates in Australian workplaces reported to be around 25 per cent and higher and affecting millions of workers, it is fair to say that there are serious shortcomings with current bullying-prevention policies and practices. Also, only a few Australian books on the topic have been published, and none recently. This book, therefore, fills an important gap in the literature.

Like John, my professional training is in social work and while, as head franchisee of The Body Shop, first in Australia and latterly in New Zealand, I've been a retailer for nearly 40 years, the business values expounded by Dame Anita Roddick, founder of The Body Shop, have always resonated with me. Her belief was that for business to prosper it had to balance creatively the financial and human needs of all its stakeholders — employees, customers, suppliers, animals, the environment and particularly the needs of the communities in which it operates.

John and I met in 1995, when we were volunteers for a small not-for-profit group in Frankston, Victoria. In addition to the work he has done in researching for and writing this book, John has a workplace record which amply equips him for the task. In his first job after leaving school at 17, he worked for 10 years in a commercial printing factory where he was a victim of bullying. After gaining an honours degree in social work, he was a caseworker with families and children and later a manager. When I first met him, he was a lecturer in social work at Monash University in Melbourne, had recently competed a PhD on the topic of job satisfaction, and was chairman of the board of the not-for-profit.

In more recent years John has worked on many creative and effective community projects with local citizens, endeavours that my community foundation has been proud to support. In these roles he has observed and experienced personally a wide range of the issues and problems that he presents in this book, including through providing support, advice and counselling to employees who have been mistreated at work. Part of his role has been to advise employers about bullying prevention.

In this book, John has approached the wide range of issues that relate to workplace bullying with fairness and balance. He has concentrated rightly on the experiences of employees with workplace bullying, and the many challenges they face in attempts to resolve the problem. However, he has also outlined the problems that employers experience, including the impact on production, profits and services when bullying is not addressed, or when occasionally employees make mistaken or dubious complaints.

As he works through the book, John clarifies the meanings of many issues which are confusing for those new to the topic. He examines the range of bullying behaviours and identifies areas which are perceived commonly by employees to be bullying, but which are not bullying according to the relevant workplace health and safety laws. He highlights the importance of employees and employers having a good appreciation of what bullying is and is not. John outlines a wide range of bullying behaviours so that their serious psychological, physical and social impacts on employees can be understood. He discusses bullying's causes.

Where John is most forthright, and maybe even provocative to some, is his discussion of what happens when bullying problems are raised openly by employees in the workplace. He discusses candidly how some employers use unethical tactics to avoid accountability, often with the support of human resources (HR). John's discussion about what happens in such situations is essential, if uncomfortable, reading for victims of bullying since they need to understand the possible repercussions when they complain. He presents valuable suggestions about how to prepare a formal written complaint.

John elaborates on complaints and other actions, including legal action, which those who believe they have been bullied might pursue. His frank and unembellished description of the process and possible outcomes will not encourage many intending complainants. This is with good reason given his reference to research that reveals most victims are reluctant to complain. This is because they believe it will be a waste of time, it will not stop their bullying and they may be punished, including possibly losing their job. On the other hand, John argues rightly, that to be forewarned is to be forearmed. He concludes with suggestions from employees who have experienced bullying and he outlines characteristics of a respectful workplace and how to achieve them. It is sound advice for employers and managers wishing to achieve a bullying-free workplace. He includes information for bullied employees on who to contact for advice and support.

Finally, this book will not be comfortable reading for some; rather, part of its intention is to convert over-optimists into realists who are able to deal competently with the challenges they are facing. It achieves this and is soundly based on many one-to-one interviews by the author with employees who have been targets of bullying in addition to an examination of both Australian and international literature on the topic. The book's focus is not narrow; while its main emphasis is on supporting victims of bullying, it provides timely advice for others, such as employers, managers, families of victims, doctors, counsellors, educators and students. The book is unique in Australian literature and will benefit a wide audience.

Barrie Thomas, Managing Director, The Body Shop New Zealand

PREFACE

This book was inspired by my involvement as an advocate in a serious case of worker abuse. 'Jane' asked me for help when she was targeted for mistreatment by her manager. It put me on a steep learning curve with the complex and insidious aspects of bullying at work.

Nearly 30 years ago I completed a doctoral thesis on job satisfaction, a related topic, and 10 years before an honours thesis on occupational health and welfare. Neither study included workplace bullying. As an issue of public interest and research, it didn't emerge until the late 1980s when it was introduced by British investigative journalist Andrea Adams. She is thought to have created the expression 'workplace bullying'.

I was on the receiving end of bullying in my first job as a junior in a printing factory. But nothing I experienced came close to Jane's cruel mistreatment at the hands of her manager, 'Michelle', aided by her minions and equally callous HR managers.

Jane was 58 years of age at the time and an office worker for a manufacturing company. She was falsely accused by Michelle of serious misconduct. Michelle was a serial bully, the worst kind, who preyed on vulnerable employees while sucking up to gullible and weak senior managers. It enabled her to mistreat subordinates with impunity. Over the years, Michelle had accumulated a long list of casualties.

Michelle's big bag of dirty tricks included ruthlessly hounding subordinates she didn't like out of their jobs by making their life at work intolerable. Her devious plan for Jane was to get her the sack for misconduct or force her to quit through the distress and humiliation of being accused of serious wrongdoing.

Jane was eventually exonerated, but it wasn't before the HR manager had conducted a sham investigation where from the start Jane was treated as guilty. This included calling her a liar when she said she didn't understand why the accusation had been made against her. After three months, the HR manager wrote to Jane informing her that 'after a fair and thorough investigation' he'd found the allegation substantiated and she was asked to show cause why she shouldn't be sacked.

Through her union, however, Jane challenged the finding on the grounds that not only was the main piece of evidence false but, incredibly, had never been presented during the investigation for her response.

An appeal by her union representative to a more senior manager resulted in the HR manager's judgement being overturned and Jane was invited back to work. But 12 months had elapsed between the allegations being made and Jane's exoneration, with no explanation or apology offered for the long delay. She had been on sick leave for all this time with escalating anxiety and depression, culminating in a diagnosis of post-traumatic stress disorder.

Although the HR manager was removed from his position shortly after Jane's exoneration, it was little consolation for her because his equally ruthless replacement gave Jane an employer-directed ultimatum — return to work immediately or resign, with six months' extra pay offered as an incentive to quit. The return-to-work option was conditional on Jane continuing to work under Michelle's supervision.

The proposed payout was subject to the imposition of a legally-binding non-disclosure contract which meant that Jane couldn't speak publicly about her terrible experience. It was also conditional that she wouldn't seek financial compensation from the employer in the future. It was the same kind of sordid and exploitative arrangement that's come to prominence recently through the *#MeToo* movement between notorious public figures and their victims.

There was no acknowledgement by her employer that Jane's failing mental health and time off work were the direct result of the false accusation of misconduct and the lengthy period the employer took to resolve the matter. It wasn't overlooked, though, by the employer's consultant psychiatrist who assessed Jane during her long period of sick leave. There's little doubt that his damning report about the cause of her condition and the possible legal implications for the employer were behind Jane's payout offer, albeit meagre, and conditional on keeping her mouth shut about the circumstances and taking no further action against the employer, including legal action.

The new HR manager told Jane that the offer would be 'off the table' by the end of the week and, under severe duress, she accepted it. Although Jane wasn't aware at the time that it was unlawful for her employer to coerce her to sign such a contract, it was clear to her that she was no longer wanted and the invitation to return to work was not genuine.

At the time of completing this book, Jane was 64. Since her resignation she was unable to obtain another job because of poor mental health, lack of confidence and self-esteem, no reference and an employment market that discriminates against older workers. As a single person not eligible for the age pension, she had struggled to survive on a low unemployment allowance. The last time I saw Jane was mid-winter when she was huddled under a blanket on the couch in her lounge room with her dog, 'Jessie', unable to afford heating.

The former employer has a long history of concealing its mistreatment of employees. I discovered and spoke to other bullying victims who'd been bribed or coerced by the employer to resign. Based on the ones I met and was told about, I estimate that over the years the employer would have spent millions of dollars on sham investigations, legal advice and confidential payouts to conceal bullying within the company.

Ironically, the employer boasted noble values such as integrity, transparency and respect, but the methods it used to cover up bullying revealed values that were the direct opposite — deceit, treachery and contempt.

Through this case, I discovered the seriousness of workplace bullying in Australia, including a 2012 Federal Government report describing it as 'the key workplace health and safety issue of our time' and costing the economy billions of dollars annually. I found many instances of serious bullying in a wide range of industries and occupations, often with dire personal consequences for victims, including suicide.

Of great concern is that well-resourced organisations, such as policing, health, emergency services and the public service, which claimed to be making genuine attempts to address their cultures of bullying, were failing according to external reviews, including by the Human Rights Commission.

Through my examination of the available legal options, I discovered that legislation on workplace bullying in Australia is complex and confusing. There is a heavy onus on victims wanting redress to make a formal complaint with less obligation on employers to protect employees from bullying. Also, generally the legislation is reactive rather than preventative in that it's only enacted after the damage has been done. Among its shortcomings is that it only covers bullying behaviour at the most serious end of the scale, but most bullying isn't at this end. An example is uncivil behaviour, most often thought to be mild bullying or not bullying at all, but which can still result in serious psychological harm for those targeted.

Importantly, the various processes available to victims to enforce legislation can incur high legal costs, be job-ending and in some instances career-ending. In most cases they prolong and worsen victims' distress.

Australian workplace health and safety regulators suggest a wide range of seemingly good advice for targets of bullying. I couldn't find anywhere in the regulators' advice, however, a caution that taking action on bullying, such as reporting it or even discussing it with managers and co-workers, can be the start of a highly perilous journey with positive outcomes rare. None says it could be job- or career-ending and none recommends that resigning may be the best option in some circumstances.

Surprisingly, unlike in the United States, United Kingdom and other parts of Europe, published research on the problem in Australia is limited and there is only a small handful of locally-produced books on the subject, and none recent. None ventures into the trickery and grubby tactics that some employers use routinely to conceal their bullying.

It was clear there was a place for a distinctly Australian book which provided a frank local overview of the problem. The book would be pitched at everyday readers, but also appeal to others such as professionals interested and involved in the field of workplace bullying, especially those new to the topic. Its aim mainly would be to inform and protect affected workers, but also to promote greater interest in the area and help those wanting to address the problem, including employers.

The book was written against the backdrop of the *#MeToo* movement, the first year of Covid-19, the exposure of wage theft and casualisation as a widespread problem for many Australian workers, and completed in the aftermath of the Australian Human Rights Commission releasing its report on an 18-month national inquiry into workplace sexual harassment.

I'm optimistic that a climate of positive change is emerging which will lead to sincere attempts by employers to develop respectful workplaces where bullying is minimised and well managed, and genuine concern for the health and well-being of employees is a high priority.

If you've been bullied at work, I'm sorry that this has happened to you. Be aware that reading this book may prompt distressing thoughts about your experience, and possibly without warning. Support is available including Emergency Services 000, Lifeline 13 11 14, Beyond Blue 1300 22 46 36, your general practitioner and the emergency department of your local hospital.

Dr John W. Murphy

INTRODUCTION

Workplace bullying is the key workplace health and safety issue of our time.[1] No one is immune from workplace bullying. Full-time, part-time and casual workers are bullied. So are volunteer workers, outworkers, contractors, subcontractors and students gaining work experience. Managers, CEOs and board members are bullied as well.

News media tell us about the mistreatment of hospitality workers who make our morning coffee and about the abuse of highly-skilled doctors who treat us when we're ill.

News media report regularly on the tragic stories about bullied workers who've reached the end of their tether. For example, pushed to the extreme, a young hospitality worker took her life after being bullied cruelly by co-workers.

Another example is a medical specialist who planned to end his life. He claimed that other doctors had made anonymous and spurious complaints about him to the hospital where he worked and to the Australian Health Practitioner Regulation Agency (AHPRA). These types of complaints can destroy the reputations and careers of medical practitioners, especially when news media get wind of them. Although cleared of every complaint, his stressful experience eventually wore him down. On the day he planned to suicide, a relative intervened.

Through news media we know that bullying among Australian school children is a serious problem. Depending on the source of statistics, the bullying rate is around one in five, or 20 per cent.[2] We know, too, that when children are bullied it can have severe and sometimes tragic consequences for them and their families. But we're only just becoming aware that adults can suffer tragic consequences from bullying as well.

In 2012 the Australian House of Representatives Standing Committee on Education and Employment described workplace bullying as 'the key workplace health and safety issue of our time' and estimated that it cost the economy many billions of dollars annually. The committee called bullying a form of psychological violence causing severe damage to workers' health and well-being and acknowledged that in some cases it pushed affected workers over the edge resulting in their suicide.[3]

It's surprising, therefore, that there are hardly any Australian books on the topic, especially recent ones, and not much research that is accessible to the everyday reader. Most books are from the United States, although the field's pioneering authors were from Europe, including Dr Heinz Leymann, Andrea Adams and Tim Field.

Dr Leymann was a Swedish researcher whose work rose to prominence in the 1990s. He said:

> *In the societies of the highly industrialised western world, the workplace is the only remaining battlefield where people can kill each other without running the risk of being taken to court.*[4]

Andrea Adams was a British journalist who investigated the mistreatment of employees and created the term 'workplace bullying'. She wrote *Bullying at Work: How to Confront and Overcome It.*[5] Tim Field wrote *Bully in Sight: How to predict, resist, challenge and combat workplace bullying — Overcoming the silence and denial by which abuse survives.*[6]

US pioneers in the field of workplace bullying prevention are Dr Gary Namie and Dr Ruth Namie who commenced campaigning in 1998 and later established the US Workplace Bullying Institute. Among their achievements are books *The Bully at Work,*[7] *The Bully-Free Workplace*[8] and the institute's website, workplacebullying.org.

The fundamentals of workplace bullying in Australia share much in common with bullying in New Zealand, the US and Britain, definitions and terminology among them, but there are some notable differences. In *The Bully at Work*, the Namies include a chapter called The World Declares War on Bullying in which they outline some of the main differences between countries.[9]

The main aim of this book is to protect the health and safety of workers employed in Australian workplaces. Therefore, the book is distinctly Australian, although literature and research from overseas in addition to local material is referenced. The laws referred to in the book pertaining to workplace bullying are Australian.

The book's intention is to help workers understand:

- what bullying is and is not
- why it happens
- the damaging health effects
- how to reduce the chances of being bullied
- what to do when it happens
- the wide range of dubious strategies that employers use to conceal bullying
- what's involved in making complaints, taking legal action and the consequences
- escaping from a bullying workplace and what to do when it's not an easy option
- the supports available.

The book's approach has been to provide an 'inside story' about workplace bullying, including information not readily available in print elsewhere. Hopefully, exposure to this information will enable workers to make better decisions about the available options and avoid some of the many pitfalls. As the saying goes, 'information is power'.

In almost all instances, being bullied saps the target's confidence and self-esteem. It's common for them to feel isolated in their workplace and somehow to blame for their bullying. But bullying can never be blamed on the target. Even when a worker is under-performing, is no longer needed or isn't liked, there are all kinds of ways that these issues can be dealt with legitimately by management. Bullying isn't one of them. An important aim of the book is to let bullied workers know that they're not alone and that bullying isn't acceptable under any circumstances.

Workplace bullying is also a major problem for employers because it results in:

- greater rates of absenteeism and turnover
- lower workplace morale
- disengaged workers
- decreased productivity
- reduced profit
- lost time for managers addressing the fallout from bullying
- legal costs, compensation payouts, increased insurance premiums
- reputational and brand damage.

The book aims to help employers appreciate the seriousness of the problem and the benefits of addressing it. It provides an overview of strategies for employers and managers. Knowing about bullying but doing nothing means that they're part of the problem. The Governor-General of Australia, David Hurley, once said, 'The standard you walk past is the standard you accept.'[10] The book highlights the benefits of a respectful workplace.

It provides health and welfare professionals with important information to share with patients and clients who've been bullied at work. While a high priority is to provide support to those closest to the front line of the problem, students and scholars new to the topic may find the book's overview a useful start for further study.

This isn't a self-help book with step-by-step tips. It's an introduction to the topic. The book attempts to present things truthfully, simply and in plain English for a general reader. While this has meant leaving out more in-depth analysis, some aspects of bullying can't be broken down entirely to simple explanations. Workplace bullying is a complex problem with many dimensions, multiple causes and a wide range of individual and organisational solutions.

The author searched out opinions and research about workplace bullying from a wide range of sources, including news media, popular and academic literature, industry surveys from the private and public sectors, and one-to-one meetings were conducted with more than 50 employees who shared their experiences about being bullied at work. Each source contributed to an understanding of the problem and the views presented in the book.

The author drew upon many years of personal work experience in Australian industry at all levels, including the not-for-profit, private, government and education sectors in management, casework, teaching, factory and labouring work, board membership and community volunteering.

The writing of this book was funded by the Triple A Foundation, which was established by philanthropist businessman Barrie Thomas to fund my work in the community — an arrangement that lasted for 25 years. Barrie is a qualified social worker who switched to a business career in 1979. With a partner, he brought the cosmetics retailer The Body Shop franchise to Australia in 1983 and New Zealand in 1989.

The book is an independent not-for-profit project which was not reliant on either explicit or tacit direction or approval from external funding sources for its content or style. This enabled a broad and candid approach to be taken with the subject.

If you're a target of bullying at work, you're not alone; in Australia there are millions of workers like you being mistreated every day. This may not be especially comforting while you're being tortured at work, on edge every minute and with all areas of your life impacted. But this book has you firmly in mind.

1

BULLYING IS SERIOUS

Bullying affects millions of Australian workers

Workplace bullying seriously affects the health and well-being of millions of workers in Australia. It impacts adversely on the productivity and effectiveness of our governments, businesses, health, welfare and other important services, and it costs the economy many billions of dollars annually.[1]

In calling workplace bullying 'the key workplace health and safety issue of our time', the Australian House of Representatives Standing Committee on Education and Employment described it as a form of 'psychological violence' causing severe damage to workers' health and well-being and resulting in suicide for some.[2]

Current estimates suggest that workplace bullying in Australia impacts on at least 10 per cent and up to 50 per cent of the working population.[3,4] Based on my examination of the literature and recent research, I estimate that it's upwards of 20 per cent or 2.4 million workers (based on pre-Covid-19 employment rates). This represents a significant number of workers exposed daily to bullying and its serious consequences. Chapter 5 Impact on Targets elaborates on the wide range of damaging psychological, physical and socioeconomic consequences for bullying victims, including anxiety, depression, post-traumatic stress disorder, unemployment, loss of income, relationship breakdowns, and suicide in extreme cases. Witnesses and families of victims are also adversely affected.

The literature on workplace bullying agrees that most employees who are bullied at work don't report it for fear of retribution or because they believe it won't stop their bullying; they either put up with it or leave. So, the real extent of the problem is always likely to be understated. Various authors refer to workplace bullying as a hidden problem or hidden epidemic. Founders of the US Workplace Bullying Institute Dr Gary Namie and Dr Ruth Namie take it a step further and call it 'the corporate sector's dirtiest secret'.[5]

Contributing to the 'secret' is that when instances of bullying are brought to the attention of employers or authorities, it's addressed away from the public eye. Some employers go to great lengths to conceal bullying at their workplaces. That's their way of addressing the problem. How and why are discussed in Chapter 11 Employers' Dirty Tactics, Chapter 12 Secret Payouts and Chapter 13 Don't Trust HR! Additionally, most claims for legal compensation for psychological injury, including workers' compensation, are settled out of court, usually accompanied by a gagging order preventing anyone from speaking publicly about the circumstances.

IN THE NEWS

The main way that the public hears about workplace bullying is through news media. These include print media (newspapers, news magazines), broadcast news (radio and television) and the Internet (online newspapers, news blogs, news videos, live news streaming). Although bullying happens across all areas of work, usually we only hear about it when prominent organisations and individuals are involved. An exception is when a possible link is suspected between an employee's suicide and workplace bullying.

Interest from news media is often prompted by an independent inquiry, such as by the Human Rights Commission, into an organisation's alleged mistreatment of its staff. Sometimes employees and trade unions go public with allegations of bullying. On other occasions investigations and subsequent fines by health and safety regulators or decisions made by the courts engage the interest of news media.

News media have revealed many well-known and some not-so-well-known employers who've been accused of bullying. Ironically, not too long ago, a State workplace health and safety authority was accused of bullying its staff.

There have been many news reports about prominent people who've been accused of bullying their staff, including those holding senior positions in government, business and the community. One of them was an Australian prime minister. Spectators have been accused of bullying champion sports people at Australian Football League games and at international cricket matches (see Chapter 9 Dehumanising and Demonising). For professional sports people, game venues are their workplaces.

Industries brought to our attention regularly by news media for alleged bullying are police and emergency services, health, business, all levels of government and not-for-profit. However, the plight of hundreds of thousands of employees bullied in smaller suburban workplaces rarely rates a mention, unless one of them is suspected of taking their life as a result of bullying.

Readers keen to examine news media reporting on workplace bullying can do their own online searches with sources such as the *Melbourne Age*, *Sydney Morning Herald* and their affiliates, the *Guardian*, ABC News and others providing a range of examples.

BULLYING PREVENTION FAILING

Little progress has been made to effectively address the problem since the Australian Productivity Commission said in 2010 that workplace bullying cost Australian employers up to $36 billion a year in lost productivity, and in 2012 the Australian House of Representatives Standing Committee on Education and Employment called workplace bullying 'the key workplace health and safety issue of our time'.[6,7]

This section draws attention to a small sample of surveys and reports revealing that bullying is endemic in some Australian industries, and that efforts to address the problem are failing.

In 2014, a national study carried out by the University of Wollongong and commissioned by Australian mental health and well-being support organisation Beyond Blue found that 50 per cent of workers would experience bullying in their working lives. The research revealed that people bullied at work have higher rates of depression, anxiety and post-traumatic stress disorder, as well as physical health problems such as cardiovascular diseases, migraines and obesity. It concluded that in Australia 'bullying at work is rife and attempts to combat it are failing'.[8]

In 2015, an independent report commissioned by the Royal Australasian College of Surgeons (RACS) discovered a deep-rooted culture of bullying and harassment in its ranks with nearly 50 per cent of surgeons surveyed across all specialties reporting experiences of discrimination, bullying or sexual harassment. Two years later, 40 per cent of surgeons had failed to complete the compulsory training mandated by the college which aimed to quash the toxic culture. The RACS vice-president said bullying and harassment were still pervasive within the profession.[9]

In 2015, the Victorian Human Rights Commission surveyed more than 5000 Victoria Police members with 40 per cent of females reporting that they'd been sexually harassed at work, resulting in serious harm to their mental and physical health. Two years later, the Chief Police Commissioner conceded, 'We're still seeing harm perpetrated in the workforce and we're still seeing considerable resistance to change.'[10]

In 2016, the Victorian Auditor-General's report into bullying and harassment in the Victorian health sector found the sector was failing to respond to the problem as a serious occupational health and safety risk. The report claimed that the sector still didn't understand the extent, causes or impact of bullying and harassment even though the issues had been given significant media coverage and caused reputational damage to organisations.[11]

In 2016, an independent study undertaken by the Australian Medical Association (AMA) surveyed 350 doctors in training across Queensland with more than 33 per cent reporting that they'd experienced bullying or harassment from another staff member during the previous 12 months.[12]

In 2017, 69,000 public service employees participated in the Victorian Public Service Commission's (VPSC) annual People Matter survey. Nearly 14,000 (20 per cent) said they'd been bullied at work over the previous 12 months and more than 17,000 (25 per cent) said they'd observed others being bullied. The report expressed serious concerns that efforts to reduce bullying in the Victorian Public Service over the previous 10 years had failed.[13]

In 2017, the chief executive of the Victorian Country Fire Authority acknowledged a toxic culture within the organisation after hundreds of responses to the interim report on gender diversity and inclusion survey in 2016 found the fire agency had a toxic culture of fear, bullying and sexual harassment.[14]

In 2018, the head of the New South Wales Ambulance Service publicly apologised to employees for years of bullying and harassment in the service. The apology came in the aftermath of a paramedic taking his life. The Health Services Union national secretary indicated that he was cynical about the response. He said that there was a 'strong paramilitary culture' in the service and doubted the apology would lead to the end of the problem.[15]

In 2018, leading doctors in New South Wales warned that a toxic culture of bullying and harassment among public health care workers was threatening the welfare of patients. A government survey of more than 65,600 health employees revealed that bullying, harassment and a distrust of managers pervades the State's public health system, with more than one in three staff reporting that they'd witnessed bullying during the previous 12 months.[16]

In 2019, an independent review of workplace culture in Canberra's public health system revealed troubling practices of bullying and harassment with most staff witnessing misconduct in the previous 12 months. Four hundred submissions from staff, consumers, non-government organisations and unions, plus 1900 responses to a staff-wide survey, were overwhelmingly negative. The report revealed a 'worrying and pervasive poor culture across the ACT public health system'. A submission to the review from the Community and Public Sector Union revealed experiences of sexism, racism and bullying, with a survey finding 75 per cent of participants had experienced bullying or harassment while working for ACT Health.[17]

The above sample suggests that the presence of firmly entrenched toxic cultures in large, complex organisations is difficult and, in some instances, impossible to change. Despite a growing awareness of workplace bullying, mainly through its regular exposure in news media, organisations still lack understanding about the extent, causes and impact of bullying, not only on employees but also on organisational effectiveness, including productivity, service quality and profits. It's an irony that so-called caring vocations such as health (doctors, nurses and paramedics) and protective and emergency services (police and firefighters) appear to be over-represented in news media reports of workplace bullying and not just in the ones included here. My selection is just a tiny sample from a much bigger collection.

It could be argued, with some justification, that the cases cited may not be representative. On the other hand, collectively they represent many thousands of cases of bullying which demonstrate a significant widespread problem.

'DIRTY SECRET' OR IGNORANCE?

As highlighted in the previous section, the founders of the US Workplace Bullying Institute, Dr Ruth Namie and Dr Gary Namie, refer to workplace bullying as the corporate sector's 'dirtiest secret'.[18] Many organisations and professions have entrenched cultures of bullying and harassment which they deny or cover up. Some organisations including some banks, religious institutions and governments have other kinds of 'dirty secrets' which they go to great lengths to conceal. Some of these organisations have been identified in news media and more is said about this issue in Chapter 11 Employers' Dirty Tactics.

There are many more organisations, however, which fail to recognise workplace bullying as a problem and are ignorant about the relevant health and safety regulations as they apply to bullying.

Ask local employers such as the hairdresser, café owner, butcher, real estate agent, community house co-ordinator, as well as the proprietors of the small factories in suburban industrial estates what they know about workplace bullying and the health and safety laws relating to it. I spoke to many employers and managers from big and small organisations during this project and discovered most knew little about the regulations.

When employers lack awareness of workplace bullying — what it is, how to prevent it and what to do when it happens — there's virtually no protection for employees, other than quitting which is not always an easy option depending on their personal circumstances. This issue is discussed in more detail in Chapter 20 Toughing It Out.

PROBLEMS WITH RESEARCH

The current absence of co-ordinated research, including large-scale, in-depth national studies, is a major obstacle to achieving a better understanding of workplace bullying in Australia.

Present sources of information are wide-ranging and include the results of small independent studies, individual industry-based surveys in business and the public service, regular reports of bullying and opinion pieces in news media, several books by psychologists (none of them recent publications), professional journal articles, information from workplace health and safety regulators, the Fair Work Commission, Human Rights Commission, other authorities, organisation websites, YouTube and Facebook.

The current limitations with Australian research deprive us of all kinds of important information about victims, employers, bullies, types of bullying, the impact of bullying on victims, their families, employers and the economy. The absence of this information prevents those who might otherwise advocate more actively for bullying prevention, such as trade unions, employer groups, professional associations, news media and others, from having strong credible evidence to support their case for change.

BULLYING AND THE LAW

There's a range of laws in Australia that relate to workplace bullying. In their 2016 critical evaluation of these laws, Monash University researchers Anne O'Rourke and Sarah Kathryn Antioch highlighted the limitations, including:

- The Fair Work Commission (the national workplace relations tribunal) is unable to award damages, impose fines or order reinstatement where a worker has been dismissed. Having greater powers would provide a stronger enforcement system and a more compelling deterrent to workplace bullying.

- Penalties for breaching the Fair Work Act are not enough to act as a deterrent to potential bullies or bring about proactive workplace strategies to address bullying cultures.
- Under OHS legislation individual employees can't commence proceedings and receive compensation for loss and suffering in the event of a prosecution being successful because only the authority or inspector can instigate proceedings.
- Proving beyond reasonable doubt that the injuries are work-related can be difficult when the bullying is insidious and underhanded and not witnessed either individually or electronically. The result is that WorkCover insurers deny workplace bullying claims, thereby forcing already vulnerable employees to abandon their claims when they don't have the financial resources required to take their matter to court.
- Under compensation law, there are problems proving the existence of injuries that are psychological in nature such as stress, anxiety and depression, unlike with physical injuries where the evidence is commonly observable and identifiable.
- There are significant limitations to bringing a bullying claim under common law relating to negligence, not the least of which are the limited definitions of 'serious injury', the difficulty of proving that the harm to the plaintiff was reasonably foreseeable, and proving that an employer had specific knowledge of an employee's level of sensitivity that exceeds what might be considered normal.
- Cases of adverse action can be difficult to prove, that is when as a direct result of an employee making a bullying complaint, their employer threatens the employee or organises their dismissal, causes injury, alters their job description to their detriment or allows the bullying to continue.
- The Victorian Crimes Act is the only legislation in Australia that includes the element of intention into the offence of bullying, that is the intention to cause physical or mental harm including self-harm, but it only addresses the behaviour of

individual perpetrators of bullying and employers can't be held liable or vicariously liable for the workplace conduct.[19]

O'Rourke and Antioch maintain that the significant costs associated with workplace bullying and the results of surveys indicate that bullying remains persistent despite the implementation of anti-bullying laws. They argue, therefore, that more severe remedies are required. They recommend standalone comprehensive anti-bullying legislation for the more serious bullying behaviours that include criminal and civil penalties corresponding to the seriousness of the conduct.

ESSENTIAL INFORMATION LACKING

Much of the information provided by those responsible for preventing and regulating workplace bullying is missing essential detail.

Authorities emphasise, for example, that workers have a right to a healthy and safe workplace and that every employer has a legal responsibility to ensure the health, safety and welfare of employees. Attention is drawn to a wide range of protections for employees, including a range of workplace safety legislation, criminal laws, fines, other penalties and, in Victoria, lengthy prison sentences for serious offenders. They strongly recommend that all employers should have bullying prevention policies which include processes for employees to safely report their bullying, and have complaints fairly investigated and resolved. They provide a range of seemingly useful advice for employees to safely report their bullying. Based on this range of reassuring information, an employee could reasonably assume that they're well protected from bullying at work or can achieve redress if they're bullied. Nothing, however, could be further from the truth.

Nowhere to be found is that:

- Generally, attempts to prevent workplace bullying in Australia are failing.
- Acting on their bullying can be highly risky for employees,

with the complaints process far from plain sailing and expected outcomes for complainants rarely achieved.

- Most employees don't report their bullying because they believe it will be a waste of time. They either put up with it or quit.
- Reprisals against a complainant from employers, alleged bullies and their supporters are common, irrespective of whether bullying allegations are proven or not.
- Many complaints about workplace bullying don't fit the definition of bullying used by Australian regulators, thereby leaving many if not most complaints invalid.
- Most bullying is carried out insidiously without witnesses and, therefore, is difficult to prove.
- Most employers have little understanding of the problem of workplace bullying, how to prevent it and how to deal with it when it happens, so it's likely they'll bungle complaints and investigation processes.
- Managers on whose watch bullying has occurred don't welcome complaints because they see them as a serious threat to their reputation and careers as do the managers who appointed or promoted a bully to a position of responsibility.
- Managers' responses to bullying complaints are likely to be influenced by their personal relationship with the alleged bully or their perceptions of who is the greater value to the workplace, the complainant or the bully.
- Because most bullies are supervisors or managers, generally they're better equipped to defend themselves against allegations of bullying.
- The accused and their supporters may increase the intensity of bullying against an employee after they've made a complaint and sometimes beforehand if they find out that a complaint is pending.
- An organisation with a culture of bullying will likely attempt to cover up the problem rather than address it. This may involve twisting the truth, blaming, sacking or

demoting the complainant, and making their work life difficult.

- A complainant may become isolated socially at work if co-workers believe that an association with them poses a personal risk to their well-being at work, including to their relationship with the bully manager.
- Even if a bullying complaint is substantiated, the complainant may be seen as a troublemaker by the employer, a 'dobber' by co-workers and especially by the accused's close colleagues. Even co-workers who were previously close to a complainant may condemn them for stirring up trouble. Life at work may become unpleasant and sometimes intolerable for them.
- Allegations of workplace bullying may place employers in a difficult legal position. Either the complainant or the alleged bully, for example, can take industrial and/or legal action against the employer if a decision doesn't go their way. Consequently, employers' decision-making in such circumstances can be based on what's best for the organisation rather than on truth, justice and protection for the victim. This is despite clichéd claims to the contrary such as 'the well-being of our employees is our highest priority' and 'we take our bullying policy very seriously'. An accusation of bullying may test an employer's otherwise strong ethical principles if they feel backed into a corner. This issue is covered in more detail in Chapter 11 Employers' Dirty Tactics, Chapter 12 Secret Payouts and Chapter 13 Don't Trust HR!
- In some instances, quitting is the safest option for a bullied worker, especially if they're employed in a toxic workplace where a culture of mistreating staff prevails. Leaving the job may not be an easy option, however, depending on an employee's personal circumstances and the availability of suitable alternative employment.

The advice provided in authorities' literature and on their websites is all positive, but it neglects an important obligation to be realistic about the possibilities, including failing to advise when caution is required.

PREVENTION NOT A HIGH PRIORITY

Earlier in this chapter evidence was presented that attempts to address workplace bullying in Australian industries have been failing. Because currently no one is presenting a strong case for bullying prevention, it's easy for governments and employers to downplay or dismiss the serious human and economic costs of the problem. For some time, bullying has been viewed as being within acceptable limits, part of the normal rough-and-tumble of work life, and the high personal costs for employees and employers are simply the price of doing business.

There's no indication that Australian governments or the authorities they fund to monitor the health and safety of workers plan to step up efforts to address the problem. The Australian Labor Party, which initiated the Federal Government inquiry on bullying in 2012, is now languishing in opposition. Historically, employer groups have opposed industrial relations reform and recently have pressed for greater deregulation.[20] Nowadays when governments speak about pursuing industrial relations reform, it's most often about eroding the rights and conditions of workers. The trade union movement, historically the champion of workers' rights, struggles to be heard with flagging membership, now only around 14 per cent of the country's workforce.[21] Conservative governments have been the traditional adversary of trade unions and are accused regularly of 'union bashing' or pursuing 'union-busting legislation'.[22,23]

At the time of writing this book, it was too early to predict with confidence how the Covid-19 pandemic would impact on these issues or on workplace bullying. It's fair to say, however, that as a social and economic problem, workplace bullying will continue to face stiff competition for government and public interest. Currently there are many urgent social, economic and environmental priorities in Australia, especially those caused or made worse by Covid-19.

SUMMARY

- Bullying happens across all areas of work and seriously affects the health and well-being of millions of workers in Australia and costs the economy many billions of dollars annually.
- The Australian House of Representatives Standing Committee on Education and Employment described workplace bullying as 'the key workplace health and safety issue of our time'.
- Upwards of 20 per cent or 2.4 million workers in Australia are exposed daily to bullying and its serious consequences.
- Although bullying happens across all areas of work, usually we only hear about it when prominent organisations and individuals are involved, or extreme circumstances such as when a victim takes their own life.
- Most workplace bullying occurs away from the public eye because victims don't report it, employers cover it up, and compensation for psychological injury is settled out of court.
- Many prominent people have been accused of bullying, including those who hold senior positions in government, business and the community.
- Because of a lack of research, we don't know just how serious bullying is in Australia, but many estimates suggest it's widespread.
- Much of the information provided by those responsible for preventing and regulating workplace bullying is lacking in essential detail.
- Despite the range of legal options for victims who've been targets of bullying, the law is limited in its ability to address the problem.

2

WHAT IS BULLYING?

Workplace bullying is a serious risk for employees

Workplace bullying is complex and there are no easy solutions. This chapter and those following will explain why and elaborate on its complexity, starting here with current definitions.

The Australian Fair Work Ombudsman says:

> ...*an employee is bullied at work when a person or group of people act repeatedly and unreasonably towards them or a group of workers and the behaviour creates a risk to health and safety. It includes victimising, intimidating, humiliating or threatening.*[1]

The Australian Human Rights Commission says:

> ...*workplace bullying is verbal, physical, social or psychological abuse by your employer (or manager), another person or group of people at work.*[2]

In Australia most workplace health and safety regulations and employers' staff conduct policies draw from these definitions.

There's a range of definitions from other parts of the world. Examples include:

The Canadian Centre for Occupational Health and Safety:

> *Acts or verbal comments that could mentally hurt or isolate a person in the workplace. Sometimes, bullying can involve negative physical contact as well. Bullying usually involves repeated incidents or a pattern of behaviour that is intended to intimidate, offend, degrade or humiliate a person or group of people. It has also been described as the assertion of power through aggression.*[3]

Employment New Zealand:

> *Workplace bullying is repeated and unreasonable behaviour directed towards a worker or a group of workers that can be physical, verbal or relational/social (excluding someone or spreading rumours).*[4]

Bullying UK:

> *Workplace bullying is a form of abusive behaviour where an individual or a group of people creates an intimidating or humiliating work environment for another. This is with the purpose of harming their dignity, safety and well-being.*[5]

Founders of the US Workplace Bullying Institute, Dr Ruth and Dr Gary Namie:

> *Health-harming mistreatment of a person by one or more workers that takes the form of verbal abuse, conduct or behaviours that are threatening, intimidating or humiliating; sabotage that prevents work from getting done or some combination of the three.*[6]

NOT JUST PAID WORKERS

The Fair Work Ombudsman says that the national anti-bullying laws cover most workplaces (or those that are constitutionally covered businesses).[7] The laws also cover:

- volunteers
- outworkers
- students gaining work experience
- contractors or subcontractors.

According to the Fair Work Ombudsman, the best way to manage the health and safety of volunteers and other workers not directly employed by an organisation is to treat them as paid employees, for example, by providing them with the same risk and safety assessments as paid workers.

For advice about their legal obligations regarding the health and safety of volunteer workers, organisations should refer to their State workplace health and safety authorities, State law institutes, volunteer peak bodies and insurance brokers. Contact details are listed in the Who to Contact section at the end of this book.

TERMINOLOGY

In Australia, New Zealand, the UK and the US, 'workplace bullying' is the favoured term to describe an employee's mistreatment at work. The reference to 'workplace bullying and harassment' is covered next. But there's a wide range of different ways used to describe workplace bullying behaviour. They include psychological violence, psychological abuse, verbal abuse, workplace violence, workplace mobbing, workplace abuse, workplace incivility, workplace cyberbullying, gaslighting and workplace victimisation.

The definitions and terms used by Australian health and safety regulators are recommended. Advice and decisions by employers, regulators, trade unions, tribunals and courts will be influenced by local definitions and terminology.

BULLYING AND HARASSMENT

Sometimes the word 'bullying' is accompanied by 'harassment', such as 'the employee was a victim of bullying and harassment'. This can be confusing because usually a distinction isn't made between 'bullying' as defined by occupational health and safety legislation and 'harassment' as defined by discrimination law. Therefore, it's not clear whether an employee has been subjected to breaches of both sets of laws or just one.

Workplace bullying, according to occupational health and safety law, has already been defined. Under discrimination legislation it's not lawful to treat a person less favourably based on protected attributes such as their sex, race, disability or age. The law also has specific provisions relating to sexual harassment, racial hatred and disability harassment.[8]

According to Australia's Human Rights Commission, sexual harassment is any unwanted or unwelcome sexual behaviour where a reasonable person would have anticipated the possibility that the person harassed would feel offended, humiliated or intimidated. It has nothing to do with mutual attraction or consensual behaviour.[9]

Examples of sexual harassment include:

- staring, leering or unwelcome touching
- suggestive comments or jokes
- unwanted invitations to go out on dates or requests for sex
- intrusive questions about a person's private life or body
- unnecessary familiarity, such as deliberately brushing up against a person
- emailing pornography or rude jokes

- displaying images of a sexual nature around the workplace
- communicating content of a sexual nature through social
  media or text messages.

In March 2020, the Australian Human Rights Commission completed the report of its 18-month independent inquiry into workplace sexual harassment in Australia. Titled *Respect@Work: National Inquiry into Sexual Harassment in Australian Workplaces*, it's available on the Australian Human Rights Commission website.[10]

From a workplace health and safety perspective, many of the inquiry's findings and recommendations are relevant to workplace bullying given that sexual harassment and bullying are about mistreating employees which risks their health and safety at work including their psychological safety. There are major differences, however, between workplace bullying and sexual harassment.

Through its inquiry, the Commission reported its findings on the way that power disparities in society, as well as in the workplace, enabled sexual harassment. And gender inequality was the key power disparity that drives sexual harassment. Gender inequality is defined as the unequal distribution of power, resources and opportunity between men and women in society, due to prevailing societal norms and structures. It's no surprise, therefore, that with sexual harassment, most victims are women and most perpetrators are men. On the other hand, with workplace bullying the gender of victims and perpetrators is more evenly distributed.

Whereas bullying is recurring behaviour, harassment can be a single incident, although often harassment behaviour is recurring.

If a person has been referred to as a victim of workplace bullying and harassment and is employed in a toxic workplace where anything goes regarding mistreating staff, it's possible they've been exposed to breaches of occupational health and safety laws as well as discrimination laws.

Both bullying and harassment relate to an employee being mistreated at work, but unless specific reference is being made to discrimination law or sexual harassment, in this book the term 'bullying' is used as it applies to breaches of occupational health and safety law.

PATTERN OF MISTREATMENT

The various definitions agree that for an employee's mistreatment to be labelled bullying, it needs to be recurring — in other words, a pattern of ongoing mistreatment.

Generally, a one-off incident that's not part of a pattern of mistreatment isn't considered bullying although it may still intimidate, humiliate, threaten, undermine and distress a target. A one-off incident could be a breach of criminal law if it involves theft of or damage to an employee's property, threats of physical violence, actual physical violence or stalking. Stalking is a form of harassment including following, loitering, watching, contacting or leaving material for another person designed to intimidate, torment and cause them fear.

Single incidences, such as swearing at a co-worker, may fall into the category of misconduct for which some form of reprimand by the employer could be warranted. Employers should not tolerate any behaviour that causes a risk to employees' health and safety, irrespective of whether it's a single incident or repeated. A single incident of mistreatment may be the precursor to a pattern of bullying behaviour.

ABUSE OF POWER

Bullying is an abuse of power, the bully's power, generally because of their senior position, but also their standing within the organisation, the community, their profession, relationships at work and/or outside of work, special knowledge, experience, skills, confidence and long service to the employer. Most bullying is top down, but it can occur between workers of equal standing. It can be bottom up, also referred to as upwards bullying. An example is an employee who regularly bad-mouths the manager behind their back or continually undermines their authority, reputation and confidence publicly or in private.

MANAGING OUT

A common form of workplace bullying is managing out. Often it involves mobbing, which is outlined in the following section. While managing-out strategies vary, most are aimed at making the targeted employee's work life intolerable, so they'll decide to leave.

A managing-out strategy is relatively easy to conceal beneath the legitimacy of reasonable management practice and not breach unfair dismissal laws. Therefore, it's difficult for those targeted to prove. For example, a manager who wants to get rid of an employee can legitimately vary aspects of their job to make it unpleasant and dissatisfying. This could include changing or reducing working hours, increasing responsibilities, removing benefits or shifting them to another work area such as one that is isolated or unpleasant. If the strategy doesn't create the desired impact, the process can be ramped up. 'Jane's' story presented in the Preface is a good example of managing out.

In Chapter 11 there's a long list of 'dirty tactics' that some employers use to bully and manage out unwanted employees. But some of the main managing-out strategies are described in more detail as follows:

Dodgy performance improvement plans

This involves putting an employee on an improvement plan with pre-determined unachievable goals. A common tactic is giving them an impossible project deadline. Sometimes an employee will pick up quickly that the performance improvement plan is setting them up to fail and they'll protest or resign. Others may toil in earnest believing that they've got a genuine chance to redeem themselves. To coerce them to resign, a brazen employer may tell an employee that they're going to fail their performance improvement plan.

Isolation

This involves psychologically manipulating an employee to resign. Examples include reducing their responsibilities so they've got insufficient work to keep them busy. This may be dissatisfying for a highly-motivated worker. Also, it may result in their incurring the disdain of co-workers who have heavier workloads.

Another tactic is re-allocating choice or high-status work tasks to others, such as the management of important customers and projects, liaison with major stakeholders, shifting them to a secluded or unpleasant work area, excluding them from work meetings and social functions. A common tactic is when a perpetrator deliberately ignores the presence of a targeted worker when they greet and farewell other workers.

Phony redundancy

Normally a redundancy involves removing job roles that the employer is unable to sustain. There are many reasons why a redundancy happens such as new technology taking over the roles of employees, a business relocating or closing down. Many employees lost their jobs during the fallout from Covid-19 simply because there was no longer work for them. Some employers, however, misappropriate the language of redundancy to get rid of a particular employee rather than their actual position. Employers may leave the position vacant for a while to mask the dodgy redundancy, then fill the position later. Often this involves giving the job another title or making minor changes to the list of job tasks while retaining the main responsibility areas. Sometimes an employer may offer an employee a confidential payout to leave. More about this appears in Chapter 12 Secret Payouts.

Threats and deception

This involves coercing and lying to get an employee to resign. Telling an employee 'we feel that your career goals would best be achieved elsewhere' are weasel words for 'we want you to go', as are 'we could put you through a formal process, but we thought you would like to leave with your dignity and reputation intact'. Another is 'if you don't resign, you'll never work in this industry again'. Threats of a miserable work life, including demotion, transfer, withdrawal of benefits and privileges and dissatisfying work are commonly used in managing out employees.

Some employers and managers talk routinely about managing out staff as if it's a legitimate management practice, but it's not. The practice is mostly a sly and unethical strategy used to bully or manipulate a disliked, under-performing or unwanted employee out of their job without going through an organisation's formal performance improvement, disciplinary, dismissal or redundancy processes and bypassing unfair dismissal laws.

MOBBING

Closely related to managing out is mobbing. It's a term that appears mainly in the overseas literature on bullying. It's defined as emotional abuse, particularly ganging up by a group of co-workers, subordinates or superiors to force someone out of the workplace through rumour, innuendo, intimidation, humiliation, discrediting and isolation.[11] Mobbing can also involve physical bullying, such as assault, by a group of workers.

What's particularly interesting about mobbing is the theory around it which generally dispels the view that all bullies are inherently bad people. According to US anthropologist Jan Harper, mobbing is distinct from bullying because the perpetrators are not just serial bullies, but can be formerly friendly, non-aggressive people who've been intentionally encouraged or deceived to see the target as a threat.[12] Explanations are grounded in the research about animal aggression and human aggression and focus on why normally good people might turn 'evil' and mob a co-worker. More is said about this in Chapter 7 Why Bullying Happens, Chapter 8 Morals and Obedience and Chapter 9 Dehumanising and Demonising.

INCIVILITY

Workplace incivility is a type of workplace bullying. Professor David Yamada, a US legal expert on workplace bullying, says that when he started his work in the area more than 20 years ago uncivil behaviours were on the bullying spectrum. He maintains that currently sharper lines are being drawn between bullying and incivility.[13] Other elements of bullying are also being scrutinised separately.

In her book *Mastering Incivility*, pioneering workplace incivility researcher Dr Christine Porath defines workplace incivility as:

> *...seemingly insignificant behaviours that are rude, disrespectful, discourteous or insensitive, where the intent to harm is ambiguous or unclear.*[14]

Sharone Bar-David, organisational consultant and author of *Trust Your Canary — Every Leader's Guide to Taming Workplace Incivility*, says that workplace incivility ranges from barely visible behaviours to blatantly rude conduct verging on harassment (bullying).[15] According to Bar-David, the definition comprises various elements such as:

- seemingly inconsequential, low-intensity behaviour where manner and body language set the tone for how the words are interpreted
- rude and discourteous behaviour where acceptability varies depending on the context, culture,* team and generation, and
- intent to harm, which can be difficult to determine such as if

rolling the eyes is an innocent expression of frustration or an intentional dismissive response.

* In this context, culture refers to a general term used in the social sciences which includes the social behaviour and norms found in human societies, in addition to the knowledge, beliefs, arts, laws, customs, capabilities and habits of individuals in these groups.

Bar-David says that because some forms of incivility are subtle, they 'fly under the radar' of organisations' bullying-prevention policies. It's not uncommon for management to be unreceptive when employees report being treated uncivilly. Complaining employees are often told to 'develop a thicker skin'. This response can also be a tactic to cover up the problem which is addressed in more detail in Chapter 11 Employers' Dirty Tactics.

According to Bar-David, one of the major differences between the bullying and incivility literature is that bullying is seen largely as intentional and incivility is based on ignorance rather than malice. The workplace bullying literature, however, suggests that the distinction isn't always clear cut. The intentional versus ignorance issue is covered in the following chapter, What Isn't Bullying. Another difference, according to Bar-David, is that bullying behaviour is repeated over months or years whereas uncivil behaviour can be a one-off event.

When people are mistreated at work, either through incivility or other forms of bullying, it negatively impacts on them. Even a single event of rudeness may be harmful to an employee's performance, focus, helpfulness and creativity. Porath's research on workplace incivility reveals that targets of recurring uncivil behaviour can experience the same types of negative health effects as targets of more extreme forms of bullying behaviour.

A feature of the workplace incivility literature is the emphasis on positive workplace cultures for effective bullying prevention. This topic is covered in Chapter 22 Respectful Workplaces. The workplace incivility literature plays an important role in helping to develop a more in-depth understanding of the types of workplace bullying that are thought to occur at the milder end of the spectrum and which often are not even considered bullying, despite the serious consequences for those who've been targeted.

CYBERBULLYING

Also called online bullying, cyberbullying occurs when the Internet, mobile phones and other devices are used to deliberately and repeatedly hurt or embarrass targets. It's especially common among adolescents and young children, but it's not exclusive to younger people even though most literature on the topic focuses on them. Despite its relative newness as a topic of public interest, cyberbullying has produced a voluminous quantity of literature on the subject.

Cyberbullying can include teasing, name-calling, threats, nasty comments, put-downs and rumours with the aim of embarrassing, upsetting, scaring or excluding targets.[16] Workplace cyberbullying is the same as traditional workplace bullying, but the bullies use electronic devices and online communication to bully their targets. The development of smartphones, apps, mobile phone cameras and immediate Internet access have provided effective tools for cyberbullying. They've also made it easy to undertake cyberbullying secretly given that stationary technology, such as desktop computers, are commonly in public view and can be scrutinised by others.

Workplace cyberbullying includes but is not limited to:

- malicious or threatening emails, text messages and tweets
- electronic communication that includes jokes about ethnicity, religion, sexual orientation or any other topics that make targets uncomfortable
- public shaming via a mass email

- sharing embarrassing, offensive or manipulated images or videos of an individual
- spreading lies and gossip, with social networking sites and blogs usually are the most common ways that people become victims of others' bullying.[17]

The impact of workplace cyberbullying on employees and employers is the same as the impact of more traditional forms of workplace bullying as outlined in Chapter 5 Impact on Targets and Chapter 6 Costs for Employers. The solutions outlined in Chapter 22 Respectful Workplaces are also the same.

GASLIGHTING

Like incivility, gaslighting is on the workplace bullying behaviours spectrum. Gaslighting is a label for a form of psychological abuse whereby the target is psychologically manipulated so they'll question their judgements and perceptions. Underpinning gaslighting behaviour is the perpetrator's quest for power and control over the target.

It's not a commonly-used term in Australia where few people outside the fields of violence against women, psychology and human resource management know about its origin or meaning. Gaslighting doesn't appear in the *Diagnostic and Statistical Manual of Mental Disorders* (the 'bible' for mental health professionals), and the bulk of literature and research on workplace bullying doesn't rate the term a mention.

There's limited dedicated scholarly research to support the assertions made by those who write about gaslighting. This is not to say, however, that their writing is without value. In the first instance, they borrow heavily from the workplace bullying literature and references on personality disorders. Secondly, the authors appear to have years of clinical experience in the mental health field, including supporting those through counselling who've been targeted for the types of sinister abuse that gaslighting involves.

The term gaslighting had its origin in a 1938 play, *Gaslight*, followed by two film adaptations in the early 1940s with the same name. The central theme of the story is a husband slowly attempting to drive his wife to insanity to distract her from discovering his criminality, including his murder of her aunt years earlier. One of his tactics is to adjust their home's gas lights in one part of their house causing the lights throughout the house to flicker while telling his wife that she's imagining it.[18]

Until relatively recently, gaslighting was used mostly to refer to the manipulation and control perpetrated by men in romantic relationships. But clinical psychologist Dr Stephanie Sarkis says that gaslighting has no gender boundaries in the workplace.[19]

In Chapter 4 Bullying Behaviours a wide range of behaviours is included. Gaslighting focuses on the insidious and drawn-out manipulative behaviours which aim to undermine co-workers. According to the Australian Human Resources Institute, the difference between gaslighting and the more overt forms of bullying is visibility.[20] As with workplace incivility, gaslighting behaviour can be difficult to identify and act on.

Clinical psychologist Dr Stephanie Sarkis says that the manipulation techniques that gaslighters commonly use include:

- using your own words against you
- plotting against you
- lying to your face
- denying your needs
- sabotaging your work
- building you up then knocking you down
- showing excessive displays of power
- trying to convince you of 'alternative facts'
- spreading rumours about your stability
- concocting stories to get you fired
- turning family, friends and co-workers against you.

Dr Sarkis says that each has the goal of watching the target suffer and consolidating the gaslighter's power over them.

Driving a wedge between co-workers is a favoured tactic to enhance the domination and control of gaslighters. According to Dr Sarkis, often gaslighters set up rivalries among co-workers to divert attention away from their own inadequacies and unethical workplace practices.

In Chapter 10 Bullying and Personality, a brief outline of personality disorders is provided which many writers in the field of workplace bullying agree underpin the behaviour of serial bullies, that is, those who regularly inflict harm on co-workers. Dr Sarkis maintains that gaslighting shares characteristics with several of the personality disorders described in the *Diagnostic and Statistical Manual of Mental Disorders (DSM-5)* as Cluster B Personality Disorders, that is:

- Histrionic
- Narcissistic
- Antisocial
- Borderline.

More about personality disorders can be found in Chapter 10 Bullying and Personality. According to Dr Sarkis, personality disorders are thought to be deeply ingrained in a person's behaviour making such an individual difficult to treat.

Information provided in this book is not a diagnostic tool for psychiatric analysis. A diagnosis of personality disorder can only be made by a highly-trained mental health professional relying on a wide range of knowledge and skills gained through many years of university study, professional supervision and experience working in the field.

HAZING

Hazing is also called bastardisation and initiation, and it refers to rituals and challenges involving harassment (bullying), abuse and humiliation used to induct a person into groups such as gangs, sports teams, schools, universities and military units.[21] Hazing can range from relatively harmless mischief to prolonged patterns of behaviour that are abusive or criminal conduct. The term is not commonly used in Australia and most references I discovered referred to US military and university initiations.

A major survey in 2007 of 60,000 athletes from 2400 US universities found that 79 per cent experienced some form of hazing to join their team, and 60 per cent indicated that they accepted hazing as a practice and wouldn't report it. Behaviours included excessive alcohol consumption, humiliation, isolation, sleep deprivation and sex acts.[22]

Hazing is not confined to overseas institutions, however. Several local examples have been reported by news media.

The Australian Defence Force (ADF) has a long history of brutality and bastardisation, including sexual assault and discrimination, sometimes with tragic consequences for victims. In more recent times, however, the ADF has made serious efforts to address the problem.

WHISTLE-BLOWER BULLYING

According to the Australian Securities and Investments Commission (ASIC), whistle-blowing is when a current or former employee or company officer, supplier or contractor to the company, spouse or family member reports fraud, defrauding the company or its customers or suppliers, or misleading people to make a sale. It also covers reporting of business practices that cause consumers harm.[23] Reports can be made to the company directly or to ASIC. Some whistle-blowers leak information to news media when their reporting has not brought the desired outcome.

Whistle-blowing involves a complaint about negligence, dishonesty or misconduct in the workplace. Employers' negative responses to whistle-blowers is a good example of the serious risks taken by employees who report wrongdoing in their workplaces. Like many employees who've been bullied, whistle-blowers can suffer serious mental health, physical, social and economic consequences as a result of their complaint. There's a range of prominent Australian examples where whistle-blowers have paid an enormous price for their actions, including the loss of their jobs, death threats, loss of friends and colleagues, depression and post-traumatic stress disorder.

Many believe that whistle-blowers are heroes for what they've been able to achieve, but not all whistle-blowing has a successful outcome for the whistle-blower. Some whistle-blowers may experience a sense of achievement based, for example, on the outcome of a Royal Commission which validates their actions. On the other hand, the disclosures of other whistle-blowers never get this far. Either their complaints can't be substantiated or are successfully covered up. Invariably, they suffer the same adverse consequences as those whose complaints are substantiated, but without any validation of their actions. Irrespective of the outcome of their efforts, many whistle-blowers eventually question whether their complaints were worth the personal cost.

As there are laws to protect employees from workplace bullying, there are laws to protect whistle-blowers from retribution by employers such as sacking, demoting, discriminating against, harassing or intimidating. Whistle-blowers can seek compensation through a court if they suffer loss, damage or injury for making a report. Also, ASIC can investigate allegations of victimising or threatening a whistle-blower.

But, as with workplace bullying, invariably the laws don't prevent initial retribution against a whistle-blower, or the major personal costs they suffer. Rather they provide opportunities for redress, including compensation, afterwards.

MISUSE OF REGULATORY PROCESSES

A form of bullying not widely known outside the occupations in which it mostly occurs is when professional regulatory processes are abused to mistreat workers. Common targets are doctors, nurses, dentists, allied health workers and other professionals. One doctor I spoke to, a surgeon, told me that his career was seriously damaged by an elitist group of old-school surgeons who he said abused the system to pursue their own selfish ends. Understandably, he did not wish to be identified, but contributed the following personal commentary for which I am grateful:

The misuse of regulatory processes is a well-utilised strategy by some CEOs and medical managers or even surgeon colleagues for disciplinary purposes, to gain market advantage or plain misuse of power.

Regulators such as the Australian Health Professional Regulation Agency (AHPRA) are informed of an 'adverse event' which is when an unexpected complication occurs. They are quite common in complex surgery and are often multi-causal with system factors frequently ignored, leaving surgeons scapegoated. Often there is misrepresentation of complication data to imply the surgeon is a risk to the public.

Even when surgeons make decision errors, there is rarely any assessment of the working conditions that may have been contributory. It is still a blame game rather than learning from adverse events.

The regulator is obliged to investigate and often this leads to the immediate standing down of the accused.

Because regulators are under-resourced and investigators not medically trained, the process can be prolonged and lead to the

*ruining of careers regardless of the findings which are often
biased by sham peer reviews.*

Advocates for reform to regulatory processes in the health care field agree and say that AHPRA is being misused with vexatious complaints made by medical practitioners in the guise of being in the public interest when the mandatory notification is abused by the complainant/s for commercial and/or personal reasons.

Health care practitioners who've suffered mental health problems face another obstacle in the way of their treatment and recovery. It's the risk of being reported to AHPRA by their treating practitioner which may result in severe restrictions being placed on their practice and the consequent damage to their reputations and careers. Health care professionals are obliged by the regulator to report fellow health care professionals who they're treating if they believe the public is at 'substantial risk of harm' based on their poor mental health. The requirement also covers intoxication and misconduct.

AHPRA argues that it's important that the regulation agency knows when patients may be at substantial risk of harm from a registered health practitioner so that action can be taken to protect the public.[24] This rationale is difficult to dispute. But not only is the system open to abuse regarding vexatious or over-zealous reporting, as described earlier, but according to doctors' groups such as the Australian Medical Association and the Royal Australasian College of General Practitioners, mandatory reporting is to blame for making health professionals too scared to seek help for a mental illness. 'We have already lost too many talented, brilliant and dedicated colleagues who felt they could not seek help because they would be reported,' AMA president Dr Tony Bartone said.[25]

An opinion piece in the *Medical Journal of Australia* (*MJA*) says that doctors and other medical professionals are more likely to die by suicide than the general population.[26] Male doctors reportedly take their own lives at 1.4 times the general rate and female doctors 2.2 times. According to the opinion piece, recent Australian studies reveal that doctors experience high levels of stress early in their training and careers. The studies found that one in five medical students reported suicidal ideation in the preceding 12 months and 50 per cent of junior doctors experienced moderate to high levels of distress.

Fear of being reported to medical authorities was highlighted as a serious problem for doctors experiencing poor mental health. The article maintained that it's not an irrational fear given studies revealing the concerns that medical practitioners have about the competency of colleagues experiencing mental health disorders. In his book *Why Physicians Die by Suicide*, psychiatrist Dr Michael J. Myers says that given the highly stressful nature of the medical profession, reticence by doctors to seek professional help with their mental health problems is a serious issue because it deprives them of the early intervention essential for effective treatment and a positive prognosis.[27]

In Chapter 1 Bullying Is Serious, a range of Australian surveys was highlighted revealing that bullying is a serious problem for doctors, including those in training, and other health care professionals with up to 50 per cent reporting that they'd been bullied during the preceding 12 months. Bullying exacerbates the many stresses inherent in the medical profession and allied professions and can be a tipping point for practitioners already on the edge.

'BULLYING' – A NEGATIVE TERM

Some writers have argued that 'victim', 'bullying' and 'bully' are negative terms which stigmatise those involved and may hinder parties' attempts to resolve problems.

It's understandable that some targets of bullying may not wish to be referred to as 'victims'. In her book *Mobbed Out of Existence*, Mary A. Lewis raises the issue of labelling and emphasises the importance of empowering people who've been bullied at work by not giving them 'weakened victim status'.[28] The empowering term 'survivor' is often used to describe a person who's experienced a traumatic event. Although when seeking compensation through the courts for personal injury resulting from workplace bullying, lawyers seem to favour more emotionally-charged terms such as 'victim' and 'bullying'. In her book *Workplace Bullying Lawyers' Guide*, Australian human rights lawyer Kathryn-Magnolia Feeley uses the term 'victim' liberally.[29] Referring to someone as a 'survivor' when seeking compensation for personal injury might imply that they've recovered from their experience or that it may not have been serious in the first place, which may undermine the outcome of a legal claim.

Clearly 'bullying' and 'bully' are negative terms, albeit at the milder end of a range of emotionally-charged language often used to describe the mistreatment of workers and its perpetrators. In Chapter 15 Preparing a Complaint, it's advised that complainants should avoid using the terms 'bully' or 'bullying' in internal complaints or even in enquiries to management about alleged mistreatment. Rather, it's recommended that the behaviours of concern be described in detail with the name/s of the alleged perpetrator/s, dates, times and witnesses included. This is because of the strong alienating potential of accusatory and name-calling language such as 'bullying' and 'bully' which are likely to immediately prompt defensive and even aggressive responses from those in the firing line, including self-protective employers not keen to concede that they're overseeing an unsafe workplace. Clearly, however, there needs to be a balance between toning down a complaint to the point where it downplays the seriousness of allegations and a highly emotionally-charged complaint that alienates everyone from the start.

In a blog titled *Workplace bullying is not incivility or mere disrespect*, the US Workplace Bullying Institute advocates strongly that the problem should be given a strong name to match the seriousness of the impact on workers' lives.[30] The institute warns against using euphemisms for workplace bullying because 'the desire to dance around a topic without honestly naming it blocks effective action'.

Professor David Yamada, in an article titled *Distinguishing workplace incivility and abrasiveness from bullying and mobbing*, agrees and argues that when someone is being savagely abused at work, it's not about 'bad manners or jerky behavior'. He adds that the distinctions need to be kept in mind, even if it makes some people uncomfortable.[31] Professor Yamada says that in the US workplace incivility, rudeness and abrasiveness are more readily acknowledged than bullying and mobbing. He believes the reason is that management is far more threatened by allegations of bullying than by claims of incivility.

In one of his popular monologues, the late American comedian and satirist George Carlin summed up the argument when he referred to 'evasion language', which is when efforts are made to 'bury people's pain under soft language'.[32] Carlin said:

> *I don't like words that hide the truth. I don't like words that conceal reality. I don't like euphemisms. And the American language is loaded with euphemisms because Americans have a lot of trouble dealing with reality. Americans have trouble facing the truth, so they invent a kind of soft language to protect themselves. And it gets worse with every generation.*

As an example, Carlin used the evolution of the name of the mental health condition 'post-traumatic stress disorder' (PTSD) to describe combat stress in soldiers. He said the term had its beginning as 'shell shock' in World War I, became 'battle fatigue' in World War II, 'operational exhaustion' in the Korean War and 'post-traumatic stress disorder' in the Vietnam War for soldiers who had 'adjustment problems' (another euphemism I discovered while researching this topic). Carlin said that over time humanity was squeezed out of the term and the pain was completely buried under jargon. He concluded pointedly:

> *If we were still calling it shell shock, some of those veterans might have got the attention they needed at the time.*

In Australia, workplace bullying is relatively new as an area of public interest and study. I believe that it will be less confusing for readers at this time if the most commonly-used terms are used here — 'bullying' and 'bully'. Workers who've experienced bullying are referred to in this book as both 'victims' and 'targets', although I acknowledge that some may see 'targets' as a euphemism.

SUMMARY

- Bullying happens when a person or group of people act repeatedly and unreasonably towards other people and the behaviour creates a risk to health and safety. It includes victimising, intimidating, humiliating and threatening.
- For an employee's mistreatment to be labelled bullying, it needs to be repeated over time which forms a pattern of behaviour.
- Mobbing is abuse described as ganging up by a group of co-workers, subordinates or superiors to force the target out of the workplace.
- Workplace incivility comprises seemingly insignificant behaviours that are rude, disrespectful, discourteous or insensitive where the intent to harm is ambiguous or unclear. While considered mild bullying, it can have the same serious impact on targeted employees as more serious forms of bullying.
- Also called online bullying, cyberbullying occurs when the Internet, mobile phones and other devices are used to deliberately and repeatedly hurt or embarrass targets.
- Gaslighting is a label for a form of psychological abuse whereby the target is manipulated so they'll question their judgements and perceptions.
- Hazing is also called bastardisation and initiation, and it refers to rituals and challenges involving abuse and humiliation used to induct a person into a group.
- Managing out aims to make the targeted employee's work life intolerable so they'll decide to leave.
- Whistle-blowers can suffer significant mental health, physical, social and economic consequences as a result of making a complaint.

- Regulatory processes can be misused to bully doctors, nurses, dentists, allied health workers and other professionals.
- The language used to describe bullying in a complaint needs to strike a balance between toning down the concerns to the point where it downplays their seriousness and a highly emotionally-charged approach that alienates everyone from the beginning and which encourages aggressive responses.

3

WHAT ISN'T BULLYING

Unhappiness at work isn't always caused by bullying

Working out whether bullying has happened or not is difficult and sometimes impossible.

Workplace health and safety authorities say that reasonable management actions carried out in a fair way aren't bullying. But they don't say anything about when management actions are unreasonable and unfair, therefore justifying them to be called bullying, but passed off by management as reasonable and fair. In this chapter the difficulties for employees and employers in distinguishing non-bullying behaviours from bullying is discussed.

It's common for employees to confuse activities and behaviours that are normal, reasonable and legitimate management actions with bullying.[1] Complicating matters is the fact that defensive employers and those accused of bullying often claim when allegations of bullying are made that the behaviour wasn't bullying but normal, reasonable and legitimate management action. Further, often employers call alleged bullying a 'clash of personalities' or 'a difference of opinion' when it's really bullying. Sometimes they genuinely don't know the difference. But it can also be part of an intentional strategy to cover up the problem by downgrading a complaint to a less serious matter.

Workplace bullying is a breach of occupational health and safety law. An employer may incur fines, legal costs, internal investigation expenses, compensation payouts, increased workers' compensation insurance premiums and reputational damage. It's not hard to appreciate, therefore, why some employers might favour a cheaper-to-deal-with 'personality clash' or a simple 'difference of opinion' involving a few confidential mediation sessions between the parties. Also, because the employer has acted on the problem, it creates an impression that they're treating the matter seriously, even though the action taken may not fit the problem.

TRIVIAL COMPLAINTS

In 2011 there were 6000 complaints to WorkSafe Victoria about workplace bullying. This was an exceptional number attributed by WorkSafe to news coverage of a high-profile bullying case where the victim took their own life. Graphic descriptions in news media reporting on the types of extreme bullying involved in this case didn't seem to deter people from making complaints to WorkSafe about the most trivial of workplace matters.

At the time, only 10 per cent of the 6000 complaints received by WorkSafe were referred to its bullying response unit because, they said, the majority fell well short of what constitutes workplace bullying under the law. Of these referrals, just one in 10 resulted in a WorkSafe inspector visiting a workplace to investigate the complaint.

A WorkSafe representative responded at the time that the term bullying was being used loosely in the community, in many instances to describe something that has 'gone against me' or 'that I haven't liked' or something that 'I haven't wanted to do'. As a result, he added, there was a mismatch between what's being labelled bullying and what would really constitute bullying under the Occupational Health and Safety Act.[2] The WorkSafe representative provided the following examples from WorkSafe's files:

- A construction worker was involved in a physical altercation with his supervisor after a discussion about poor work performance. The supervisor suffered facial injuries and the worker was sacked on the spot. The worker alleged his termination was bullying and unfair because the manager deserved a punch in the face.
- A retail worker was caught by her manager stealing money from the cash register and was sacked and reported to police. The worker admitted theft, but said that being sacked and reported to police was bullying.
- A freight and logistics worker had been working the same shifts for two years when the employer implemented rotating shifts for all staff. The worker said he would prefer to retain his shifts, but was told he needed to move to the rotating roster. He alleged that he was being singled out.

In 2013 Commissioner Cloghan of the Fair Work Commission issued a caution regarding the misuse of bullying complaints, placing a relatively high threshold on whether workplace bullying exists. He said:

> *The Commission should guard against creating a workplace environment of excessive sensitivity to every misplaced word or conduct. The workplace comprises of persons of different ages, workplace experience and personalities — not divine angels. Employers are required to pursue inappropriate behaviour but need to be mindful that every employee who claims to have been hurt, embarrassed or humiliated does not automatically mean that the offending employee is guilty of bullying and gross misconduct.*[3]

According to WorkSafe Victoria, generally an employee's dissatisfaction or grievances with their organisation's management practices by themselves aren't workplace bullying. A worker may experience job dissatisfaction, feel undervalued or inappropriately treated at work, but this doesn't mean that they're actually being bullied.[4] WorkSafe doesn't say, however, that feelings of dissatisfaction can also be the consequence of bullying.

WorkSafe Victoria says that reasonable management actions carried out in a fair way aren't bullying, such as:

- allocating work and setting performance goals, standards and deadlines
- restructuring the organisation and changing work responsibilities
- informing and warning a worker about unsatisfactory work performance or behaviour
- undertaking performance management processes and providing constructive feedback.

Part of the solution to the problem of employees misinterpreting legitimate and reasonable management practice for bullying is to have a clear, documented indication of what bullying is and what it's not.[5] While this makes sense, a difficulty is that almost every so-called reasonable management action can be manipulated or camouflaged to bully a worker, a point that appears continually lost in the literature and advice provided by regulators and employers. Each of the four legitimate management actions used above as examples by WorkSafe Victoria can be manipulated to punish, inconvenience, pressure or make the employee look bad in relation to their work performance or conduct.

BULLYING ISN'T CONFLICT

Referred to earlier was the practice of employers attempting to resolve workplace bullying with conflict resolution strategies, including mediation, either with a professional mediator or the employer or their representative, such as a manager, acting as mediator. Both bullying and personality clashes have an undesirable effect in the workplace and should be dealt with promptly to improve staff morale, emotional safety and productivity. But bullying isn't a conflict-based personality difference implying fault on both sides. Therefore, the ways that bullying and conflict should be dealt with are different due to the different dynamics involved.[6]

Generally, the person being bullied has nothing to do with, nor can avoid, being targeted. Bullying UK says that if an employee is being systematically belittled, excluded or intimidated, they're not just clashing with someone — it's bullying.[7]

Research on workplace bullying commissioned by 24-hour telephone crisis support agency Beyond Blue found that mediation is often misused and overused as a strategy to address the problem of bullying and can exacerbate the situation, particularly when an imbalance of power already exists.[8] Founders of the US Workplace Bullying Institute Dr Ruth Namie and Dr Gary Namie state categorically that bullying is a form of violence and should never be mediated.[9] They say that it doesn't work for domestic violence, which is similar to workplace abuse in several ways, and it compromises those who've already been compromised.

Australian human rights lawyer Kathryn-Magnolia Feeley emphasises that bullying isn't about a difference of opinion at work. She says that bullying ostracises, marginalises, demeans, intimidates, threatens and injures the employee to the extent that they doubt their self-worth and their ability to function.[10] She adds that given that commonly workplace bullying is an abuse of an employee's greater power over another, mediation simply provides a bully with the opportunity to escalate their bullying and exacerbate their target's distress.

Professor Loraleigh Keashly, from Wayne State University in Detroit in the US, is an expert in dispute resolution, with many books and professional journal articles on the subject to her credit. She highlights mediation's shortcomings with respect to workplace bullying as follows:

- There's clearly a power imbalance in bullying cases; one person is a victim and the other isn't.
- One party is unable to defend themselves and because the victim was severely compromised beforehand, mediation's attempts to meet in the middle disempowers them even further.
- Mediation doesn't punish past behaviours, so the victim can't gain justice for the harm they've already suffered.
- Because in mediation procedures are kept confidential, other members of the organisation can't learn about the evidence presented which prevents organisational progress in reducing bullying.[11]

Additionally, employees and alleged bullies can find themselves in a quandary if they refuse to participate in an employer-initiated solution that involves mediation. Employees who report bullying but then refuse to participate in efforts at resolution will likely be accused of being obstructive or not serious about their complaint. An alleged bully's refusal to participate in mediation may be interpreted as them having something to hide when, in fact, they may simply be disputing that they've done anything wrong.

Mediation has been criticised as being tied to HR-led solutions which means that it's not the ideal solution for bullying.[12] It's argued universally that HR denies that bullying exists within their organisational culture. Instead they use options that make it appear that they're doing something, such as mediation, but in reality they're simply disguising the problem which makes victims more powerless and lets the perpetrator get away with their mistreatment. There's more about this in Chapter 13 Don't Trust HR!

JOB DISSATISFACTION

Although being targeted for bullying is a major cause of an employee's unhappiness at work, being unhappy at work doesn't necessarily mean that the cause is bullying.

There's no such thing as the perfect job and workers require a certain amount of tolerance and resilience to manage the everyday rigours of work life, including unpleasant aspects of their jobs. Most jobs have dissatisfying parts, and each worker must decide what individual job satisfaction factors are important for their quality of work life.

The factors contributing to a satisfying job vary for different employees. The most common job satisfaction factors relate to job content, supervision, financial rewards, promotion opportunities, co-workers, company and management, health and safety, job security and hours of work.[13] A worker doesn't have to have a high level of satisfaction with each of these factors to be satisfied overall with their job, just the ones that are particularly important to them.

For example, an employee with considerable financial commitments may be more concerned with their job's salary and security than a worker with fewer financial obligations. A highly-skilled and experienced worker may value working independently rather than be closely supervised, whereas an inexperienced worker lacking confidence may value greater supervision and support.

Also impacting on employees' job satisfaction are personal factors including age, abilities, training for the job, personality, occupational level, ethnicity, culture, community, needs and values.

Examples of dissatisfying aspects of jobs which may not qualify as bullying include:

- a belief that you're being underpaid
- feeling unappreciated
- a disorganised supervisor

- working with staff you don't like
- working with staff who don't like you
- an aloof supervisor or colleague
- loss of privileges/bonuses
- regular performance evaluation
- changes to the organisation
- feeling insecure during organisational change
- changes to work responsibilities
- being asked or not asked to work overtime
- departure of close colleagues
- incompetent, unco-operative or lazy co-workers
- having requests for time off refused
- being caught up in office politics
- increases in workload through absenteeism, resignations or terminations
- feeling excluded from social conversations at work
- being relocated to another office, section or region
- receiving constructive criticism
- being disciplined for poor work performance/tardiness/making a serious mistake
- being asked to do tasks that are demeaning/below your position
- physically unpleasant work environment
- being overlooked for promotion
- not being invited to the office party
- having to travel a long way to work.

The difference, however, between bullying behaviour and non-bullying behaviour isn't always obvious and, as indicated earlier, many of the dissatisfying aspects of jobs listed above can be manipulated or camouflaged to bully employees. Additionally, some dissatisfying aspects of jobs can be the result of poor management rather than bullying. They may still need to be addressed by the employer, especially if they impact on workplace safety or productivity, but not necessarily within a workplace bullying problem-solving framework.

All employees must decide what their level of tolerance is for working conditions that they don't like. Maintaining a high level of job dissatisfaction is likely to result eventually in mental and physical health problems for employees, a negative impact on their work performance, as well as an adverse impact on their life outside of work, especially with personal relationships. Leaving the job may be an option, but it isn't always a convenient option (see Chapter 20 Toughing It Out).

The possibility of changing unsavoury aspects of a job or resolving problems through discussion with management should be considered. This option may not be realistic in every instance. Consulting a professional counsellor may help to get to the bottom of why an employee is unhappy at work when the reasons are not obvious (see Chapter 18 Counselling).

BLAMING THE VICTIM

Some employers and co-workers who are accused of bullying resort to the 'he/she's got personal problems' excuse, which is a blame-the-victim or fault-the-victim defence. This implies that an employee's grievance is prompted by over-sensitivity created by their personal problems and stresses originating away from the workplace rather than by anything the employer or anyone else at work has done.

Worries from outside the workplace invariably impact to varying degrees on an employee's ability to experience happiness at work and their capacity to do their job well. Employers can't ignore a troubled employee's deteriorating work performance when it results in:

- reduced productivity and quality of work
- poor reliability
- friction with other employees including bullying co-workers
- negative impact on staff morale
- workplace accidents through forgetfulness/lack of concentration

- inappropriate behaviour at the workplace
- increased absenteeism.

Some employers still believe that their employees should keep their work lives and personal lives separate. But workers aren't robots and the old employer's mantra 'keep your family problems at home' is obsolete in modern workplaces. In Chapter 22 Respectful Workplaces, dealing with employees' personal problems is discussed. A worker's personal problems, however, are neither a justification for bullying them nor an excuse when it happens.

In Australia, case law is that an employee's previous mental or physical condition caused by life issues not related directly to work are not a defence against bullying when bullying has aggravated a pre-existing condition.[14] In other words, if it can be established that workplace bullying has been significant, substantial and the major cause of the employee's present mental and/or physical condition, then pre-existing personal problems aren't a defence by the alleged bully or employer.

Exceptions are when the employee's present mental and/or physical health condition has been aggravated by their failure to obtain a promotion or benefit in connection with their employment.

Kathryn-Magnolia Feeley's *Workplace Bullying Lawyer's Guide* is a helpful general reference on the legal aspects of workplace bullying, and particularly the section 'Disease' (pp. 43–44) for a more detailed explanation of the issues discussed in this section.[15]

UNINTENTIONAL BULLYING

In the previous chapter the idea of 'unintentional bullying' was introduced. Given that many writers in this field emphasise that bullying behaviour is predatory and intentional, 'unintentional bullying' appears to be a contradiction of terms.

In *Business Ethics* magazine, Gael O'Brien explains the idea of 'unintentional bullying' being about a perpetrator's personality — namely their lack of self-awareness, poor emotional intelligence, excessive passion, assertiveness or forceful expression.[16] The article says that some people don't always hear how they sound to other people when they come across as confronting and angry and they can be surprised when their behaviour is called bullying.

A person may call someone derogatory names, for example, without any appreciation that the target finds it offensive. Some people have little appreciation of where good humour stops and insensitivity begins. As a consequence, it's common for perpetrators to dismiss concerns about their behaviour as the claimant having a 'thin skin'.[17]

A lack of understanding about what bullying is and its serious impact on targets is a major cause of so-called unintentional bullying. A study of more than 5500 workers from over 70 organisations in England found little evidence that people who engage in bullying behaviour are doing so deliberately to harm the recipient.[18] Management consultants Caitlin Buon and Tony Buon maintain that their work in investigating or mediating allegations of bullying and harassment found the majority of bullying experienced by employees is unintended.[19] While acknowledging the presence of some individuals who are predatory with a desire to harm their targets, they claim that the majority who are accused of bullying are unaware of the true impact of their behaviour on others.

However, one of the main difficulties in establishing the intentions of alleged bullies is their reluctance to confess wrongdoing. More likely is a rigorous defence with the following responses common:

- outright denial, that is, 'it never happened'
- saying the alleged bullying was reasonable management action
- portraying the complainant as difficult to get on with
- turning the tables and claiming the complainant is the bully

- saying the complainant is over-sensitive caused by their personal problems
- saying the claimant has misunderstood the situation
- saying if the claimant is upset; it wasn't intentional.

In later chapters the manipulation skills of serial bullies are highlighted. Often managers, who comprise most bullies, are adept at quoting workplace health and safety and other organisational policies and using bureaucratic language to confuse claimants and portray themselves as innocent of bullying accusations. Generally, managers can connect with and charm senior management and external investigators better than the distressed subordinates who are their bullying targets.

As indicated earlier, confounding the issue of intentions is that most complaints about bullying may fall short of what constitutes workplace bullying under the law. It would follow, therefore, that the majority of those accused of bullying may be innocent and their claims about not intentionally trying to harm a complainant are true. This context provides considerable scope for individuals who genuinely desire to harm their targets to claim unintentionality and be believed.

The Australian Fair Work Commission says that it's bullying when:

> ...a person or group repeatedly behaves unreasonably towards a worker or group at work and the behaviour must create a risk to health and safety.[20]

In this definition there's no reference to the perpetrator's intention, just the outcome — the creation of *a risk to health and safety*. Proving bullying is difficult, however, and because defendants can be more skilled at presenting their case than their targets, a claimant will need to be able to establish through documented records that there's been a pattern of mistreatment over time which breaches occupational health and safety laws.

In Chapter 15 Preparing a Complaint, the importance of a complainant keeping a detailed record of alleged mistreatment is emphasised, including the event, place, time, date and witnesses. In genuine cases of bullying, it will be more difficult for those accused to claim that their bullying behaviour was unintentional when the claimant's detailed evidence of a pattern of mistreatment is presented convincingly.

WHAT DOES 'REASONABLE' MEAN?

The various Australian definitions of workplace bullying contain the word 'reasonable' in the context of assessing whether bullying has happened or not. Although it's clearly an important term, no one provides a clear explanation of what 'reasonable' means. It's one of those terms like 'common sense' that we take for granted; we never ask what it means when it's being used, for example, 'use your common sense'.

When we tell someone to use their common sense there's an assumption that they think exactly like us and use the same criteria to make a sound judgement. However, people's capacity for sound judgement varies considerably because they're influenced by a wide range of factors. They include their age, gender, culture, education, socioeconomic circumstances, life experiences, state of mind, state of health, emotional intelligence, confidence, self-esteem, etc. It would be silly, therefore, to expect someone else to use the same decision-making criteria as us to make a judgement, even on a matter where we think the conclusion or answer seem obvious.

Much of this type of reasoning also applies to the issue of what's reasonable or unreasonable. For example, the Australian Fair Work Ombudsman says:

> ...for behaviour to be considered unreasonable it depends on whether a reasonable person might see the behaviour as unreasonable in the circumstances.[21]

The Fair Work Ombudsman continues:

> *...reasonable management action that's carried out in a reasonable way isn't bullying and that management action that isn't carried out in a reasonable way may be considered bullying.*

WorkSafe Victoria says:

> *...reasonable management actions carried out in a fair way are not bullying.*[22]

But what does reasonable mean in this context? If an employee believes that they're being bullied, how do they establish if there's a reasonable basis for their concerns? How does an employer know if there are reasonable grounds for the employee's concerns? Importantly, who and where is a reasonable person who can provide unbiased advice on such matters?

The Merriam-Webster online dictionary defines a reasonable person as:

> *...a fictional person with an ordinary degree of reason, prudence, care, foresight or intelligence whose conduct, conclusion, or expectation in relation to a particular circumstance or fact is used as an objective standard by which to measure or determine something such as the existence of negligence in law.*[23]

According to this definition, reasonable or unreasonable behaviour comprises actions that a reasonable person in the same circumstances would see as reasonable or unreasonable. Sometimes this is referred to as the *reasonable person test*. It has some principles in common with the *pub test*, except in the pub test the reasonable person's capacity for sound judgement may be impaired by the quantity of alcohol consumed, potentially making the pub test less reliable.

Almost certainly when an employee complains about being bullied at work, the alleged bully will see their accuser's concerns as unreasonable. But is the bully a reasonable person in this situation? They have a lot to lose if they accept the allegations against them as reasonable. Therefore, this raises another question — can a reasonable person be biased? For example, can an employer's judgement in an internal investigation of an employee's bullying complaint be considered reasonable if the employer's good reputation could be tainted, or if they're at risk of incurring considerable legal expenses if the allegations are proven?

If it's still not clear, take some comfort from the fact that *Wikipedia*, normally the go-to reference for non-experts, commences its entry to *reasonable person* with:

> *This section may be too technical for most readers to understand. Please help improve it to make it understandable to non-experts...*[24]

John Ventura's *Law for Dummies*, another favourite for non-experts, uses the term without explanation.[25]

Employees who believe they're being bullied at work should seek advice from their union, their State's workplace health and safety regulator, Fair Work Australia or a lawyer. They're more likely to be reasonable than the alleged bully or employer. Read Chapter 13 Don't Trust HR! before consulting someone from the human resources department about bullying matters.

———

SUMMARY

- It's difficult for employees and employers to tell apart what's bullying from what's not.
- Most concerns employees have about being bullied at work aren't bullying, according to occupational health and safety law.
- Some employers downgrade complaints about bullying to a less serious problem to avoid costs, protect against possible litigation and to protect their reputation.
- While employers may use a blame-the-victim defence, according to Australian case law, an employee's previous mental or physical condition caused by life issues not related directly to work is not a defence against bullying.
- A person's intent is not the main determinant of whether bullying has taken place or not; it's whether the behaviour has caused a risk to another's health and safety according to occupational health and safety law.

4

BULLYING BEHAVIOURS

Bullying is a pattern of mistreatment

Bullying is when a person or group repeatedly behaves unreasonably towards a worker or group at work and it creates a risk to their health and safety. It takes many forms. The list presented here is just a sample.

A single instance of one of the behaviours listed wouldn't fit the definition of bullying, but if it's one of a range of bullying behaviours used to mistreat an employee over a period of time, it could be bullying. 'Dan's' experience is an example.

'Dan'

Travis, one of Dan's co-workers at the warehouse, intentionally drove a forklift at Dan and veered away at the last moment. This, by itself, was highly dangerous and intimidatory behaviour and would normally warrant discipline for misconduct or even dismissal but, in this instance, Dan didn't report it to management. Travis, however, engaged in other intimidating activities that formed a pattern of bullying behaviours which created a clear risk to Dan's health and safety. Examples included:

• While Dan was seated eating his lunch, Travis swung a heavy iron bar at his head then stopped just a few centimetres away.

• He regularly parked his car up against Dan's car so that Dan couldn't drive away after work.

• He would intentionally block Dan's way in the corridor and glare at him menacingly.

• He put a rotting fish in Dan's locker.

• He hid Dan's daily work schedule.

• He took Dan's lunch from the fridge and threw it in the garbage.

• He called Dan derogatory names to his face and behind his back.

• He enlisted co-workers to join the abuse (mobbing).

• He stalked Dan in the car park and threatened to kill him when Dan said he would report the bullying.

While Dan's unfortunate circumstance is a clear-cut example of bullying, most bullying isn't as clear cut. As indicated in the last chapter, it's common for employees to confuse activities and behaviours that are normal and reasonable management actions with bullying. By itself, a decision that hasn't gone an employee's way may not qualify as bullying. For example, rejection of a suggestion or refusal to approve preferred annual leave time. Something that has not met with the approval of an employee may not be bullying. For example, a change to a work roster or changes to responsibilities. Something that the employee didn't want to do may not be bullying. For example, being relocated to another part of the workplace or being directed to do an unpleasant task.

If over a period, however, there's been a clear pattern of seemingly poor treatment directed towards an employee, then it could be bullying through victimisation. For example, a succession of decisions going against them, or being allocated multiple unpleasant tasks that other staff in equal positions haven't been asked to do.

It's important, however, before jumping to any conclusions that they're being bullied and making a formal complaint, that an employee consults an independent authority for advice, such as their State's health and safety regulator, trade union or a lawyer.

Because of the confusion about what bullying is and what it isn't, a relatively large sample of bullying behaviours is provided. The list, however, doesn't take into account the unique circumstances of individual employees. Readers must make their own assessment of its relevance for their purposes and should obtain any appropriate professional guidance before taking action. Advice from books, including this one, and the Internet should always be combined with individual guidance from informed people familiar with an employee's personal circumstances such as a general practitioner, counsellor, trade union representative, workplace health and safety authority or lawyer.

Bullying openly

The following are examples:

- humiliating the target through criticising, shouting or swearing at them
- constantly nit-picking the target with unjustified criticisms
- making unfounded comments or threats about the target's job security
- falsely accusing the target of making mistakes
- excessive and unwarranted supervision of the target

- giving impossible deadlines, undue interruptions, last-minute requests
- underworking the target to make them feel not needed
- sending the target critical/insulting emails
- unnecessarily copying in the emails to other staff, including management, to undermine the target's reputation
- falsely accusing the target of workplace misconduct
- giving the target demeaning tasks or ones not relevant to their position level
- changing the target's work responsibilities, roster or work location to inconvenience them
- undermining or deliberately impeding the target's work
- criticising the target while withholding constructive feedback or deserved praise
- allocating the target excessively awkward or repetitive tasks to deliberately make their job boring or less satisfying
- withholding necessary resources such as information, tools and equipment so the target will struggle or fail
- allocating tasks that are beyond the physical ability or experience of the target
- making the target do humiliating or inappropriate things as part of an initiation
- constantly changing work guidelines
- belittling the target's opinions
- making fun of, criticising or disadvantaging the target based on their ethnicity, culture, gender, age, religious beliefs, sexual disposition, stature, physical disability/state of health, lack of education, etc.*
- making inappropriate sexual advances to the target*
- using aggressive behaviour with the target such as banging the desk, slamming the door, finger pointing, standing over, getting 'in their face', throwing or smashing things in a rage
- stalking, for example pestering, following, lurking with the intention of causing the target discomfort/distress

- threatening the target with physical violence or inflicting actual violence
- engaging in uninvited physical contact with the target*
- making disparaging comments about the target's family members
- greeting or farewelling others, but not the target
- using 'ambush' meetings to discuss performance concerns with the target where the agenda is more serious than portrayed beforehand or having more people/managers present than was previously indicated to the target
- using humour that is vulgar/in poor taste in front of the target
- intimidating the target during meetings to discuss their bullying complaints by outnumbering them with management and/or legal personnel
- criticising or disciplining the target but allowing other staff to get away with the same thing
- manipulating disciplinary processes to pressure or manage out the target
- giving the target the silent treatment
- teasing or mocking the target
- excluding the target from work social functions such as lunches, drinks, parties and staff farewells.

*Note: These behaviours may be in breach of discrimination law.

Bullying stealthily

Examples include:

- taking credit for the target's work achievements or ideas
- bad-mouthing the target to management and other employees with baseless criticisms
- spreading or condoning gossip, rumours and innuendo about the target
- threatening other employees who are supporters of the target

- discouraging co-workers from social interaction with the target
- making false poor-performance entries in the target's personnel file
- manipulating a performance-improvement plan so the target fails
- invading the privacy of the target by prying into their emails or personal belongings
- without justification, blocking the target's applications for annual leave, promotion and training
- compelling the target to be assessed by an occupational psychiatrist and/or physician, including on multiple occasions, with the aim of eventually acquiring an unfit-for-work medical report and/or as part of the process of pressuring the employee to resign (managing out)
- colluding with other staff, including management, to get rid of the target
- boasting to other workers about sexual encounters with the target
- betraying the target's confidences to other workers, including management
- unwarranted monitoring of the target's telephone conversations and emails
- tampering with the target's personal belongings or work equipment
- damaging or stealing the target's personal property.

The workplace incivility literature includes many of the behaviours listed above, but has a range of additional behaviours consistent with the following definition:

Workplace incivility involves seemingly inconsequential, low intensity behaviours that are rude, disrespectful, discourteous or insensitive where the intent to harm is ambiguous or unclear and where manner and body language set the tone for how the words are interpreted.[1]

Examples include verbal and non-verbal behaviours, such as:

- sarcasm
- eye-rolling
- smirking in disapproval
- head shaking and other judgemental body language
- dismissive sounds
- disrupting meetings by arriving late
- asking for input, then ignoring it
- having side conversations during meetings
- constantly interrupting during meetings
- interrupting conversations
- inappropriately changing the subject
- adopting a belittling attitude
- answering phone calls during meetings, sending texts and emails, using Facebook, Twitter, etc.
- walking away from a conversation without explanation.

Incivility is in the eyes of the target and varies from person to person, but is also influenced by culture, generation, gender, industry and organisation. What an employee considers uncivil behaviour may differ from what a co-worker or their manager thinks. Often incivility is not considered bullying at all, but rather just part of the rough and tumble of everyday work life.[2] Because of the ambiguity of most uncivil behaviours, the intention to harm is difficult to prove despite the target experiencing the behaviour as rude, disrespectful or hurtful. Complicating matters is that much uncivil behaviour is associated with commonly accepted personality traits such as bluntness, grumpiness, moodiness and sarcasm.[3] Therefore, when complaints are made by employees about uncivil behaviour, often there are unsupportive responses such as:

- He's a grumpy old bugger; just ignore him.
- She's under a lot of pressure right now.
- Don't let it bother you so much.
- Try to keep it in perspective.
- You're over-sensitive.
- Just get on with it and stop whinging.

Despite workplace incivility continuing to be seen at the so-called milder end of the workplace bullying spectrum, or not bullying at all, research on the subject reveals that it may have the same negative impacts on targets as bullying occurring at the so-called more serious end of the bullying scale. More about this appears in the following chapter, Impact on Targets.

Given the difficulties in proving that bullying has happened, an employee who believes that they've been targeted and who wants to lodge a formal complaint with their employer or external authorities will need to provide a detailed record of their alleged bullying, including a description of each bullying event, the time, date and names of witnesses. I say more about this in Chapter 15 Preparing a Complaint.

Information provided in this chapter is a guide only and does not consider the wide range of factors that might have a bearing on a target's unique circumstances.

SUMMARY

- Most bullying isn't clear cut, which can lead employees to think they're being bullied when they're not, and employers to confuse bullying behaviours with reasonable management actions.
- When there's a clear pattern of victimisation such as decisions regularly going against an employee or being given unpleasant tasks that other staff in equal positions aren't given, then it could be bullying.
- Before jumping to any conclusions about bullying, an employee should consult an independent authority such as their State's health and safety regulator, trade union or a lawyer.
- Workplace incivility involves seemingly inconsequential, low-intensity behaviours that are rude, disrespectful, discourteous or insensitive where the intent to harm is ambiguous or unclear.
- Because of the ambiguity of most uncivil behaviours, the intention to harm is difficult to prove.
- Employers and managers not familiar with the serious consequences of incivility may see the behaviour as inconsequential.
- Research on workplace incivility reveals that it has the same negative impacts on targets as other forms of bullying.
- If an employee wants to lodge a formal complaint about bullying, they'll need to provide a detailed record including a description of each bullying event, the time, date and names of witnesses.

5

IMPACT ON TARGETS

The effects of bullying can creep into every part of a worker's life

Workplace bullying impacts on the health and well-being of employees in many ways. The experience of being a witness to bullying can also be a traumatic experience.[1]

Many of the psychological symptoms listed below are related to stress, anxiety and depression. Physical and social symptoms are also included. The list has been compiled from the literature on workplace bullying and my work over many years providing support to employees who've been bullied. It includes the results from the more than 50 one-to-one interviews I conducted with employees who'd been bullied at work.

Psychological

- distress
- humiliation
- loss of confidence and self-esteem
- feeling constantly on edge
- inability to stop thinking about the situation
- poor concentration

- bursting into tears regularly
- feeling irritable
- depression
- post-trauma stress
- difficulties with memory
- panic attacks
- fear of leaving safety of home (agoraphobia)
- sleeping excessively to escape distressing thoughts
- homicidal thoughts about killing the bully and/or the bully having a grisly death
- suicidal thoughts and attempts to suicide
- difficulty trusting others
- ongoing anger.

Physical

- major changes in eating patterns resulting in weight gain or loss
- stomach aches
- tension headaches
- skin reactions
- shaking and palpitations
- back and neck pain
- vomiting and dry retching
- frequent illness
- increased tiredness
- loss of sleep
- nightmares
- sexual dysfunction
- hair loss
- cardiovascular and gastrointestinal disease
- overuse of alcohol and tobacco
- abuse of prescribed and over-the-counter medication
- dependence on illegal drugs.

Work and Social

- damage to reputation
- isolation from work colleagues
- deterioration of work performance
- loss of commitment to work/the organisation
- intentional or unintentional decrease in work effort
- work accidents through concentration loss
- increase in mistake-making
- reduction in positive risk-taking
- loss of creativity and problem-solving
- adopting getting-even tactics
- taking out frustration on co-workers, customers, clients and patients
- involvement with the justice system such as convictions, fines and custodial sentences
- vandalising the workplace, stealing
- physical assault of the bully
- problems with relationships outside work
- loss of interest in outside-work activities
- job loss and loss of income
- unemployment
- inability to pay bills/maintain assets.

STRESS, ANXIETY AND DEPRESSION

Stress, anxiety and depression can be inseparable for people who experience serious bullying at work. A brief outline of each is included below:

Stress — some form of stress is normal and can be a motivator to get things achieved, but for most people this type of stress is temporary. It's when stress is excessive, prolonged and builds up such as with workplace bullying that it may lead to anxiety and depression along with various physical ailments or medical conditions.

Anxiety — the causes of anxiety disorders are complex, but are thought to originate from genetic, environmental, psychological and developmental factors. When a person has a genetic predisposition to anxiety disorders, the excessive stress from workplace bullying can hasten the onset.

Some degree of anxiety is normal, but it's when it becomes prolonged that it can become a serious problem.

For a person to be diagnosed with an anxiety disorder, their fear or anxiety needs to be out of proportion to the situation that they're reacting to or incompatible with their age. In his book *Anxiety*, psychiatrist Dr Mark Cross, who has suffered from anxiety most of his life, says that in Australia anxiety is common, with around 11 per cent (2.6 million) of the population reporting anxiety-related conditions.[2] He says that anxiety accounts for the majority of mental health conditions. The most common anxiety disorders are outlined briefly below:

- *Generalised anxiety disorder* — continually worried about something bad happening. Affecting more women than men. Can come on at any time, be overwhelming and can lead to a panic attack. It causes a distraction from the sufferer's day-to-day activities. Physical symptoms include insomnia, stomach aches, restlessness and fatigue.
- *Panic disorder* — most often referred to as panic attacks, people with the condition describe being overtaken by powerful feelings of physical and psychological distress, mostly without warning. Women are more prone to panic disorders than men. Symptoms include palpitations, pounding heart, rapid heart rate, chest pain, sweating, trembling/shaking, feeling of shortness of breath/smothering sensations, dizziness/light-headedness, feeling of choking, numbness/tingling, chills/hot flushes, nausea, and abdominal pains.
- *Post-Traumatic Stress Disorder (PTSD)* — caused by

personally experiencing or witnessing highly distressing life events. Initially associated with traumatic stress experienced by soldiers at the front line. First called shell shock, then battle fatigue and now PTSD. *DSM-5* (*Diagnostic and Statistical Manual of Mental Disorders*) includes it under Trauma- and Stressor-Related Disorders. Symptoms include flashbacks to the causal events, acute anxiety, nightmares, uncontrollable thinking, social withdrawal and hyper-vigilance.

- *Social anxiety disorder* — fear of being seen negatively or humiliated by others in social or performance situations. People with the condition can feel overwhelmed with worry and self-consciousness about everyday social situations. In severe cases, people avoid social situations altogether.

- *Agoraphobia* — fear of open or crowded places. Sufferers experience panic attacks when exposed to these situations. It can lead to their being terrified to leave their house.

- *Obsessive compulsive disorder* — OCD is a personality disorder that's characterised by extreme perfectionism, order and neatness. People with OCD feel a strong need to impose their own standards on their outside environment.

- *Compulsive hoarding* — characterised by collecting many possessions with ongoing difficulty in disposing of them regardless of their value. Hoarders can amass so many possessions that their homes can become difficult to live in through lack of space.

- *Specific phobias* — extreme fear associated with objects and situations usually triggered by the feared object or situation. Common phobias include fear of the dark, being confined in small spaces, flying (planes), heights, spiders, reptiles, failure, public speaking, and many others. On the website fearof.net there's a list of 100 phobias suggesting that there are many things people are afraid of.

- *Illness anxiety* — sometimes called hypochondriasis or health anxiety, sufferers worry excessively that they are or may become seriously ill. While they may not have any major physical symptoms, they believe that normal body sensations or minor symptoms are signs of severe illness, even though a thorough medical examination may not reveal a serious medical condition.

Depression — a common but serious medical condition that negatively affects how a person feels, thinks and acts. It causes feelings of sadness and/or a loss of interest in activities previously enjoyed. It can lead to a range of emotional and physical problems and can reduce a person's ability to function at work, home and elsewhere.

Symptoms of depression can range from mild to severe and include:

- Feelings of sadness, tearfulness, emptiness or hopelessness
- Angry outbursts, irritability or frustration, even over small matters
- Loss of interest or pleasure in most or all normal activities, such as sex, hobbies or sports
- Sleep disturbances, including insomnia or sleeping too much
- Tiredness and lack of energy, so even small tasks take extra effort
- Reduced appetite and weight loss or increased cravings for food and weight gain
- Anxiety, agitation or restlessness
- Slowed thinking, speaking or body movements
- Feelings of worthlessness or guilt, fixating on past failures or self-blame
- Trouble thinking, concentrating, making decisions and remembering things
- Frequent or recurrent thoughts of death, suicidal thoughts, suicide attempts or suicide
- Unexplained physical problems, such as back pain and headaches.[3]

A diagnosis of clinical depression requires five or more of the above symptoms to persist over a two-week period causing clinically important distress or impairing work, social or personal functioning with depressed mood or decreased interest or pleasure as one of the five. Like most mental and physical health conditions, there's a spectrum that ranges from minor to major.

Many employees who are targets of bullying resign from their jobs eventually, but many stay. Katherine Williams, social worker and author of *Workplace Bullying: A Survival Guide*, recommends that the safest option for targets of bullying who are struggling to cope with their mental health is to find another job as quickly as possible.[4] But for many, this isn't a realistic option. In Chapter 20 Toughing It Out, there's a long list of reasons why employees remain in their jobs and endure bullying.

Most of the bullied employees I interviewed reported symptoms of depression and/or post-traumatic stress disorder. Some remained in their bullying workplaces with their mistreatment continuing. Irrespective of whether they left or stayed, they reported the same basic PTSD symptoms. Only a third had sought treatment such as medication or counselling.

As this wasn't an in-depth study of bullying's impact on mental health, there was no comparison of the differences between those who left and those who stayed. Irrespective of whether targets of bullying leave or remain in their workplaces, however, if left untreated their mental health is likely to deteriorate over time.

Some of those I interviewed, for example, were left with a long-term incapacity to work. This was particularly the case for older employees close to the end of their working lives suffering anxiety and depression, and lacking confidence, self-esteem and trust after their ordeal, and knowing that most likely they would face rejection by an ageist employment market. It also applied to employees with a pre-existing mental health condition, many of whom appeared to have the capacity to cope well with the pressures of their work if left to it, but struggled when they were seriously mistreated.

As former local government employee 'Anna', 63, explained:

It's hard enough to get a job when you're my age, let alone when you wear the emotional scarring from your bullying like a flashing sign on your forehead. In my interview for a new job, I broke down when they asked me why I left my old job. I wasn't offered the job. It was clear they saw me as a risk.

The information provided in this chapter is general information only and not a diagnostic tool for mental health conditions that may be caused or exacerbated by workplace bullying. Information and advice from books, including this one, and the Internet should always be combined with individual guidance from qualified professionals such as a general practitioner and a qualified counsellor.

Consulting a GP is an important first step in seeking support for stress, anxiety and depression.

SUMMARY

- Workplace bullying is the cause of a wide range of psychological, physical and social problems.
- For many people workplace bullying is the worst or among the worst experiences of their lives.
- Common psychological consequences are stress, anxiety and depression.
- Common physical consequences are headaches, sleeplessness and gaining/losing weight.
- Common work/social symptoms are reputation damage, relationship problems and poor work performance.
- A good starting point for employees who are worried about their mental health is a consultation with their GP.

COSTS FOR EMPLOYERS

The serious impact that bullying has on workers is only one part of the problem

The serious impact of bullying on employers is presented in this chapter.

Over the last 10 years Australian authorities have produced a range of estimates about the serious impact of workplace bullying on employers and the economy. The Australian Government's House Standing Committee on Education and Employment, for example, estimated that workplace bullying cost the economy up to $36 billion annually.[1]

Safe Work Australia reported that compensation costs are much higher for workplace bullying than for workplace physical injuries. Also, the average time lost from work because of workplace bullying was 25 weeks while the average time lost from work from all other claims was seven weeks.[2]

The Australian Workplace Barometer Report on Psychosocial Safety Climate and Worker Health in Australia reported the estimated cost to employers of job strain and bullying was nearly $700 million annually with absence through sickness and presenteeism costing $8 billion annually.[3]

Presenteeism is when a worker has ongoing health issues or personal problems that prevent or distract them from being fully productive at work. It includes the stress and accompanying distractions that result from being bullied. But presenteeism isn't just about working at a slower rate or doing lesser-quality work. It's been estimated, for example, that 60–80 per cent of workplace accidents are caused by personal stress when workers are distracted.[4]

Individual employee reactions to bullying can cost employers dearly, in direct and indirect ways. They include how targeted employees approach their work, their time, each other, customers, their commitment to the organisation and their willingness to put in extra when required.[5]

In Chapter 2 What Is Bullying? readers were introduced to workplace incivility as a form of bullying. It is:

> *...seemingly insignificant behaviours that are rude,*
> *disrespectful, discourteous or insensitive, where the intent to*
> *harm is ambiguous or unclear.*[6]

Because some forms of workplace incivility are subtle, they fly under the radar of organisations' bullying-prevention policies with employees' concerns about being treated uncivilly often dismissed by employers as petty. While incivility may be perceived as being at the softer end of the bullying continuum, targets can experience the same types of adverse health effects as targets of bullying at the so-called serious end of the scale.

In an article in the *Harvard Business Review*, workplace incivility researchers Christine Porath and Christine Pearson outlined the results of their survey of 800 managers and other employees across 17 industries in the US.[7] It revealed that targets of incivility often punish their offenders and their employer. This is while commonly hiding or suppressing their feelings and not necessarily thinking of their actions as revenge. The survey found:

- 48% intentionally decreased their work effort
- 47% intentionally decreased the time spent at work
- 38% intentionally decreased the quality of their work
- 80% lost work time worrying about the incident
- 63% lost work time avoiding the offender
- 66% said that their performance declined
- 78% said that their commitment to the organisation declined
- 12% said that they left their job because of uncivil treatment
- 25% admitted to taking their frustration out on customers.

There's a wide range of ways that bullying impacts negatively on employers. They're divided into three often overlapping categories.

1. Production losses

Caused by:

- absenteeism
- employees working slower than usual
- stress-related workplace accidents
- suspension of projects while key workers are on sick leave
- employees looking for another job during work time
- preparing their bullying complaint or defence in work time
- administering investigations
- participating in investigations
- administering staff resignations
- recruitment of new staff
- replacement workers settling in
- orienting/training new staff.

2. Financial losses

Caused by:

- employees taking full sick leave entitlements

- replacing employees on sick leave, including paying higher duties
- delaying the completion of work/projects
- stress-related workplace accidents
- redundancy payouts/financial settlements
- replacing staff (administration, advertising and selection)
- investigating bullying complaints
- implementing investigation recommendations
- supporting victims, the accused and witnesses/observers
- training new employees
- retaliation by aggrieved employees, such as theft and vandalism
- legal advice/representation
- fines for breaches of workplace health and safety regulations
- psychiatrists'/physicians' reports on affected employees' fitness to work
- increased insurance premiums resulting from claims.

3. Intangible losses

Caused by:

- departing employees' skill, experience and institutional wisdom
- reduced employee morale
- reduction in motivation and commitment
- erosion of trust and loyalty
- breakdown in work relationships, communication and co-operation
- exposure to risk of litigation
- damage to reputation/company brand
- difficulties recruiting the best workers from outside the organisation because of poor employer reputation
- appointing second-rate internal applicants to important management/other positions because the best candidates want

to avoid being in the direct firing line of a bullying
manager/co-worker
- loss of stakeholder goodwill
- loss of customers.

The following is an example of an employer who spent a fortune on its
workplace bullying problem; not with attempts to address it, but on
efforts to conceal it.

Employer X

*Employer X, a large health care provider, was the epitome of a
bullying organisation that ticked most of the boxes on the
unnecessary costs-to-employers list because of its failure to
address its bullying problem. Over the last 10 years workplace
bullying and concealing the problem would have cost the
company millions of dollars directly and indirectly.*

*Over many years workers were subjected to bullying by
supervisors, managers and CEOs. Two of the last three CEOs
were serial bullies and, as is often the case, bullying was role-
modelled at the top.*

*Most employees targeted for bullying put up with it or resigned.
Staff turnover was high. Commonly employees took extended sick
leave prior to resigning, with some using the time productively to
look for another job. A couple of years ago a senior company
manager confided that at the time there were around 20 staff on
extended sick leave attributed to bullying-related stress.
Generally, bullied employees use all of their allocated sick leave
and when that's used up, they eat into annual leave and long-
service leave, and then sometimes take leave without pay.*

*Some of Employer X's employees reported their bullying,
resulting in internal investigations usually accompanied by
extended sick leave for the employees. A small number reported*

their bullying to WorkSafe. Some took their cases to the Fair Work Commission and some applied for workers' compensation. A small number sought compensation through litigation for the psychological injuries caused by their bullying. Each of these options incurred costs for the employer.

All internal complaints about bullying were scrutinised by the company's lawyers and advice provided to the employer about individual courses of action. Lawyers' fees commonly range from $350 to $650 an hour.[8] One documented complaint was more than 100 A4 pages in length, which would have taken a lawyer many hours to carefully examine, take notes and document advice for the employer. All letters to employees prepared by HR on matters relating to their alleged bullying were scrutinised first by the company's lawyers. In some instances, the employer's legal firm charged $5000 to write a letter on the employer's behalf, which included reading the case file and consulting with the employer.

Internal investigations into employees' allegations of bullying were undertaken by a consultancy firm engaged by the company's lawyers. Most complaints were conveniently found unsubstantiated. But sham investigations still took weeks to assess complainants' allegations, interview complainants, witnesses, the accused and management. In one case, witnesses reported that the investigator seemed to be just going through the motions and asked hardly any relevant questions. In another case, some of the complainant's witnesses weren't even interviewed.

In one instance, an external investigator revealed to three complainants that she believed there were clear grounds for their complaint and her final report would reflect this. Subsequently, however, the employer notified the complainants that their bullying complaint had been found unsubstantiated.

The complainants asked for more details, but the employer refused citing client legal privilege. Client legal privilege is a rule of law protecting communications between legal practitioners and their clients. According to the Law Council of Australia, however, the chief purpose of client legal privilege is not to confer a right for the benefit of the client, but to facilitate the administration of justice.[9] In this case, however, it was a highly dubious process which may have supported a miscarriage of justice.

It was common practice for the employer, when it felt there was a risk of litigation and/or bad publicity, to offer complainants a financial settlement (hush money) to resign subject to a legally binding non-disclosure contract (gag arrangement), including an agreement not to seek further compensation from the employer. There were instances when the alleged bullies were also offered financial settlements to resign.

SOME EMPLOYERS DON'T GET IT

It's a grave mistake to believe that the serious damage done to bullied workers, the financial costs and production losses for employers are incidental and their impact on the bottom line is simply the price of doing business. There's often a huge cost for employers, employees and the economy.

Many employers approach workplace bullying on a superficial level. They engage in posturing about the seriousness of their code of conduct policy, especially when they're in damage control after bullying has been alleged. 'We take our bullying policy very seriously' and 'we're committed to the health and safety of all our employees' are the most common among a range of glib responses.

Little is usually done by these employers, however, to equip managers and other employees to recognise and handle bullying situations.

Through their company values they claim to promote respectful workplaces, but when a strong culture of bullying exists, especially one that they've gone to great lengths to conceal, they're simply values fraudsters. I say more about this in Chapter 22 Respectful Workplaces.

Ill-advised and unethical employers prepared to risk the health and safety of their employees believe that it's a better option for the organisation to conceal bullying rather than prevent or address it properly. But like Employer X, once they start sliding down the slippery slope of deceit and treachery for organisational problem-solving, it's difficult to turn things around.

An employer's failure to develop a proactive strategy against bullying in favour of dubious cover-up practices can eventually cost them hundreds of thousands of dollars and, in some cases, much more. Legal fees, secret payouts, costly lawsuits, a reduction in staff morale and productivity, high staff absenteeism, turnover, reputational damage and their resulting inability to recruit and retain the best staff, strongly challenge the belief that covering up workplace bullying is a good option.

However, when an organisation digs itself into this type of deep toxic hole, with a disproportionate number of villains and second-rate leaders, it's difficult and in some cases impossible to achieve positive change.

———

SUMMARY

- Employers are adversely affected by workplace bullying and, in some cases, it can destroy a business.
- Workplace bullying costs the Australian economy up to $36 billion annually.
- The annual cost to employers of job strain and bullying in Australia is nearly $700 million with absences through sickness and presenteeism costing $8 billion.
- 60–80 per cent of workplace accidents are caused by personal stress when workers are distracted, including by bullying.
- Targets of bullying often punish the offenders and their employer.
- There's a wide range of ways that bullying impacts negatively on employers including production losses, financial losses and intangible losses.
- Short-sighted employers believe that the losses are simply the price of doing business.
- Dubious bullying cover-up practices can cost employers much more than the costs of developing effective anti-bullying strategies.

WHY BULLYING HAPPENS

It's not just a bad person mistreating a co-worker

While writing this book, I met with more than 50 employees who'd been targeted for bullying. Nearly all of them described their mistreatment as the worst or among the worst experiences of their life. Many had extended periods of sick leave because of anxiety and depression. Almost all of them remained puzzled about the reasons for their bullying.

It's not possible here to examine in detail every conceivable cause of bullying, so just a sample is included. The aim of this chapter and the following two is to dispel the popular myth that workplace bullying is simply about a bad person mistreating a co-worker. There's a range of causes, many of which are interwoven.

HARD TO KNOW

Unfortunately, there's no straightforward answer to why bullying happens because every bullying situation is different.

There are so many different types of bullying that range from being unkind to being malicious. It can be carried out openly or slyly. In an organisation there can be a culture of bullying where almost no one is immune from being a bully or being a target. Sometimes the bully can act alone or with others. Bullying can occur with the approval and even at the direction of management. In some instances, when employees are disliked or underperforming, some managers and co-workers think that it's justified to bully them out of the workplace rather than go through their organisation's official performance improvement, disciplinary, dismissal or redundancy processes and bypassing unfair dismissal laws.

Bullying can be a deliberate attempt to harm a target. On the other hand, some people who are characteristically insensitive and abrasive don't always hear how they sound to others when they come across as confronting or angry, and they can be surprised when their behaviour is labelled bullying.

Irrespective of the accused's intentions, however, if the behaviour causes a risk to the target's health and safety, it could qualify as a breach of occupational health and safety law. Whether ambiguous lower-intensity bullying/uncivil behaviour would be considered bullying by Australian authorities and employers at this time is another matter. Seemingly trivial complaints about co-workers not saying hello or eye-rolling, for example, may be rejected by an employer and such complaints frowned upon.[1]

It seems that many successful actions taken by targets of bullying have been for behaviours perceived to be at the more serious end of the spectrum, that have been experienced by multiple targets and can be verified by witnesses. However, most bullying doesn't happen this way.

THE ORGANISATION

An organisation's culture and leadership are important in understanding why bullying happens. Factors in an organisation's external environment are important, too, such as political, economic and social influences; they can help the organisation to prosper or threaten its survival, with each having the capacity to bring all kinds of pressures and stresses to staff that can lead to bullying.

For example, the pressures and stresses that are created by the restructuring of an organisation with demands for improved employee performance can lead to bullying. Workplaces undergoing rapid change can have higher levels of frustration, anxiety and stress among employees.[2]

Work environments that are hypercompetitive where employees are pitted against one another for promotions, commissions and bonuses may lead to bullying. In these circumstances, bullying behaviours may be aimed at eliminating or reducing the competition.[3]

Imminent redundancies can create rivalries among employees as they desperately attempt to avoid selection for severance. Examples include taking credit for others' achievements, denigrating them to management with baseless criticisms, and spreading gossip, rumours and innuendo about them.

Previous research and writing on the causes of workplace bullying suggest that the social and economic fallout from Covid-19 will likely create the preconditions for an increase in the problem, including:

- emotionally vulnerable work groups (including employers)
- on-the-run and poorly handled re-organising/downsizing
- job stress through remaining workers being asked to do more
- job insecurity and competition between employees to keep their jobs
- casualisation of the workforce/erosion of working conditions such as unfair dismissal regulations
- worker anxiety and depression
- outside-of-work stresses spilling into the workplace
- distrust, over-sensitivity and incivility among stressed workers
- an increase in stress-related absenteeism
- psychologically fragile employees becoming easy prey for bullies.

Bullying in these circumstances isn't inevitable, however. It's unacceptable and preventable. A bullying-free workplace requires a strong workplace culture that fosters respect and trust for employees. Putting a high value on the health and well-being of workers raises expectations about standards of behaviour in the workplace.[4] More about this appears in Chapter 22 Respectful Workplaces.

Generally, employees want a respectful workplace where:

- they know what's expected of them
- they're safe and treated fairly
- their contribution and skills are recognised and valued
- they can work in harmony with co-workers
- their work performance and careers are enhanced though training and support.[5]

The further an organisation strays from these ideals, the more likely it is that bullying will happen. An extreme example is a toxic workplace. The term 'toxic workplace' is often used but rarely explained.

Basically, a toxic workplace is a dysfunctional workplace with multiple chronic problems. The following is based on Dr Linnda Durré's list of characteristics from her book *Surviving the Toxic Workplace*.[6] I've added to the list. Characteristics include:

- a weak board of directors
- incompetent/unmotivated management
- unrealistic production or service targets resulting in overworking staff
- underpayment of staff/wage theft
- external pressures from an unstable political, social or economic environment
- a culture of bullying and sexual harassment, involving cover-up, fear and silence
- discrimination based on gender, age, race, sexual preference, disability, etc.

- low morale, conflict and poor teamwork
- high rate of transfers to other departments, divisions or branches
- high staff turnover
- employees taking maximum sick days to avoid coming to work
- high rate of extended stress leave because of bullying-related illnesses
- excessive workers' compensation claims
- escalation of problems when managers fail to address issues raised by staff
- widespread gossip and rumour
- ongoing conflict between employees including potential for workplace violence
- a culture of rudeness, vulgarity and general offensiveness
- petty enforcement of company policies relating to breaks, social interaction, dress code, etc.
- odd habits of co-workers that may be distracting, disgusting or illegal
- management's failure to support staff with alcohol and drug problems, mental illnesses, suicidal or homicidal tendencies
- vague job descriptions and/or delegation of responsibilities
- unclear restructuring plans to consolidate or terminate positions
- poorly-handled staff redundancies
- dangerous physical work environment, such as flouting of building codes/health and safety regulations/poor security allowing access to unauthorised people.

Commonly in these types of organisations denial, minimisation and procrastination are among the coping mechanisms used by management, with problems such as bullying going largely unchecked. There's little opportunity for redress for employees who wish to act on their bullying, and for those who do it's a perilous journey with expected outcomes rarely achieved. Most likely are processes that intensify an employee's bullying with unfavourable outcomes exacerbating their anxiety and depression. I say more about this in Chapter 11 Employers' Dirty Tactics.

No organisation is immune from bullying, even respectful ones, but a respectful workplace will address it as soon as it happens aided by an established anti-bullying policy and processes, including investigations that are genuine, prompt, impartial and undertaken competently. Employees who report their bullying will be protected from reprisals and the outcomes will be based on the pursuit of truth and justice rather than solely on manager self-protection or protecting the organisation from litigation and reputational damage.

POOR LEADERSHIP

Inadequate leadership plays a key role in creating and maintaining bullying workplaces. These types of workplaces typically have managers lacking in the following attributes:

- education, experience and skills — ability to do the job
- modelling behaviours — able to lead by example
- passion — committed, enthusiastic and active
- recruitment — capacity to hire staff who possess the appropriate education, training, experience and skills and whose personal values are compatible with the values of the organisation
- realistic workloads — able to organise staff workloads compatible with their abilities and the time available
- problem-solving — adept at resolving difficulties promptly and effectively
- clear expectations — letting staff know what's expected of them
- fairness — treating staff equally and without favouritism
- skills development — providing staff with tools, resources and opportunities

- accountability — helping staff understand their responsibilities
- mission, vision and values education — explaining what they mean for the organisation and staff
- team participation — involving employees in planning and decision-making
- feedback — providing positive recognition and constructive criticism
- empathy — showing consideration and compassion to employees
- appreciate barriers — understanding the obstacles to achieving assigned tasks and deadlines
- worker safety — ensuring employees' health and safety, including their psychological well-being.

The list of leadership attributes is extensive, and just some of the main ones have been included here. The possible role of a leader's personality in bullying is covered in the following chapter. The confusion, frustration, tensions, and conflict between co-workers and the consequent reduction in morale resulting from poor leadership can set a volatile scene which is often a precursor to bullying behaviour. The following is an example:

'David'

Senior manager 'David' worked in a large department with more than 200 employees where workplace bullying was common. The department was part of a bigger organisation which had around 1000 employees. David wasn't a bully, but he inherited a department that had a tradition of bullying in an organisation that maintained an entrenched toxic culture.

A major hindrance to addressing bullying was the existing cohort of largely untrained and incapable managers who lacked knowledge and skills in planning, problem-solving and people management. It was one of those organisations where almost anyone could obtain a supervisory or management position if they stayed around long enough. Nepotism was prevalent with staff recruitment and it wasn't unusual for supervisory and management positions to be given to the relatives of executives. It wasn't uncommon for people in basic clerical positions without tertiary qualifications to be given team leader positions in multi-disciplinary teams comprising all tertiary-qualified professional employees. Among the responsibilities of these unqualified and inexperienced team leaders was to supervise the professional work of their subordinates.

Managers were strongly resistant to change and David's efforts to address the department's bullying problem were continually undermined.

Making matters worse was that the organisation's CEO was a bully, too, so attempts by David to implement effective anti-bullying strategies were unsupported. The CEO believed that having a brief section on bullying in the organisation's staff conduct policy was sufficient. As in many organisations, it was a token policy with little substance. No bullying complaint had ever been substantiated and staff with concerns about bullying either put up with it or resigned. When bullying did occur it was concealed using dubious tactics.

Eventually David resigned because of his despair about the possibility of positive change and being bullied regularly by the CEO.

In Chapter 22 Respectful Workplaces, the difficulties of changing the culture of an organisation are highlighted, especially when bullying is firmly entrenched.

Employees who remain employed in an unsafe workplace, depending on the combination of toxic factors, may simply be delaying the inevitable — becoming a target of bullying, their resignation, dismissal or early retirement, anxiety and depression and/or inability to work because of deteriorating health.

WHY EMPLOYEES BULLY

A veteran union official I know says that generally bullies mistreat co-workers because they can. He says that if someone has a strong predisposition to bully, they'll do it if they're not constrained by effective staff conduct policies and stiff penalties for breaches.

But the specific answer to why bullies bully is complex. The fields of psychology, sociology, social work, history, neurosciences, philosophy, genetics, biochemistry and anthropology are all interested in human behaviour. In the field of workplace bullying, attempts to understand the bully appear to be influenced mostly by the behavioural sciences — psychology, sociology and anthropology.

As raised earlier, researchers have difficulties locating and profiling workplace bullies. The inability of people to recognise themselves as bullies or their reluctance to 'come out' for participation in research are just some of the problems. It means that most profiling of bullies originates from the anecdotal descriptions of victims and their counsellors.

This doesn't mean that current profiling is without value, however, as social science researchers regularly make sense of complex social phenomena through observation and anecdotal evidence. In psychiatry, for example, theories of personality disorder have been developed through historical observation rather than scientific study. Importantly, many of the books on workplace bullying are written by highly experienced professionals with backgrounds in clinical counselling and academic research. Generally, they're in a good position to draw reasonable conclusions from their clinical, research and consultancy work about bullies.

The following is a summary of the different explanations from the literature about why bullies bully:

- Serial bullies are inadequate, defective and poorly developed people. They've failed to confront their innermost feelings of personal inadequacy and self-loathing. Inventing failings in others helps them to feel better about themselves.[7]
- Serial bullies experience no remorse, feel justified in their actions, and they lack the knowledge and skills to do things differently. They're not interested in getting on with targets; rather they're obsessed with controlling them.[8]
- Most bullying experienced by employees is unintended. Most of those who are alleged to have engaged in bullying behaviour are unaware of the true impact that their behaviour is having on someone else and do not intend for the other person to be harmed.[9]
- Unintentional bullies lack self-awareness, have poor emotional intelligence, excessive passion, assertiveness, or forceful expression. Some people are unaware how they sound to other people when they come across as confronting and angry and they can be surprised when their behaviour is labelled bullying.[10]
- A study of 5500 workers from over 70 organisations in England found little evidence that bullying was deliberate. The study recommended more research before labelling people who mistreat their co-workers as bullies.[11]
- Serial bullies possess a range of anti-social characteristics, including they:

  – crave power which they experience as exhilarating and reinforcing
  – desire to harm the victim
  – gain pleasure when exerting power over the victim
  – enjoy seeing their victims' fear and distress
  – display abnormal behaviour and behaviour patterns

– use power to destroy a person or their confidence.[12]

- Bullies have no effective organisational restraints to curtail their mistreatment of co-workers.[13]
- Employees may follow direct or inferred advice from managers to mistreat co-workers (see 'Managing out' and 'Mobbing' in Chapter 2 What Is Bullying?) because they:

– are highly competitive and want to gain personal advantage
– are poor performers and want to redeem themselves
– work for an organisation with a culture of mistreating staff
– are gullible and easily convinced that bullying is justified
– are unaware of the serious impact on the target
– fear job loss or other punishment if they fail to follow directions to bully others
– have an excessive need to please, even if it means hurting others
– have flexible moral standards (the next chapter looks at this).

Despite the range of explanations about why people bully co-workers, including the ones about personality, ignorance and pressure from others, any form of bullying behaviour which psychologically or physically injures people at work is unacceptable. Workplace health and safety laws define bullying as behaviour which causes a risk to an employee's health and safety. The perpetrator's intentions or external pressures to inflict harm on co-workers are interesting for the analysis of organisational behaviour, but they're not an excuse.

TARGETS OF BULLYING

No one is immune from being mistreated at work, but some people seem to experience it more than others. Included in this section is a range of employees' personal characteristics which in some workplaces may increase their chances of being treated badly. They include:

- are hard-working, skilled and competent which co-workers interpret as competition
- are popular with co-workers and/or management which incites jealousy among co-workers
- are a poor performer or not a team player
- are difficult to get on with
- are a bully themselves
- are non-confrontational people disinclined to stand up for themselves when mistreated
- are not socially connected to or respected by co-workers
- have low confidence and self-esteem
- speak candidly about their frustrations with co-workers or the job
- reveal desperation to keep their job
- are vulnerable because of a personal crisis or illness
- expose vulnerabilities by sharing information about their personal problems
- are inexperienced, naive and gullible
- have bigoted co-workers intolerant of people's differences.

Bullying can be random and indiscriminate, so an employee's personal characteristics or behaviour may have little to do with their being targeted for bullying. Serial bullies can be conniving, but can also be spontaneous or irrational with their decision-making about who they target. An employee, for example, may be bullied by a co-worker simply because they remind them of someone they dislike outside of work or from their past or because they are avid supporters of a disliked football team or political party. However, bullying as defined in health and safety regulations can't be justified under any circumstances.

It was interesting that a handful of the 50 workers I met with to speak about their bullying pinpointed its start to a time when they had a public or private disagreement with the co-worker who became their bully, including in some instances on issues unrelated to work. Some co-workers may interpret any kind of disagreement with them as a criticism and, as a result, forever dislike and punish the person perceived to be their critic.

AM I THE PROBLEM?

Following on from the previous section, being bullied is a major attack on an employee's confidence and self-esteem and blaming oneself is a symptom. 'What did I do wrong?' is commonly asked by targets of bullying. But bullying may have little to do with a target's own behaviour. Psychiatrist Roy Lubit in his book about toxic managers says that they're commonly clueless about the negative impact they have on others. Some don't care if they hurt others. Some even enjoy it. And some managers bully because they're simply overwhelmed with stress.[14]

Workplace bullying is always an unjustified and uninvited assault, even when the target has done something wrong. Therefore, 'Am I the problem?' shouldn't necessarily be the first consideration for an employee trying to make sense of their bullying experience. But before acting on their perceptions about being bullied, such as making a formal complaint or even making an initial enquiry about a complaint, employees should reflect on how they behave at work and how it might affect or be seen by others.

An employee can't escape the possibility that they're seen as a problem employee, which attracts negative reactions from co-workers. Maybe they're the kind of person who would exasperate even the most competent, patient and fair manager. We hear about some people being their own worst enemy. An employee shouldn't ignore the possibility that this applies to them. I emphasise again that none of this justifies an employee being mistreated, but it may be the reason that they're disciplined more often than others, supervised more closely, subjected to stricter boundaries, excluded socially and even ignored by frustrated co-workers.

It can be difficult to consider that we're a problem in any social situation. Many of us build up some solid emotional defences to protect ourselves from old negative emotions, hurts and fears. This type of defence can be activated when we feel someone is casting aspersions on our character and behaviour, including work performance, even when criticisms may be fair and constructive.

When an employee decides to make a complaint about their bullying at work, it will be helpful and, in some instances vital for them to be aware of their standing in the organisation. In other words, what their co-workers and managers think of them. To defend against accusations of bullying, it's likely that in their defence the bully will dig up every bit of dirt on their accuser that they can. Alleged bullies may claim that the employee making accusations of bullying is the problem, including being difficult to get on with or being a bully themselves.

The alleged bully may even claim to be the victim. Because often the employee will end up having to defend themselves against counter-accusations, it will be helpful if they can anticipate beforehand the negative things that the bully or employer might say. This can only happen if the employee can engage in honest self-reflection.

Of course, anticipating the possible defence, including lies, that could be used against them may be difficult. Lying can figure prominently in a defence about bullying. For example, it's not unusual for a manager accused of bullying to fabricate poor performance concerns as part of their defence against the complainant. It may even include retrospectively creating false entries in the complainant's personnel file.[15] The euphemism for this unethical practice is 'file reconstruction'. An example is when a manager lies about giving the complainant information, support and disciplinary warnings in the past and invents false file entries such as copies of emails and letters that cast aspersions on the complainant's performance and character.

If an employee has a poor performance record, has experienced disciplinary action previously, is lazy, unco-operative, makes too many mistakes, is unpunctual or unreliable, and has poor relationships with co-workers, these will likely be used by the bully to counter-attack. Usually, poorly-performing employees not held in high regard by co-workers and management aren't in a strong position to complain about bullying, or anything else, unless it's at the most serious end of the spectrum. Even employees with squeaky-clean performance records find the process of complaining about their bullying an uphill battle.

Despite their legal obligations to provide a safe workplace, employers may be reluctant to empathise with or be receptive to a complaining employee who they see as a poor performer and a liability to the organisation. They may feign concern initially, but do nothing.[16] Sometimes a passive response or no response to an unwanted employee's grievance about bullying can be an intentional strategy to encourage them to abandon their complaint or resign.

If an employee fails to engage in honest reflection about their own behaviour and reputation at work, they're unlikely to be prepared for the bully's and/or employer's attempts to deny or counter their complaint. Self-reflection can be aided by asking co-worker confidants for an honest opinion about their reputation in the workplace. Usually, employees who are bullied are emotionally fragile, so their first inclination may be to avoid more criticism, especially from co-workers they consider to be their allies. However, the risk may be worth taking if it means being better prepared for the possibility of a vigorous defence from the accused and their supporters.

SOCIETAL INFLUENCES

Most literature on workplace bullying focuses on organisational culture, managerial competence and the presence of workers predisposed to mistreating co-workers for the reasons why workplace bullying happens. However, there's a wider range of reasons to do with our society that influence why bullying happens. It's beyond the scope of this book to examine these reasons in detail, but more in-depth analysis might give consideration to issues including the impact on workplaces of global economic instability and other major world and local influences such as Covid-19 (included earlier); declining standards of ethical behaviour from some world leaders, major institutions, especially governments, business and religious organisations; the development of extreme conservative values and politics; and whether a higher societal threshold for human suffering has emerged because of regular exposure through news media to the pain and suffering experienced by people caused, for example, by war and breaches of human rights by oppressive governments.

SUMMARY

- Workplace bullying is a complex experience which can't be explained simply as a bad person mistreating a co-worker.
- The health of an organisation's culture has a major influence on the incidence of bullying.
- In bullying organisations, denial, minimisation and procrastination are the ways used by management to solve the problem.
- In respectful workplaces, bullying will be addressed immediately supported by an established anti-bullying policy with regular staff training and clear reporting processes, including investigations that are genuine, impartial and undertaken competently.
- Incompetent managers play a key role in creating and maintaining bullying workplaces.
- Those with a strong predisposition to mistreat others have free rein in the absence of effective prevention policies and penalties.
- Some people seem to attract bullying more than others, but bullying as a response to an underperforming or disliked co-worker can never be condoned.

8

MORALS AND OBEDIENCE

Can good people do wicked things?

This chapter expands on one of the more complex aspects of workplace bullying which was presented briefly in the previous chapter. It examines the moral conundrum 'Can usually good people do bad or even wicked things?'

So why are morals and obedience relevant to workplace bullying? Well, one of the most disturbing aspects of bullying is when formerly friendly and trustworthy workmates turn on a co-worker and become a bully or side with a bully. The latter can mean workmates actively joining in the bullying or looking the other way, which can include depriving their bullied co-worker of much-needed support.

Most often bullied workers are shocked, confused and disappointed when previously trusted and kind-hearted workmates appear to undergo a radical character change and become aloof, disrespectful and even cruel. This chapter examines what might be going on in the minds of these 'turncoats' through morals and obedience explanations.

NOT AN EXCUSE TO BULLY

The aim of this chapter, like the rest of the book, is to enhance readers' understanding of workplace bullying so they'll be better prepared to prevent it, avoid it, manage it if it happens, and deal with the possible health, social and economic fallout. Throughout the book attempts have been made to dissect most aspects of workplace bullying and from varying vantage points. The previous chapter highlighted that workplace bullying is always an unjustified and uninvited assault. Attempts here to break it down even further may lead some readers to conclude that explaining bullying is the same as excusing bullying, which is not correct. Bullying can never be excused.

BAD PEOPLE DOING BAD THINGS

Some of the literature on workplace bullying accuses bullies of being bad people acting out psychological flaws. Colourful but negative character descriptions are used on book covers such as 'jerks', 'weasels', 'snakes', 'monsters', 'demons', 'assholes' and 'psychos'. These and other disparaging labels may seem fitting, especially by those who've been on the receiving end of a co-worker's cruel treatment. Knowing that highly-trained psychologists, the authors of many books on bullying, refer to bullies in this way may provide some readers with comfort and redress. The fact that the colourful names on book covers are used by publishers for marketing rather than expert psychological profiling doesn't seem to matter to readers who've been bullied at work. As emphasised in the previous chapter, however, and in the following one on personality, the bully's character is only part of bullying's explanation.

ACCIDENTAL BULLYING

In Chapter 7 Why Bullying Happens, it was suggested that some bullies may be unaware of the negative impact that their behaviour has on others.[1] Writers with this view, while acknowledging that a minority of bullies are intrinsically bad and set out to hurt others intentionally, say that 'accidental bullies' can lack self-awareness, have poor emotional intelligence, excessive passion, assertiveness or forceful expression.[2] It's not surprising, though, that those on the receiving end of mistreatment are sceptical about the idea of bullying being unintentional and it being used as an excuse. Workplace health and safety regulations support this scepticism. For example, the Australian Fair Work Ombudsman says:

> *An employee is bullied at work when a person or group of*
> *people act repeatedly and unreasonably towards them or a*
> *group of workers and the behaviour creates a risk to health and*
> *safety. It includes victimising, intimidating, humiliating or*
> *threatening.*[3]

The bully's intentions don't rate a mention. It's the end result that matters — when the behaviour causes a risk to a worker's health and safety, irrespective of whether the perpetrator meant it.

The notion that people of solid moral character can lapse into bad and even wicked behaviour is difficult for most of us to get our head around, regardless of whether we've been bullied or not. This is partially because of the traditional view that a good person's principles are unwavering. Many writings on morality explain a high-principled person as someone who believes and sticks to the golden rule to treat others as they themselves want to be treated.

It's a common belief that there's a clear line of separation between good people and bad people. It follows that people who bully others while claiming to be good people, are either lying or kidding themselves. However, you don't have to venture too far into the morality and social psychology literature to discover that this position is on shaky grounds. An exception, perhaps, is the bully who has psychopathic (anti-social personality disorder) traits who can switch from saint to demon in an instant and with no remorse when others are hurt. The next chapter says more about this.

Following is a basic examination at what morality is and then in the context of social psychology, obedience and workplace bullying.

WHAT ARE MORALS?

Morals are widely shared communal standards about right and wrong. There's been considerable research on morality. Naomi Ellemers and her co-writers, for example, reviewed more than 1200 research articles on the topic published between 1940 and 2017.[4] Ellemers and her colleagues state that morality plays an important role in creating an orderly society where individuals know and depend on one another. For example:

- Moral principles indicate what is good, virtuous, just, right and ethical.
- Moral guidelines focus on not doing harm and encourage individuals to display behaviour which may have no obvious practical use or personal benefit, for instance, when it involves showing empathy, fairness and altruism.
- Moral rules and sanctions are used by communities to discourage dissenters from selfish behaviour, especially to dissuade them from lying, cheating and stealing.

Some people have strong moral beliefs and defend their views robustly while being dismissive of opposing beliefs. But while morals may vary from person to person, religion to religion, and culture to culture, many moral principles are shared because they arise from universal basic human emotions.

WHAT IS SOCIAL PSYCHOLOGY?

Social psychology helps us to understand why many forms of social influence are so powerful. It's the scientific investigation of how the thoughts, feelings and behaviours of individuals are influenced by the actual, imagined or implied presence of others.[5] There have been thousands of social psychology studies on human behaviour, with some findings useful in explaining how an individual's or group's behaviour, including bullying, can be strongly influenced by others. Several of the more prominent ones are highlighted here.

MILGRAM'S OBEDIENCE EXPERIMENT

Dr Stanley Milgram's experiment was carried out in 1961 at Yale University in the US. He wanted to know if normally good people could do bad and even wicked things.

Dr Milgram was the child of Jewish parents and grew up in the US during World War II. Like most of his generation, he was consumed with how the Holocaust could have happened. The Holocaust was the systematic extermination of six million European Jews by Nazi Germany and its collaborators between 1941 and 1945 during World War II.[6] The dominant view was that it was the brainchild of a handful of wicked people committing horrendous acts of violence in pursuit of their own evil ends. But Dr Milgram thought that by itself this was too simple an explanation.

Leading Nazis, including officials, high-ranking military officers, industrialists, lawyers and doctors, were charged with crimes against peace and humanity and, when found guilty, were imprisoned or executed.[7] Adolf Eichmann, who headed Nazi Germany's Jewish extermination unit, spent many years on the run but was caught eventually in South America, tried in Israel in 1961 and executed in 1962.[8]

As a social psychologist, Dr Milgram's interest was triggered by the Nazis on trial who portrayed themselves as quietly spoken, obedient bureaucrats who claimed merely to be carrying out their assigned duties. 'I was just carrying out orders' became known as the 'Nuremberg Defence'.[9] He was attracted to the works of controversial Jewish German-born American political philosopher Dr Hannah Arendt (1906–1975).[10] She wrote about how ordinary people become pawns in tyrannical political systems, where those in power have complete control and don't allow people freedom to oppose them.

Through his experiment, Dr Milgram wanted to test how far people might go in obeying an instruction from an authority figure if it involved harming another person.[11] His study's research subjects comprised 40 males, aged between 20 and 50, from a range of occupations and socioeconomic backgrounds. They were instructed by an experimenter to give electric shocks to people they were led to believe were other research subjects.

These other research subjects, however, were really Dr Milgram's assistants. While connected to fake electric wires, the assistants posing as research subjects were asked a series of questions by the real research subjects and when they gave a wrong answer the real research subjects were instructed by an authority figure (another of Dr Milgram's assistants) to administer a shock. The pretend shocks were progressively increased from 15 volts (Slight Shock) to 375 volts (Danger: Severe Shock) to 450 volts (XXX).

The assistants receiving the pretend shocks were in another room and gave audible signs of distress when shocks were administered, but when higher-voltage shocks were given they went silent. Some of the research subjects protested at continuing to give shocks when the receivers seemed to be experiencing severe distress, but they were ordered to continue. Sixty-five per cent of research subjects continued to administer shocks at the highest voltage when instructed, even when the receivers' silence suggested that maybe they'd collapsed or even died.

Dr Milgram concluded:

- Ordinary people are likely to follow orders given by an authority figure, even to the extent of killing an innocent human being. Obedience to authority is ingrained in us all from the way we are brought up.
- People tend to obey orders from other people if they recognise

their authority as morally right and/or legally based. This response to legitimate authority is learned in a variety of situations, for example in the family, school, and workplace.[12]

Psychologists continue to debate whether Dr Milgram's research helps to explain what happened during the Holocaust and with other wartime atrocities. However, Dr Milgram's biographer, Professor Thomas Blass, said that his experiments on obedience to authority are among the most important psychological studies of this century. This is because of the enduring significance of the findings — the remarkable ease with which ordinary people can be ordered by a legitimate authority to harm an innocent individual.[13]

Despite his admiration for Dr Milgram's work, Professor Blass highlighted an important limitation of the experiment was that it was conducted in a controlled laboratory setting and, therefore, doesn't provide a fully adequate explanation of the Holocaust.[14] Professor Blass explains:

> *While it may well account for the dutiful destructiveness of the dispassionate bureaucrat who shipped Jews to Auschwitz with the same degree of routinization as potatoes to Bremerhaven, it falls short when one tries to apply it to the more zealous, inventive, and hate-driven atrocities that also characterized the Holocaust.*

Professor Blass also raised the issue of the experiment's failure to adhere to important ethical research guidelines, namely those which cover deception, protection of participants involved, and the right to withdrawal. In relation to the latter, the research subjects were given assertive verbal prods from the experiment supervisor which strongly discouraged their withdrawal. They were (1) Please continue, (2) The experiment requires that you continue, (3) It is absolutely essential that you continue, and (4) You have no other choice; you must go on.

The purpose of Dr Milgram's experiment was to test how obedient an average person would be to instructions from an authority figure when the requests are unreasonable or immoral. But there were still important ethical issues that emerged during the experiment, namely that some subjects experienced psychological distress. While Dr Milgram disagreed with the criticisms, almost every commentary on the experiment since that time has raised the same ethical concerns.

Despite these concerns, Professor Scott Lilienfeld agrees with Professor Blass and says that there's much to be learnt from Dr Milgram's experiments on obedience. In addition to showing that the power of authority figures is greater than anyone thought before, they challenge the view that obeying orders to hurt others doesn't typically result from individual sadism.[15] Dr Milgram found no evidence that participants in his study followed orders to hurt others because they enjoyed it, although other evidence reveals that some concentration camp guards enjoyed torturing prisoners, including children.[16]

Professor Lilienfeld adds that obedience involving harmful consequences for people on a monumental scale probably requires not only an authority figure providing official approval, but also a core of 'truly wicked people' attracted to roles where unethical use of power is acceptable.

ZIMBARDO'S EXPERIMENT

Dr Philip Zimbardo is a US social psychologist who first became known for his controversial Stanford Prison Experiment.[17] Since that time he's built a strong reputation for authoring psychology textbooks, other notable works and his involvement in various humanitarian work.

Dr Zimbardo's experiment was conducted in 1971 at Stanford University in the US where 24 volunteers who were students at the university were recruited as research subjects for a two-week study of prison life. Dr Zimbardo was interested in the dehumanising conditions in many prisons and whether they originated from the personalities of prison employees or from the roles they were required to carry out. He wanted to know if ordinary people played the roles of guards and prisoners in a controlled experiment, would they assume the identities assigned to them?[18]

The research subjects were randomly assigned to be either guards or prisoners. On the second day of the experiment, the guards began to treat the prisoners cruelly, giving them harsh and sadistic punishments.[19] Over following days, the guards forced the prisoners to perform humiliating line-ups, push-ups, strip naked, simulate sodomy, clean dirty toilets with their bare hands and have bags placed over their heads. On the sixth day the experiment was abandoned when research subjects started to break down emotionally.

According to Dr Zimbardo and his colleagues, the Stanford Prison Experiment revealed:

- People will readily conform to the social roles they are expected to play, especially if the roles are strongly stereotyped, such as those of the prison guards. If the guards are placed in a position of authority, they will act in ways they would not usually behave in their normal lives.
- The prison environment was a major contributor to creating the guards' brutal behaviour rather than personality factors. None of the participants who acted as guards showed sadistic tendencies before the study and each had been given personality tests beforehand to screen for normal adjustment.[20]

As with Dr Milgrim's experiment, Dr Zimbardo's study has been criticised, including because the guards and prisoners were merely acting in their assigned roles, which means that their behaviour may not be influenced by the same factors which affect behaviour in real life. Consequently, the study's findings can't be reasonably generalised to real life, such as prisons and other settings.[21]

Ethical criticisms included the lack of fully informed consent by participants because Zimbardo himself didn't know what would happen in the experiment. Participants playing the role of prisoners were not protected from psychological harm, experiencing incidents of humiliation and distress. One prisoner, for example, had to be released after 36 hours because of uncontrollable bursts of screaming, crying and anger. Dr Zimbardo argued at the time that the benefits gained about our understanding of human behaviour and how we can improve society should outweigh the distress caused by the study.[22] But this remains a contentious issue among researchers and it's unlikely that his experiment in its original form would be approved by universities today.

ZIMBARDO AND ABU GHRAIB PRISON

Dr Zimbardo's book, *The Lucifer Effect: Understanding How Good People Turn Evil*, was inspired by his experiences with the Stanford Prison Experiment and his involvement on the legal defence team of one of the US guards at Abu Ghraib Prison during the Iraq War (2003 – 2011).[23] With other soldiers, the guard was charged with committing atrocities against prisoners.

Over a three-month period the guards inflicted horrific torture on prisoners after receiving orders from US intelligence officers to soften them up for interrogation. It included physical and sexual abuse such as electric shocks, food and water deprivation, rape, sodomy, forced public masturbation and murder. Sickening photos of the torture, taken by the guards themselves, showed them smiling and appearing to enjoy torturing the prisoners.

Eleven soldiers were convicted of their crimes in military trials involving courts martial and custodial sentences. However, a report from a two-year investigation by the US Senate Armed Services Committee concluded that the physical and mental abuse of detainees in Iraq, Afghanistan and Guantanamo Bay Naval Base were the direct result of government policies and should not be dismissed solely as the bad work of guards and interrogators.[24]

US administration officials had publicly blamed the abuses on low-level rogue soldiers — an assertion the report called 'both unconscionable and false'. The report said that the abuse of detainees in US custody can't simply be attributed to the actions of 'a few bad apples' acting independently. It maintained that senior officials in the US Government solicited information on how to use aggressive techniques, redefined the law to create the appearance of their legality, and authorised their use against prisoners. The committee chair said that the message from top officials was clear — it was acceptable to use degrading and abusive techniques against prisoners.

Dr Zimbardo formed the view that normally good people can be led to act in ways that are:

> ...irrational, stupid, self-destructive, antisocial and mindless when they're immersed in total situations that impact on human nature in ways that challenge our sense of the stability and consistency of individual personality, of character, and of morality.

He says that he's reluctant to define people as good or evil because all people have the capacity to act as both in certain situations. He believes that in some circumstances, especially when under the direction of strong authority figures, good people can be 'induced, seduced and initiated into behaving in evil ways'.

There are criticisms of Dr Zimbardo's conclusions. Professors Lee Ross and Richard Nisbett, for example, say in their book *The Person and the Situation,* that situational causes can be attributed only when everybody, or almost everybody, in a situation does the same thing.[25] At Abu Ghraib Prison the guards who committed the atrocities weren't the majority and there were guards who not only refused to participate, but also reported the atrocities to their superiors. Importantly, the abuses didn't happen when other soldiers were on duty in the same locations with the same detainees under the same conditions.

The criticisms don't invalidate Dr Zimbardo's situational explanation, but build upon it by arguing that it's important to carefully consider the relative contribution of both personal and situational influences in determining the behaviour of the individuals involved.

Dr Milgram's and Dr Zimbardo's theories continue to be popular and they appear in most introductory psychology and social psychology textbooks as examples of how generally good people can be transformed to engage in bad and sometimes horrendous behaviour. Their work has prompted further research on why many types of social influence are so powerful.

MORALS AND BULLYING

The review of the research on moral decision-making by Naomi Ellemers and her colleagues, as well as other research, helps with our understanding of workplace bullying. This section describes how.

- Attempts to understand moral behaviour and determination of what's right and wrong must consider that people define right and wrong differently based on their differing political, cultural or religious beliefs.[26] There are major differences of opinion about what workplace bullying is and isn't. Usually the cause is a combination of differing values about what's good and bad and ignorance about the legal definition provided by workplace health and safety authorities. People have different principles that impact on their moral reasoning about what's right and wrong, so what one person may see as wrong, such as treating a co-worker badly, another may see as acceptable.
- People have differing thresholds for engaging in bad behaviour.[27] With bullying, there's a spectrum of behaviours

— incivility at one end, and at the other end physical assault, threats of assault, and stalking.

- People can have their good or bad behaviour reinforced by the approval or disapproval of co-workers and authority figures.[28] With workplace bullying, it may vary from workplace to workplace, including in the same organisation. For example, in a toxic workplace or department where bullying behaviour is common, people may be encouraged and even pressured to engage in bad behaviour or to ignore it if witnessed.

- People feel disconnected from their actions and their values when they comply with orders, even though they're the ones committing the act.[29] With managing-out strategies, for example, where bullying is used to coerce the target to resign, the cronies of the main bully who's often a manager, believe that they're immune from condemnation and potential discipline because they're just following orders, including orders that are implied but not spoken. Also, some employers see bullying as an effective management tool to manipulate employees and increase their productivity and motivation.[30] Managers, therefore, may be actively or indirectly encouraged to incorporate workplace bullying into their style of management.[31]

- Some people may switch their moral principles depending on the circumstances, which challenges the premise that people are driven by moral standards which remain constant over time.[32] While people's personalities, genes and upbringing are generally thought to be the main sources of moral values and disagreements about morality, people can change their moral values to benefit themselves over others. While most people tend to show some concern for others, other people demonstrate moral opportunism where they still want to appear moral, but are keen to maximise their own benefit. An example of moral flexibility is when a staff member wants to gain favour or advantage over another by damaging their reputation through rumour, innuendo and lies. Joining in or ignoring the bullying of a co-worker to curry favour with a bully-manager is another example.

- Instinctively, people accused of workplace bullying are highly protective of their positive self-view because of the negative personal psychological fallout from perceiving themselves as a bad person, such as loss of self-esteem and confidence. They avoid self-criticism, even when they fail to live up to their own standards of moral behaviour.[33]

To ensure they qualify as a moral person, they activate a mental self-defence process to preserve internal beliefs about their moral selves. Strategies involve:

- redefining their behaviour from bad to not bad
- deflecting responsibility to others for what happened
- disregarding the impact of their behaviour on others
- excluding others from good moral treatment
- forgetting the moral rules that they didn't adhere to
- failing to recall their moral transgressions
- disregarding others whose behaviour appears morally superior
- posturing with symbolic acts of selflessness such as showing kindness, sensitivity, empathy and altruism, thus distancing themselves mentally from their wrongdoing, that is 'I must be a good person because I'm doing good things.'

COGNITIVE DISSONANCE

The psychological term for the mental self-defence process described above is 'cognitive dissonance'. It refers to the mental conflict that occurs when a person's behaviours and beliefs don't align. People attempt to reduce mental conflict to ease their discomfort. Cognitive dissonance is not instinctive when a person holds opposing beliefs, so they need to be aware of the inconsistency to feel discomfort. Not everyone experiences cognitive dissonance to the same extent though.

Some people have a higher threshold for uncertainty and inconsistency than others.[34]

Common situations where cognitive dissonance might occur include:

- Smoking despite awareness of the adverse health effects.
- Lying despite thinking that you're an honest person.
- Purchasing a new car that's not fuel efficient, despite being environmentally conscious.
- Eating meat while disliking the thought of mistreating animals.

An example that's relevant to workplace bullying is joining in the mistreatment of a co-worker while believing that you're an ethical and compassionate person.

Although cognitive dissonance seems like a negative thing, it can also help people change and grow in positive ways. When people are aware of their conflicting beliefs and behaviour, they can align their thinking and behaviours with their values. The mental self-defence process to preserve internal beliefs about their moral selves, listed in the previous section, appear to be less about changing thinking and behaviour to grow in positive ways, and more about resolving cognitive dissonance through conning oneself psychologically that the bad behaviours causing mental conflict either aren't bad or don't exist.

WHAT'S TRUMP GOT TO DO WITH IT?

Now, if after reading the previous section you've formed the opinion that cognitive dissonance is 'psychobabble', the following is an example that might resonate. In the months just prior to completing this chapter, US President Donald Trump had lost his re-election bid and he and his supporters were struggling to accept the result because they couldn't give up their deeply held belief that he was 'the best president since Abraham Lincoln' and was deserving of a second term in office. It was reported by the *New York Times* that he told the governor of South Dakota that his dream was for his likeness to be immortalised on Mt Rushmore alongside legendary former presidents George Washington, Thomas Jefferson, Theodore Roosevelt and Abraham Lincoln.[35] He tweeted that the *New York Times* article was another example of fake news, but added:

> *...based on all of the many things accomplished during the first 3½ years, perhaps more than any other Presidency, it sounds like a good idea to me.*[36]

A week after the US presidential election a survey carried out by *Politico* and *Morning Consult* found 70 per cent of Republicans believed that the election was not 'free and fair', with most thinking there had been ballot tampering and extensive voter fraud with mail-in ballots. Donald Trump and his supporters continued to strongly promote these beliefs on news and social media without offering any substantiating evidence.[37]

Columnist Jay Michaelson from the *Daily Beast*, a US news publication focused on politics, media and pop culture, wrote an article titled *The Mentality That Explains Trump's Dead-Enders* and said that Donald Trump spent the last four years distorting reality to serve his own ends, and his 'rabid followers' have lapped up his lies because they're compatible with their own beliefs with cognitive dissonance ruling their world.[38]

Jay Michaelson said of cognitive dissonance:

> *In 1954, social psychologist Leon Festinger embedded himself in a cult called The Seekers, whose leader, Dorothy Martin, preached that a UFO would rescue them before destroying the planet on December 21 of that year. When that didn't happen, many sect members left. But most of the inner circle remained, inventing all kinds of rationales for why the prophecy didn't come true, for example, their faith persuaded the aliens to give Earth a second chance, and redoubled their devotion.*

From this research, Festinger developed the theory of cognitive dissonance — that human beings will do just about anything to resolve contradictions between their deeply held beliefs about the world and the reality of the world itself. Cognitive dissonance is so unpleasant, so disordering and catastrophic for the ego, that no amount of absurd, tortured reasoning is worse than reality contradicting a deeply held belief.

All of us try to resolve cognitive dissonance, but the Trump movement has been a years-long exercise in it. Election denial is its latest manifestation. But before that came COVID denial, science denial, climate denial, 'alternative facts' and the inability of Trump's most devoted fans to see him for the obvious conman that he is.

Cognitive dissonance is also a primary reason that people resort to conspiracy theories, which Trumpworld increasingly resembles, especially with the allegation of widespread fraud in the presidential election which, of course, has no factual basis whatsoever and is simply another conspiracy theory propagated by Trump.

As with most psychological theories, there are alternatives to cognitive dissonance as an explanation for attitude change — *self-perception theory* and *impression management theory* among them.[39]

FINAL COMMENTS

There are many ways to explain morals and behaviour, of which only a small sample has been presented here. Of particular interest is consideration of the moral conundrum relevant to workplace bullying — can normally good people do bad and even despicable things? My aim wasn't to provide a categorical answer; rather it was to suggest that there isn't one, and that a wide range of ideas and opinions is likely to influence the possible answers. For an enquiring mind, the chapter might lead to more reading and more questions. Importantly, it will point to the conclusion that hardly ever is there just one explanation for complex problems, and especially workplace bullying.

What is clear, however, is that research has shown that a person's morals are more flexible than was originally thought with apparently strong-principled people able to switch their moral principles depending on the circumstances. Sometimes their decision-making may be influenced by the possibility of gaining or losing jobs, careers, money and relationships. In extreme circumstances, it could mean imprisonment or losing their lives if they reside in countries with oppressive governments. The research findings presented in this chapter may go some way to explain why people that we like and respect sometimes surprise us by doing things that we find morally objectionable and even offensive. Here it's a contribution to explaining an aspect of workplace bullying. It's not meant to be an excuse or defence of those who bully their co-workers.

The following chapter looks at the role of dehumanising and demonising in bullying.

SUMMARY

- Our understanding of workplace bullying can be enhanced by examining bullying behaviour through moral philosophy, social psychology and obedience theories.
- Morality plays an important role in creating an orderly society where individuals know and depend on one another.
- Social psychology helps us to understand why many forms of social influence are so powerful.
- It's been suggested that 'accidental' bullies can lack self-awareness and have poor emotional intelligence, excessive passion, assertiveness and forceful expression, but the idea of bullying being unintentional is hard for those on the receiving end to appreciate.
- The traditional view that a good person's morals are firmly embedded in their psyche and are unwavering makes the notion of people with solid moral principles lapsing into bad and especially wicked behaviour difficult for most people to get their head around.
- Through his experiment in 1961, Dr Milgram concluded that ordinary people are likely to follow orders given by an authority figure, even to the extent of killing innocent human beings.
- Dr Zimbardo's Stanford Prison Experiment in 1971 led him to conclude that normally good people can be led to act in ways that are '…irrational, stupid, self-destructive, antisocial and mindless when they're immersed in total situations that impact on human nature in ways that challenge our sense of the stability and consistency of individual personality, of character, and of morality'.
- Cognitive dissonance causes feelings of unease and tension, and people attempt to relieve this discomfort in different ways

such as explaining things away or rejecting new information that conflicts with their existing beliefs.

- The aim of this chapter wasn't to provide a categorical answer to whether good people can do bad and even despicable things; rather it was to suggest that there isn't a clear answer, and that a wide range of ideas is likely to impact on possible answers.
- What is clear is that studies have shown that a person's morals are more flexible than was originally thought, with apparently strong-principled people able to switch their moral standards depending on the circumstances, especially those which advantage them personally.

9

DEHUMANISING AND DEMONISING

Rumour, innuendo and lies

A common way to reduce people's discomfort with and opposition to the inhumane treatment of others is to dehumanise and demonise them. With workplace bullying, it includes the perpetrators discrediting the target mostly through deceit using rumour, innuendo and lies, often to force them out of the workplace.[1] (See 'Managing out', Chapter 2 What Is Bullying?)

Dehumanising portrays people as lacking the culture and civility which distinguish them from animals and involves viewing their mistreatment as if they lack the mental capacities and rights that are commonly attributed to humans. Dehumanisation has been used to encourage genocide, lawful and unlawful killing, slavery, the denial of voting and other rights, and to attack enemies or political opponents.[2]

Demonising involves portraying someone as evil or deserving of contempt, blame or punishment.[3]

Some of the most extreme examples are from wartime where the technique is used to create a mindset among military and civilians that justifies killing or torturing the enemy.[4] For example, a source from the

US special operations community said of the people targeted by drones:

> They have no rights. They have no dignity. They have no
> humanity to themselves. They're just a 'selector' to an analyst.
> You eventually get to a point in the target's life cycle that you
> are following them, you don't even refer to them by their actual
> name. The practice contributes to dehumanising the people
> before you've even encountered the moral question of 'is this a
> legitimate kill or not?'.[5]

Additionally, the accidental killing of innocent people by drones is not recorded separately. Everyone killed in a drone strike is classified as EKIA (enemy killed in action). They're not even recorded as 'collateral damage', that is the accidental killing of innocent bystanders. This is because drone strikes are notoriously inaccurate, and it would be highly embarrassing for the military if it were known how many innocent bystanders were killed during drone strikes.[6]

INDIGENOUS PEOPLE

In Australia's history there are many instances of dehumanising and demonising our First People that extend to the present day. Only a few examples are presented here. Whenever I think about this topic, the first graphic images that come to mind are those sickening historical photographs of Indigenous men tethered together with neck chains like animals. The British legal concept of terra nullius (nobody's land) allowed British colonists to regard Australia as an empty continent, to disregard Indigenous ownership and rights, and to take the land without ever negotiating a treaty with the first occupants.

Settlers had no appreciation of Indigenous people's culture, especially their strong spiritual connection to the land.[7] This made it easier for settlers to mistreat them, including murder and attempts at extermination. Commencing in 1794, for example, only six years after

European settlement began, there were at least 270 frontier massacres over the next 140 years.[8]

Terra nullius was overturned on 3 June 1992 after a 10-year battle led by Indigenous activist Eddie Mabo when the High Court decreed that Indigenous people had ownership of the land long before European settlement, therefore voiding terra nullius. In 1993, the Federal Parliament passed the Native Title Act which recognises that Indigenous Australians have rights and interests to their land deriving from their traditional laws and customs.[9]

But the dehumanisation of Indigenous people back then wasn't just an Australian phenomenon. There was a prolonged insidious practice, most notably in Europe and the US, of what historians call 'scientific racism' — the spread of bogus theories of fictional black inferiority in an attempt to rationalise slavery and centuries of social and economic domination and plunder.[10] In 1837, Professor Friedrich Tiedemann, a German anatomist, physiologist and expert on the anatomy of the brain, was one of the first academics to scientifically challenge the common view that black people had more in common intellectually with monkeys than humans. He wrote an article in which he disputed that 'there is any innate difference in the intellectual faculties of these two varieties of the human race'.[11]

Professor Tiedemann's view has been universally supported by modern DNA science which has shown race to be essentially a social structure rather than a scientific structure. This means that humans share almost 100 per cent of their DNA with each other, and external physical features such as hair texture and skin colour, about which racists have long obsessed, occupy just a minute part of the human genetic and DNA makeup.[12] Despite the findings of modern science, however, racist references to blacks as inferiors and animals persist.

ADAM GOODES

A shameful recent example of dehumanising and demonising of an Indigenous person was the workplace bullying and racial vilification of Australian Rules footballer, dual Brownlow Medallist and 2014 Australian of the Year Adam Goodes. For sportspeople, the playing field is their place of work, and for Goodes it was workplace bullying through racial abuse on a massive scale when, during football matches, he was repeatedly booed by spectators, called an 'ape' and told to 'get back to the zoo'.[13] It was even suggested on breakfast radio that Goodes could be used to promote the stage musical *King Kong*.[14]

When spectators were challenged about their abuse of Goodes, commonly they denied being racist and attempted to demonise him through criticism, such as 'I'm not booing him because he's black; it's because he stages for free kicks' (penalties), and 'he's political', which is a reference to Goodes advocating for the rights of Indigenous people and calling out racism from the crowd.

Goodes was criticised for using his Australian of the Year award as a political platform to speak up for the rights of Indigenous people. Nowadays, it's a given that winners will use their status to promote the cause for which they've been honoured with an award. Many winners before and after Goodes have done this with the blessing of the Australian community, but Goodes was singled out for abusing the honour. He responded at the time to the criticism of his social activism:

If people only remember me for my football, I've failed in life.[15]

Another demonising technique used by spectators against Goodes was to accuse him of being a thug on the field — 'he's a sniper who takes cheap shots'. Even if the top 100 on-field thugs in the history of the game were ranked, Goodes wouldn't make the list. No player, in any code of football or in any sport in Australia, has been subjected to such a sustained campaign of intimidation by spectators.[16]

Spectator attacks on Goodes were fuelled by a small group of conservative and influential media personalities. He was portrayed by them as the problem rather than the victim. One implied that people aren't booing Goodes because he's black; they're booing him because he's a sook, a provocateur and they simply don't like him. It was suggested that he was playing the victim over trifling matters like people calling him an ape.[17] No other player has ever been subject to such malicious attacks from the media.[18]

The captains of all 18 AFL clubs jointly pleaded with spectators to stop their abuse of Goodes. The then Prime Minister urged fans to treat him with civility and dignity, and even Goodes' mother begged them to stop. But the groundswell of abuse was too strong, and they didn't stop. Goodes had to endure the abuse for two years. It was all too much for him and finally he quit, just like many other workers who've been bullied at work. It took the Australian Football League four years to apologise to Goodes, in 2019, for failing to stand up for him and acknowledge that his abuse was racially motivated.[19] In 2021 Goodes declined an invitation by the AFL to be inducted into the Australian Football Hall of Fame.[20]

ASYLUM SEEKERS

Australian writer Ruby Hamad says that when we speak about human beings in language that changes them into objects, we start to believe they're objects and can rationalise the cruelty we inflict on them.[21] She adds that we've been seeing the dehumanisation and demonisation of asylum seekers in Australia ever since the 'children overboard scandal' in 2001 when the government falsely accused them of throwing their children into the sea in a presumed ploy to secure rescue and passage. Since that time, governments have referred to asylum seekers arriving by boat as 'threats', 'illegals', 'queue jumpers', 'criminals' and 'terrorists'. It was an effective strategy with 60 per cent of Australians in a 2014 poll wanting the government to increase the severity of treatment to asylum seekers.

It didn't seem to matter to them at the time that people living in Australia unlawfully after arriving by plane and overstaying their visas totalled more than 60,000 according to government statistics, with 12,000 of them remaining here for more than 20 years.[22] It didn't seem to matter that it's not a crime to enter Australia without authorisation to seek asylum. Asylum seekers don't break any Australian laws simply by arriving on boats. There's no orderly resettlement 'queue' to join, so queue-jumping isn't a 'thing'. The resettlement system works more like a lottery than a queue, with very few resettlement places available globally and most refugees, even people in highly vulnerable situations, can't realistically expect to be resettled in the near future, if ever. Many refugees lack access to the United Nations High Commissioner for Refugees (UNHCR) resettlement processes and simply don't have resettlement available to them as an option.[23]

For some people, the negative labelling and stereotyping of people without good reason is all they need to hold them in contempt.

WORKPLACE BULLYING

The above examples of blame and stereotyping of various individuals and groups demonstrate that workplace bullying occupies a disturbing place in the way some people are treated so poorly in our society. These instances show how readily we can cast people as the villains, when frequently they're the victims.

With workplace bullying, especially when it involves managing someone out (see Chapter 2 What Is Bullying?), it's common for the initiator to psychologically manipulate co-workers and/or management to be onside with their perverse plan by using techniques related to dehumanising and demonising. They involve denigrating the target's character, work performance, commitment to their job and to the team. The aim is to get co-workers and/or management to unite against them based on the belief that they're not worthy of respect as a human being and their bullying is justified. It invites co-workers to join in or at least refrain from interfering.

Further denigration of the bullied worker happens when they make a formal complaint about bullying, either internally to their employer or externally to workplace health and safety authorities, the Fair Work Commission, or seek financial reparation for psychological injury through workers' compensation or the courts. Commonly the victim is branded by employers as a troublemaker, villain, revenge-seeker, poor performer covering their tracks, and over-sensitive because of personal problems that have nothing to do with work.

Employers, their lawyers or workers' compensation insurers defend against claims by attempting to discredit the worthiness of the complainant by not only demeaning their complaint but also their character (see Chapter 11 Employers' Dirty Tactics).

The following chapter examines the role that personality plays in workplace bullying.

———

SUMMARY

- A common way to reduce people's discomfort with and opposition to the inhumane treatment of others is to dehumanise and demonise those targeted.
- Dehumanising portrays people as lacking the culture and civility which distinguish them from animals and views their mistreatment as if they lack the mental capacities and rights commonly attributed to humans.
- When we speak about human beings in language that changes them into objects, we start to believe they're objects and can rationalise the cruelty we inflict on them.
- Demonising involves portraying someone as evil or deserving of contempt, blame or punishment.
- With workplace bullying, it includes discrediting targets mostly through deceit using rumour, innuendo and lies, often to force them out of the workplace.
- There are many examples of dehumanising and demonising our Indigenous people, especially the perception that they had no rights, which made it easier for European settlers to mistreat them, including murder and genocide.
- A recent example of dehumanising and demonising was the disgraceful workplace bullying and racial vilification of Indigenous Australian Rules footballer Adam Goodes by spectators and some sections of news media.
- We've been seeing the dehumanisation and demonisation of asylum seekers ever since the 'children overboard scandal' in 2001 when the government falsely accused them of throwing their children into the sea.
- Workplace bullying occupies a disturbing place in the way some people are treated so poorly in our society and shows how readily we can cast people as the villains, when frequently they're the victims.

10

BULLYING AND PERSONALITY

There's more to it than just the bully's disposition

When attempting to make sense of a distressing experience, it's not unusual to be drawn towards simple explanations. Those traumatised by workplace bullying are no exception, with the perpetrator's behaviour commonly explained in the context of personality flaws and character weaknesses.

As highlighted in the previous chapter, some of the popular literature on workplace bullying engages in this practice too. Authors refer to perpetrators as 'psychos', 'monsters', 'weasels', 'snakes' and 'assholes', and that bullies are inadequate, defective and poorly-developed people. However, attempts to understand why people mistreat co-workers will fall short if their personality is the only consideration. Personality does play a role, so I've covered it briefly in this chapter, but I emphasise that it's not the only factor.

WHAT IS PERSONALITY?

Personality is the unique characteristic patterns of thoughts, feelings and behaviours that make each of us who we are. We share some personality characteristics with other people, and we have unique personality traits. But personality is complex and even personality psychologists don't always agree on what makes up personality which is confounded by the wide range of personality theories.[1]

Biological theories, for example, maintain that we inherit our personality from our genes. Behavioural theories say that our personality is determined by our interaction with our surroundings. Psychodynamic theories say that our personality is determined by childhood experiences and how we progress through significant stages. Humanist theories focus on free will, individual experience and the quest for personal growth as shaping our behaviour. A modern view is that a range of plausible factors influences personality development.

Historically, the core aspects of our personality were believed to have been 'hard-wired' or set during the earlier years of life. More recent thinking, however, is that the brain has greater flexibility than was first thought and it can adjust the personality throughout life, although not dramatically and not quickly.[2]

PERSONALITY DISORDERS

Someone who has destructive thinking and behaviour, unpredictable moods, poor impulse control, and an inability to interact well with others probably has a personality disorder. Serial bullies (repeat offenders) are likely to have personality disorder traits.[3]

According to the 'bible' for mental health professionals, the *Diagnostic and Statistical Manual of Mental Disorders (DSM-5)*, a personality disorder can be diagnosed if there are significant impairments in self and interpersonal functioning together with one or more pathological personality traits.[4] These features must be:

- relatively stable across time and consistent across situations
- not typical for the individual's developmental stage or socio-cultural environment, and

- not solely due to the direct effects of a substance or general medical condition.

An understanding of personality disorders, however, is vague and imprecise because it's the result of historical observation rather than scientific study. Professor of Psychiatry at the University of Kentucky Dr Jose de Leon says more about this topic in an interesting article titled 'Is Psychiatry Scientific? A Letter to a 21st Century Psychiatry Resident'.[5]

DSM-5 lists 10 personality disorders, allocating each to one of three groups or clusters — A, B or C. Rarely do they present as a clearly-defined condition, but rather they can possess traits of several different categories of personality disorder with the intensity and severity varying as well. The division into three clusters is intended to reflect this tendency, with any given personality disorder most likely to overlap with other personality disorders within its cluster.

The three clusters are:

A (odd, bizarre and eccentric) — covers paranoid, schizoid and schizotypal personality disorders.

B (dramatic and erratic) — covers antisocial, borderline, histrionic and narcissistic personality disorders.

C (anxious and fearful) — covers avoidant, dependent and obsessive-compulsive personality disorders.

Psychologists Alan Cavaiola and Neil Lavender provide a brief description of each of the disorders:

Paranoid: Chronic and pervasive trust of others, suspicious of being deceived or exploited.

Schizoid: No desire for closeness with others and with little understanding of people and their needs.

Schizotypal: Odd and even bizarre with a tendency to say and do strange or offbeat things. Weird dress sense.

Anti-social: A mental condition in which a person consistently shows no regard for right and wrong and ignores the rights and feelings of others. People with antisocial personality disorder tend to antagonise, manipulate or treat others harshly or with callous indifference. They show no guilt or remorse for their behaviour. Sociopaths and psychopaths are included in this category, although they're not referred to in *DSM-5* as 'sociopaths' and 'psychopaths' (see the following section on psychopathy).

Borderline: Moody, angry, intense, unstable and stormy relationships. Predisposition to impulsive behaviours.

Histrionic: Excessive emotionality, shallowness and attention seeking with dramatic and flamboyant behaviour.

Narcissistic: Self-centred and grandiose. Inflated sense of their own importance. Not interested in others' points of view unless they complement their own position. Others' importance is based on their perceptions of how useful they are. If not at the extreme end of narcissism, they can be effective and usually aspire to leadership.

Avoidant: A pattern of social inhibition and risk taking fuelled by fears of inadequacy and criticism by others.

Dependent: Fear of being alone, often causing them to do things to get others to take care of them. Struggle with individual decisions and need continual reassurance.

Obsessive-compulsive: Preoccupation with orderliness, perfection and control of relationships. Over-conscientious, nit-picky, fanatical with details and timelines.[6]

Personality disorders often emerge in adolescence or early adulthood, continue for many years and cause much distress. Potentially, they can cause enormous conflict with other people, impacting relationships, social situations and the achievement of life goals.

Often people with personality disorders don't recognise that they have problems and are confusing and frustrating to people around them.

It's important, though, not to be too hasty to make an amateur diagnosis about serial bullies and their personality. Personality disorders are complex and a diagnosis of personality disorder can only be made by highly-trained mental health professionals. Even mental health professionals can struggle with the diagnosis, management and support of their patients with personality disorders.

PSYCHOPATHY

Psychopaths are from the personality's dark side. *Star Wars'* Darth Vader, commander of the Death Star, comes to mind. He was evil, all-powerful and could control and even slay his enemies just by using the power of his mind. I've heard employees refer to their employing organisation as the 'Death Star' and their bully as 'Vader'. Although real-life psychopaths don't have as much power as Darth Vader, they can still inflict serious damage on their targets.

There's a range of books devoted to psychopaths and workplace bullying. In particular, *Snakes in Suits: When Psychopaths Go to Work* by Paul Babiak and Robert Hare;[7] *Working with Monsters: How to Protect Yourself from the Workplace Psychopath* and *The Pocket Psycho* by John Clarke.[8,9] These books and their graphic titles suggest that workplace bullies are psychopaths. But the authors are quick to highlight that only 1–3 per cent of the population are psychopaths. This may seem reassuring, but according to Tim Field, author of *Bully in Sight*, a high proportion of workplace bullying is perpetrated by serial bullies, most of whom demonstrate some psychopathic/anti-social personality disorder traits.[10]

The words psychopath and sociopath are sometimes used interchangeably, but they aren't the same. A sociopath is a person with antisocial inclinations attributed to negative social or environmental circumstances in their childhood, whereas psychopathic predispositions are thought to be an innate part of a person's psychological makeup.[11]

Because sociopathy appears to be learned rather than inborn, occasionally it's thought that sociopaths can empathise in a limited way with some people. Psychopathy, on the other hand, is the most dangerous of all antisocial personality disorders because of the way psychopaths dissociate emotionally from what they do, irrespective of how horrendous their behaviours might be.

According to the experts, and contrary to popular opinion, psychopaths aren't mad; they're rational and often highly intelligent, but when combined with their impulsiveness, narcissism, lack of empathy and irresponsibility, they're particularly dangerous for workplaces and society in general. Their pretence of respectability is aided by their lying, cheating, smooth-talking, superficial charm and mastering workplace jargon.[12,13,14]

PSYCHOPATHS IN BUSINESS

Dr Robert Hare, designer of the Hare Psychopathy Checklist, maintains that in the ruthless world of modern business some of the personal characteristics of a psychopath are valued and encouraged. He says that the organisational chaos that typifies many of the current rapidly-downsizing and merging companies provides the ideal environment for the psychopath to thrive.[15]

Because their behaviour is not governed by moral standards and integrity, they can smooth talk and lie their way through merger negotiations and other business dealings. Their lack of conscience and feelings for others means that they can efficiently reduce staffing numbers without hesitation or regret in relation to the likely serious psychological, social and financial impacts on targets and their families.

Psychopaths can build up a network of relationships with powerful and influential people. Only the sharpest and most insightful employers can eventually see through a psychopath, although rarely in the beginning. Psychopaths can manipulate unsuspecting employers and managers easily who unwittingly can become their accomplices. Psychopaths have no loyalty and will cast aside accomplices once they've outdone their usefulness.

After a psychopath has consolidated their position in an organisation, there's not much an employee can do if they're being bullied by one. Professor of Psychology at the University of London Adrian Furnham says that psychopaths have strong but devious survival strategies such as deliberately creating conflict between individuals to prevent them comparing notes about the psychopath.[16] If a psychopath is challenged openly or accused of being a bully, they're able to neutralise their accuser by cunningly raising doubts about their integrity, loyalty, competence and state of mental health. Because usually psychopaths have the ear of the most influential people in the organisation, the odds can be stacked against employees who accuse a psychopath of bullying.

It's common for psychopaths to ingratiate themselves with senior management by presenting as hard-working, reliable, co-operative, honest, caring and a valuable asset to the company. Therefore, when a complaint is received by management about them which seriously contradicts this carefully-crafted image, it's an uphill battle for the complainant to be believed. Also, it's not unusual for decisions in bullying investigations, especially when the case is not clear cut, to find in favour of the employee perceived to be the more valuable asset to the organisation. Psychopaths can excel at positioning themselves to achieve this outcome.

Tim Field agrees that there's little protection from workplace psychopaths. He adds that legislation and policies don't deter them, but rather provide challenges to discover more devious ways of expressing their psychopathy.[17] According to Australian psychologist Dr John Clarke, the more you recognise them for what they are, psychopaths will make you a bigger target, and he advises getting out before the damage is done.[18]

It's important that bullied employees resist the temptation to conclude that their bully is a psychopath or possesses psychopathic tendencies. A proper diagnosis of antisocial personality disorder can only be obtained by mental health professionals conducting a full mental health evaluation. When feasible, however, it's advisable to steer clear of dangerous people at work. This is not always possible, of course, especially when they're an employee's direct supervisor, manager or a member of the same team.

There are several publications that provide insights and survival strategies such as *The Asshole Survival Guide — How to Deal with People Who Treat You Like Dirt*,[19] *Working with You is Killing* Me,[20] *Toxic Co-Workers — How to Deal with Dysfunctional People on the Job*,[21] and *Coping with Toxic Managers, Subordinates and Other Difficult People*.[22] While these kinds of books don't have the answers for every situation, they can provide useful insights.

Some words of caution, however. Most of the books are written by authors who've got many years of work experience in psychology, psychiatry, academia and other fields of professional practice. Generally, the authors have experience, insights, abilities and confidence in the areas of their advice that many of us don't have and, therefore, we may struggle to put the advice into practice effectively and safely. Also, the advice given is general and may be totally unsuited to an employee's individual circumstances.

Self-help books or advice on the Internet should not be the only sources of guidance for employees' problem-solving on workplace bullying. Trade unions, workplace health and safety authorities, the Fair Work Commission, Human Rights Commission and lawyers may be able to provide information, advice and support particular to an employee's unique circumstances. A guide about where to seek help is provided at the end of this book.

———

SUMMARY

- Consideration of a bully's personality is important, but attempts to understand workplace bullying will be lacking if they exclude a range of other important factors.
- Serial bullies are likely to have personality disorder traits of some sort.
- A diagnosis of personality disorder can only be made by highly-trained mental health professionals via a full mental health evaluation. None of the information provided in this chapter constitutes a diagnostic tool that would enable such an evaluation.
- An understanding of personality disorders is vague and imprecise because it's the result of historical observation rather than scientific study.
- While only 1–3 per cent of the population are psychopaths, most serial bullies demonstrate some psychopathic/antisocial personality disorder traits.
- Many of the current rapidly-downsizing and merging companies provide the ideal environment for a psychopath to thrive.
- The more you recognise them for what they are, psychopaths will make you a bigger target.
- It's important that bullied employees aren't hasty to conclude that their bully is a psychopath.

11

EMPLOYERS' DIRTY TACTICS

Some employers use a big bag of dirty tricks to cover up bullying

'The corporate sector's dirty secret' is how prominent US bullying prevention advocates Dr Gary Namie and Dr Ruth Namie describe workplace bullying.[1] This chapter examines the deceitful methods used by some employers to cover up bullying.

Not all employers and their managers are stereotyped as users of dirty tactics. The focus here is on those who bully, protect bullies or cover up bullying.

BAG OF DIRTY TRICKS

Some methods are in common practice such as lying, manipulation, bribing and threatening victims and their bullies to keep quiet about their bullying experiences. Others are unique to individual organisations and managers. Some managers have developed an extensive arsenal of devious and often treacherous strategies for self-promotion, self-protection, money making/saving, negotiation and the speedy resolution of problems at work which involve bypassing the organisation's official problem-solving processes. A bag of dirty tricks is particularly useful for covering up bullying.

Managers can use dirty tactics to protect themselves when they've been accused of bullying. But they can also use them when bullying has been reported on their watch and if proven would likely reflect poorly on their performance and reputation as a manager. Senior managers who've appointed bullies to positions of responsibility may not come out looking good either if accusations are proven.

BULLIES – A PROTECTED SPECIES

A common saying among employees who've been targeted for bullying is 'bullies are a protected species'. The saying comes from employees' perceptions that bullies get away with their bullying because they're protected by their employer and managers.

An employer may be aware of an employee's predisposition to mistreat co-workers but can be in a quandary when the bully is viewed as an indispensable member of the organisation. Overlooking or covering up their misconduct may be viewed as crucial for the organisation's continued prosperity. Often these bullies have special knowledge, skills and relationships with stakeholders that are not easily replaceable, but also because they:

- maintain a respected position through major achievements and/or long and loyal service
- are a senior manager and/or have close relationships with the organisation's decision-makers, including being a friend or relative
- are personally identified with the organisation's good reputation or brand
- are 'whip-crackers' valued for their ability to get employees to work harder
- are perceived to be a formidable opponent by the employer because of their capacity to challenge efforts to discipline or dismiss them, including their preparedness to use industrial or legal processes which may be costly for the employer, cause

public embarrassment, and damage to the organisation's reputation and brand.

It's not uncommon for organisations or departments within organisations to experience high staff turnover because of a so-called valued employee's bullying behaviour. There are occasions, however, when an otherwise valued employee may eventually fall out of favour because of their bullying, including when:

- production and/or services are disrupted regularly by attending to the fallout from the employee's bullying
- the costs of legal advice about their ongoing bullying are mounting for the employer
- their bullying becomes a potentially costly litigation risk for the employer
- there have been multiple confidential financial payouts by the employer to victims of their bullying
- the organisation has been publicly embarrassed by their bullying
- the groundswell of complaints has reached a concerning level that can no longer be ignored or covered up.

DUBIOUS TACTICS

Some of the devious ways that employers cover up bullying are to:

- maintain a strongly worded workplace bullying policy, but it's for show only
- downplay the seriousness of an employee's concerns about being bullied
- obstruct an employee's plans to make a complaint, including by preventing/impeding their access to independent advice
- acknowledge an employee's concerns about bullying, but then deliberately take no action in anticipation that they'll lose interest or resign

- lie about there being no other complaints about the alleged bully
- bully the complainant into withdrawing their complaint or resigning
- downgrade an employee's concerns about bullying to a potentially lesser problem such as an everyday personality clash or a misinterpretation of normal management practice
- use mediation because it's cheaper, when they know the problem is bullying and requires a formal investigation which is potentially costly and reputation-damaging
- withhold information and advice from an employee about how a formal bullying complaint should be prepared properly so that allegations are likely to be poorly presented and easier to defend against or dismissed outright
- intimidate the employee who's asked to discuss their bullying confidentially by inviting them to an 'ambush meeting' with multiple managers, including the alleged bully
- intimidate the employee by conducting meetings with them to discuss their bullying concerns in the office of the employer's lawyer
- tell the employee that the alleged bully is a more valuable asset to the organisation than the employee
- imply or say openly that if the employee proceeds with their complaint, it will fail and that the employee's standing in the organisation will be irreparably damaged
- conduct a sham investigation of an employee's allegations with a predetermined 'unsubstantiated' outcome
- leak confidential details about the employee's concerns or intention to make a complaint to other staff, but in a way that suggests that the employee is at fault or a troublemaker
- rather than address an employee's concerns about being bullied, pacify them by offering them an alternative job away from the bully/bullies
- make phony attempts to offer a bullied employee an alternative position by presenting them with a selection of

unattractive job options, including those for which they are unsuited or not qualified to do

- transfer a complaining employee to an isolated or unpleasant area of the workplace or to another region to punish them/encourage them to resign
- make or threaten to make a false misconduct/bullying accusation against a complainant to discourage them from pursuing their grievance further, or pressure them to resign

---

'Dianne'

Dianne lodged a bullying complaint with her employer about being mistreated by her supervisor, a long-term employee popular with management.

One of Dianne's workmates from another section rang her at work to ask how the complaint was progressing, to which Dianne responded that she was frustrated at the lack of progress. Another supervisor, a friend of the alleged bully, overheard Dianne's comment, and reported her to HR for breaching confidentiality.

Subsequently, HR informed Dianne that she was facing an allegation of misconduct and there would be an investigation and possibly disciplinary action. The HR manager said that he was open to 'creative options' to resolve the matter which included Dianne 'reconsidering the status of her bullying complaint', that is withdrawing it. He added, 'Alternatively, we can see how the misconduct allegation plays out.'

Dianne decided that it was a no-win situation for her and withdrew the bullying complaint and commenced looking for another job.

- reduce the complainant's hours of work and/or offer them

less-appealing work times, for example, nights and weekends, to encourage them to resign
- use a false redundancy to get rid of the complainant, claiming that their position is no longer required
- cast aspersions on a complainant's mental health, work performance, morality, ethics and relationships both in and outside of work to distract from, discredit or imply that there are non-bullying reasons for their complaint
- send complainants who maintain they are suffering from anxiety and depression because of their bullying to psychiatrists and physicians contracted by the employer to discredit their claims

---

From Crikey.com 5 February 2013

The Australian Taxation Office has been accused of sending employees to 'hired assassin' psychiatrists to silence dissent, discredit whistle blowers and terminate their employment. Taxation professionals say the ATO has not only ignored calls for tighter regulation of these powers but appears to have intensified its use of psychiatry to label targets as 'high conflict people'.

Steve Davies, the founder of OZloop, who is active in the open government sphere, says the actions of the ATO lawyers mirror the adversarial nature of the legal profession. '(It) provides a mechanism to label employees who object to their bullying as "high conflict people" with personality disorders,' he told Crikey.

'The perspective being advocated medicalises conflict and in doing so provides a mechanism for ATO lawyers and HR staff to mandate psychiatric intervention where they lack the medical qualifications to make such judgments. This gives rise to a direct conflict of interest.'[2]

- place phony entries in a complainant's personnel file to discredit them, including records of meetings or conversations that never took place, especially about bogus performance or disciplinary concerns
- claim to use an independent investigator to reinforce the credibility of an investigation when the investigator is another staff member such as the HR manager, a senior manager from another department, the CEO, the managing director or the employer's lawyer/their representative, none of whom is independent because of their strong conflict of interest as an employee or contractor paid by the employer
- discredit the allegations during the investigation process by using bureaucratic language, obscurely-worded or trick questions to confuse and intimidate the complainant
- use aggressive cross-examination techniques to get a complainant to break down or discredit their complaint

---

'Robyn'

Robyn, a base-level administration worker in local government, had lodged a complaint about being bullied by her manager. The complaint arose from an attempt to manage out Robyn with false misconduct allegations. Robyn was exonerated after an unnecessarily long and incompetently handled investigation, but she suffered severe anxiety and depression as a result. She was on sick leave for a year.

The first meeting with the employer to discuss Robyn's complaint was conducted in the big city office of the employer's lawyer with the HR manager and lawyer on one side of a large boardroom table and Robyn on the other by herself. The employer's lawyer outlined the investigation process, describing it as a highly distressing process for employees. He asked Robyn several times if she wanted to reconsider continuing with her complaint.

The employer's lawyer appointed an investigator to examine Robyn's allegations. At the first interview the investigator aggressively interrogated Robyn about her bullying allegations, taking no account of Robyn's fragile mental state, clear evidence of which was provided by doctors in her detailed bullying complaint.

Robyn broke down during the first interview and resigned shortly after, which voided her complaint.

- ignore or refuse requests to provide information to a complainant about the progress of an investigation or deliberately delay notifying them about the outcome to exacerbate their stress and anxiety, thus putting additional pressure on them to withdraw their complaint or resign
- provide ambiguous progress reports during an investigation that imply that things aren't going the complainant's way
- delay decision-making on an internal investigation so that a complainant's sick leave runs out, putting them under serious financial pressure leading them to withdraw their complaint and return to work or resign to get another job, which voids their complaint
- accuse the employee of making a vexatious (false/mischievous) complaint, being a troublemaker or that their complaint constitutes misconduct for which the employer is considering taking disciplinary or legal action
- secretly overturn an independent investigator's finding that favours the complainant
- conceal details from the complainant about why their allegations were found unsubstantiated
- bribe the complainant to resign with a financial inducement
- make it a condition that employees who are bribed to resign are legally sworn to secrecy about the circumstances
- threaten a bullying victim with a miserable work life as a

disincentive to return to work if they refuse to take a payout and resign

- offer an alleged bully a payout and a good reference to resign, telling them that the evidence against them is strong and likely to result in their dismissal without a reference, which may be career damaging and make it difficult for them to find another job

---

'Louise'

Employed as the manager of an aged care nursing home, Louise was accused of bullying staff. A number of staff had resigned because of her bullying.

The hospital administrator appointed an external consultant to investigate the allegations. The consultant was overwhelmed by the number of staff who came forward to corroborate the accusations.

Within a couple of weeks Louise resigned. The hospital CEO sent an email to all staff advising them of Louise's resignation accompanied by a strong commendation attesting to her 'outstanding service'.

Louise told a colleague 'the CEO made me an offer to leave that I couldn't refuse'.

- exploit a complainant's vulnerability and desperation to escape their distress by offering them a payout that's only a fraction of the amount likely to be awarded by a court for damages
- prevent an employee from seeking a fairer compensation amount later when they're feeling stronger and better able to negotiate by making the financial settlement conditional on them not seeking further compensation

- insist that bullying victims who accept a payout to resign agree to a legally-binding agreement to keep their mouths shut about the circumstances.

UNFAIR CRITICISMS?

If the reader is finding the criticisms about employers being shifty and ruthless hard to believe, well, of course not all employers are devious, cruel and hypocritical. It's fair to say that most aren't. But the aim of this chapter is to identify the devious tactics used by employers who are.

However, identifying the dodgy ones from the honest ones can be difficult sometimes because most of them espouse noble principles such as integrity, openness and respect.

All of them claim to take their bullying policy seriously, even the ones who've been exposed publicly as having firmly-entrenched cultures of bullying. Many of our prominent and previously most trusted institutions have been exposed as falling well short of the lofty principles that they stand for or hide behind — governments, banks and religious organisations among them. Research carried out by public relations company Edelman and titled *2018 Edelman Trust Barometer* discovered that a significant number of Australians believe that our most prominent institutions are untrustworthy.[3]

SUMMARY

- Some employers use lies, manipulation, bribes and threats to conceal bullying.
- A big bag of dirty tricks is particularly valuable for covering up bullying.
- Bullies are a protected species when they have special expertise or special relationships with important stakeholders which are not easily replaceable.
- Employers' underhandedness in covering up bullying is consistent with the exposure of some of our previously most trusted institutions as dishonest.
- Not all employers and their managers behave in the unethical ways described here. The focus is on those who bully, protect bullies or who know about but avoid dealing with the problem.

12

SECRET PAYOUTS

'Our HR manager refers to secret payouts as 'f--- off money'

Payouts to bullying victims and perpetrators to cover up the problem aren't well known outside legal and corporate circles. This is because they're steeped in secrecy with those involved legally bound not to speak publicly about them. Despite the best efforts of employers to justify them as a legitimate management process and a win-win for all, because of the secrecy surrounding them they come across as a dodgy attempt to bribe dissenters with hush money.

If one was looking for a succinct definition of these types of secret payouts, *Wikipedia*'s definition of hush money would be it:

> *A form of bribery in which one person or party offers another*
> *an attractive sum of money or other enticement, in exchange for*
> *remaining silent about some illegal, stigmatic, or shameful*
> *behaviour, action or other fact about the person or party who*
> *has made the offer.*[1]

Secret payouts have proven to be a particularly valuable tool for employers wanting to either protect or get rid of an employee who's guilty of serious wrongdoing, while avoiding their share of the blame for the misconduct. Political, sports, religious, public service and business institutions use them. A cursory search of news media on the Internet reveals many examples.

Secret payouts have come to greater public prominence in news media recently, particularly through the *#MeToo* movement involving infamous public male figures bribing their victims to keep quiet about sexual abuse or paying for the discretion of former lovers. Also, the recent worldwide pursuit of justice for victims of clergy sexual abuse has revealed that to protect their reputations, religious institutions have routinely used secret payouts to silence victims.

Not all confidential payouts to do with workplace bullying are necessarily unethical, and I'll say more about this shortly. But my interest here is on the types of payouts that are accompanied by a range of devious practices, especially bullying, which are designed to silence a bullying victim who's complained about their mistreatment.

Those likely to seek redress externally, such as through workplace health and safety authorities, workers' compensation, the Fair Work Commission, litigation or news media are particularly targeted by employers for payouts. In most instances, payouts are accompanied by legally-binding restrictions designed to silence the recipient. The reputation of the employer is then protected and a further claim by the employee against the employer later is prevented.

The secret payout process itself can be a bullying experience for employees when employers use manipulation, intimidation, exploitation, coercion and threats to get them to accept an offer. The reluctance of some employees to accept a payout which is conditional on their resignation is understandable. Depending on their qualifications, experience, work skills, age, personal finances, the availability of suitable alternative employment and a range of other social and cultural factors, resigning may not be their favoured option. Also, depending on the nature and extent of their bullying, in the aftermath of a payout an employee may not be in great mental shape to present themselves well to prospective new employers.

Importantly, a payout equivalent to six or 12 months' salary, and often less, won't sustain an employee and their family for long if they're unable to secure another job before their payout money runs out.

Many of these employees would prefer their bullying to stop rather than give up their jobs. But when an employer's motivation for a payout is to cover up bullying rather than address it, this option isn't on the table by the time a payout is offered.

The process may be presented as a legitimate management practice but, as emphasised in Chapter 3 What Isn't Bullying, every so-called legitimate management practice can be manipulated easily to bully employees. Payouts are a good example.

ETHICAL PAYOUTS

Not all payouts are dodgy, although the secrecy surrounding them may tempt some employers to violate their own ethical standards.

Sometimes secret payouts are used when an employer's best efforts to resolve a workplace bullying problem have failed. For example, an employer might make a payout to an employee with a grievance or a grudge who's mistakenly or falsely claimed to have been bullied. In Chapter 3 What Isn't Bullying, it was highlighted that it's not unusual for employees to mistake for bullying something 'that's gone against me', 'that I haven't liked' or 'that I haven't wanted to do'. When an employer fails to satisfy an employee that they haven't been bullied and believes the employee will likely escalate the matter, the employer may opt for a payout even when they believe that they've got no case to answer.

Some employees can be unwavering in their determination to achieve redress including when their grievance has a weak foundation. When an employer reaches a financial agreement with the employee, generally it's a quicker, cheaper and much less stressful ending for the employer than some of the other options involving industrial and legal action. Depending on how the payout process is handled by the employer, it can also be less distressing for the employee.

Even when an employee's bullying claim fails, the resulting demands on and consequences for the targeted employer may be substantial. Disruption to operations, damage to their reputation, and negative impact on profitability are just some. Importantly, just as bullying can take a serious personal psychological toll on those targeted, a mistaken or sham complaint can seriously impact on employers. Some employers I spoke to were highly distressed by their experience with mistaken or sham complaints. Those strongly committed to the health, safety and well-being of their staff appeared to be the most affected when an 'ungrateful' employee turned on them. The following is an example:

'Maria'

Restaurant franchisee Maria said, 'Even though I genuinely believed that there was no wrongdoing on our part, my restaurant manager who had been accused of bullying was losing sleep over the matter. It was affecting his work and was distracting other members of his team. It was also taking up more and more of my time and I was losing sleep too. I went to bed angry, woke up angry and didn't sleep much in between.

The employee who claimed he had been bullied went to a lawyer who asked me for six months' salary as a payout. The lawyer said that his client was considering reporting me to WorkSafe and applying for workers' compensation. I couldn't believe it was happening because none of his claims was true, but the lawyer twisted it all around and made it sound like his client was employed at the workplace from hell.

I felt I was being bullied by the lawyer. It was a really distressing experience.

After some haggling, they accepted three months' salary. Although I was really annoyed because we had done nothing wrong, the payout got rid of the problem and the employee...and the lawyer. It cost me around $15,000 all up.

The experience has left all of us with a bad taste in our mouths. I don't think my manager has ever recovered. He's still taking anti-depressants and two years later regularly talks to me about the experience like it happened last week. It made me realise just how vulnerable we all are to this kind of thing.

I always trusted my employees and thought of them as assets, but after this experience I'm not so sure.

DODGY PAYOUTS

With workplace bullying, often employees see payouts as compensation for the distressing ordeal they've endured at work, sometimes over years. On the other hand, employers who fear bad publicity and being sued are reluctant to call payouts compensation or anything else that might imply an admission of liability. For them it's simply an efficient and discreet financial strategy to get rid of the problem.

With secret payouts, like many forms of bullying, there can be a fine line between a legitimate management process and a dodgy one. The motivation behind dodgy payouts to victims or perpetrators of workplace bullying is less about protecting the health and safety of employees, and more about:

- ensuring that production, services and profits are not impacted
- protecting the bully and/or the bully's manager who are valued staff members
- safeguarding the employer's and other key stakeholders' reputations

- avoiding industrial or costly legal action and escaping public scrutiny.

Commonly these types of payouts are referred to as 'commercial settlements', 'financial settlements', 'settlements', or in casual conversation 'go-away money' and 'hush money'. One of the employees I met with to discuss their bullying experiences said his HR manager referred to them privately as 'f--- off money'.

WEASEL WORDS

Like many other examples of management jargon, 'commercial settlement' can be a misleading term. Management language is filled with euphemisms which are soft expressions used to substitute for other terms and practices considered harsh or offensive. They are used particularly to downplay the seriousness of mistakes. Australian author Don Watson in his cynical take on bureaucratic jargon and the overuse of euphemisms in public language refers to them as 'weasel words'.[2]

For example, 'downsizing', 'rightsizing' and 'restructuring' are common management euphemisms for multiple staff dismissals. These dubious euphemistic terms depersonalise the often-terrible personal costs for employees who are fired from their jobs while making the process sound righteous. 'Managing out', which was included in Chapter 2 What Is Bullying?, also sounds like a legitimate organisational activity. But it's a sly process which bypasses an organisation's official performance appraisal, disciplinary and redundancy processes. It aims to get rid of unwanted staff by making their life at work miserable so they'll resign voluntarily.

In Chapter 2 What Is Bullying? the issue of 'evasion language' was raised, and particularly the criticism by prominent bullying prevention advocates that the increasing use of euphemisms in the workplace bullying field 'dances around topics without honestly naming them'.[3] Referring to serial bullying as a 'personality clash' or 'incivility' are examples which can play down serious bullying behaviour.

Weasel words are in common use by employers who cover up organisational wrongdoing. Good examples are the predictable responses from employers when they've been accused publicly of workplace bullying, 'We take our bullying policy very seriously' and 'We maintain a strong commitment to the health and safety of our employees'. Even the most toxic organisations with firmly-entrenched cultures of bullying routinely trot out this type of euphemistic drivel.

RISKS FOR EMPLOYERS

As well as the perceived benefits, there are also drawbacks for employers and employees. Not the least of them is that covering up bullying using secret payouts to get complainants to resign can allow remaining employees to remain exposed to the health and safety risks of the bullying problem remaining unaddressed. In Chapter 6 Costs for Employers, the range of production, financial and other losses for employers were highlighted when they fail to address workplace bullying directly. It's not uncommon, therefore, for employers who pay a complainant to resign with a confidential payout to also take steps to address their workplace bullying problem.

Additionally, while payouts are steeped in secrecy, there's always the risk that an employer's attempts to cover up bullying will be exposed, with those responsible incurring the ire of stakeholders who've intentionally been kept in the dark. These stakeholders may include board members, investors, taxpayers, ratepayers, the general public and news media. Covering up organisational wrongdoing is a risky business, especially when it involves endangering the health and safety of employees and misappropriating the organisation's funds to maintain the deception. I'm aware of several CEOs, HR managers and other senior staff who've been demoted, dismissed, forced to resign (often with a secret payout), or their contracts not renewed because of involvement with dodgy settlements.

While the secrecy surrounding secret payouts may aim to deter other employees from asking for a settlement, it can have the reverse effect if word gets out that an employer has paid off victims or the perpetrators of bullying. Sometimes enterprising employees attempt to scam their employer into giving them a financial settlement to resign. During the preparation of this book, I discovered several instances where employees had used bogus bullying complaints to pressure their employer into giving them a payout. They weren't all successful, but a number of employers gave in and offered a payout when they believed that it was the simplest, quickest and least-costly solution.

'BENEFITS' FOR EMPLOYEES

Employers often present payouts as 'mutually beneficial' and 'win-win outcomes'. The following are some examples:

- **Payouts allow employees who've been targeted for bullying and/or sexual harassment to resign with an extra payment on top of their normal entitlements.** This can be useful to enable the employee to pay their bills while they look for another job. But rarely does the amount offered by an employer provide adequate compensation for a bullied employee's ordeal. Nor does it consider that an employee may have suffered a long-term psychological injury from their bullying. Sometimes it can be so serious that they're unable to work. Also, alternative employment opportunities may be limited.
- **A confidential settlement from their employer allows an employee to avoid the stresses of a prolonged complaint or legal process.** But it's not true to suggest that they've avoided having to jump through difficult hoops and experience significant distress to reach the stage where they've been offered a payout. Usually, employers only offer a payout to an employee as a last resort after everything else, including devious tactics, has been tried to make the problem and the employee go away. A wide range of employers' dubious

strategies was highlighted in Chapter 11 Employers' Dirty Tactics.

- **The confidentiality requirement allows a former employee to apply for another job without the former employer revealing the details why the applicant resigned.** A former employer may, however, display restraint in a reference or make subtle comments which cast aspersions on the applicant's value as an employee. Commonly, an employee who complains about their bullying is seen as a troublemaker and a liability to the organisation, and this may be reflected in the tone of an employer's reference. Also, despite confidentiality agreements, word often gets around an industry about why individual employees leave their jobs.

Often, employees who resign from their jobs under a cloud are not provided with a good reference. A statement of employment that includes the job title, start date and finish date is useless as a recommendation to a future employer, who will likely read it as a negative. On the other hand, sometimes problematic employees are given a good reference just to get rid of them. In Chapter 20 Toughing It Out, more is said about applying for another job after resigning because of bullying.

- **Being offered a financial settlement by their employer may give some employees a sense of vindication and closure.** Rarely, however, do bullied employees feel that they've been adequately compensated financially for their ordeal. Later the issue of employers making absurdly low offers with secret payouts is raised. Also, irrespective of how much employees receive, their closure will be incomplete if they're left with an enduring mental health legacy from their bullying, such as depression and post-traumatic stress disorder.

DEED OF RELEASE

Payouts are usually accompanied by a non-disclosure agreement (NDA) or a gag order, written up in a legal document called a deed of release or deed of settlement in which the employer and employee agree to legally-binding conditions. As indicated earlier, a major advantage for the employer is that should a former employee attempt to bring any legal proceedings against them in the future, the deed of release can be referred to the court to prevent the application from continuing. It excludes workers' compensation claims. The following is a sample future-claims clause from a deed of release:

> *The employee acknowledges that the payment provided to the employee under the deed is in full and final settlement of claims that the employee has or may have had against [company name].*

LOW OFFERS

Often employers and workers' compensation insurers make ridiculously low payout offers even when they strongly suspect that should a case go through an industrial or judicial process, the employer will be found liable.

The arrangement works especially well for employers when bullied employees don't have the support of union or legal representation. Generally, a bullied employee will accept a lower financial offer when they're distressed and desperate to end their ordeal. It's not unusual for some employers to help the process along with intimidation and deceit. It's common for employees to conclude later that they were duped by their former employer into accepting a low amount with restrictive terms. But by then they've signed a legally-binding agreement saying that they agree not to make another claim against the employer.

An employer I know instructed their lawyer that they were prepared to pay a bullied employee a commercial settlement equivalent to a year's salary. But the lawyer was told to make the first offer an amount equivalent to three months' salary. The employee had been unable to work for six months because of anxiety and depression, the culmination of being targeted for bullying at work for several years. He accepted the first offer because he was grateful to be offered any amount given that he was at the end of his tether and planning to resign anyway. He didn't have the advice and support of legal or union representation.

The properness of lawyers accepting these types of instructions hasn't gone unnoticed within the personal injury law field as an ethical hot spot.[4] While the behaviour may not be in breach of professional conduct rules for lawyers, from an 'everyday ethics' perspective it's not a good look.[5]

All but one of the recipients of a commercial settlement who I spoke to while researching for this book had accepted the first low offer, but later believed they were cheated and taken advantage of by their employer. The employee who received the highest payout, a year's salary, was first offered a month's salary, but through her lawyer held out for more.

In Chapter 16 Having an Advocate, the advantages of having a union representative or a lawyer to assist in employee/employer negotiations are emphasised.

BREACHING AN NDA

When a commercial settlement is offered, employers or their lawyers make it clear to the intended recipient that a violation of the terms by the employee may result in the employer suing for a breach of contract.

Employers are highly protective with their reputations. They may be reliant for their prosperity on the goodwill of and strong relationships with a range of individuals and organisations, such as customers/clients, employees, governments, businesses, communities, sponsors and so on. It can take many years to build the trust and confidence of those on whom an employer depends. The following is a standard clause from a deed of release aiming to protect the employer's reputation:

> *The employer and the employee must not make any statements (whether written or oral) or encourage, incite, participate in or authorise the making of such statements by any other person, about [company name] or the current or former board members, employees or agents of [company name], which will or may harm their reputation, or which may discourage any current or prospective business partner, customer, clients, supplier, contractor or employee from dealing with [company name].*

Another important role of NDAs is to keep an organisation's secret information secure. Sometimes former employees leak important information to their new employer or others, such as confidential customer or client data, intellectual property to do with copyrights, trademarks, patents, industrial design, trade secrets or simply ideas. The following are typical of confidentiality clauses in a deed of release:

> *The employee must:*

> - *Not disclose confidential information, except as required by law, in the performance of the employee's duties or as permitted or required by [company name].*
> - *Not misuse confidential information.*
> - *Take whatever measures are reasonably necessary to prevent the disclosure or misuse of confidential information.*

INVALID NDA

In some circumstances it may be possible for an employee who has signed a deed of release impulsively or who felt pressure from the employer to sign, to apply to the court to have the deed of release set aside. If successful, this may enable them to seek further compensation from their employer. Legal firm McDonald Murholme outlines the grounds for an application to the court for a deed of release to be set aside:

- **Duress.** This is the most obvious course of action where a deed of release should be set aside. It includes physical and economic duress where the employer places excessive pressure on the employee to sign the deed of release. It may include threats of physical violence against the employee or someone known to the employee. With economic duress the employer might promise more severance money if the employee signs, or attempt to deceive the employee into believing that they're not lawfully entitled to more money.

- **Undue influence.** This method can be deceptive as on face value it may appear that the deed of release was validly entered into. In fact, the employee may have entered into the agreement willingly, believing it to be a fair bargain for all parties concerned. However, the nature of the relationship between the parties may mean that a fair agreement can never be reached.

Some relationships are regarded in law as inherently imbalanced and an agreement will be presumed unfair and be set aside upon application to the court. The employer/employee relationship is not deemed automatically to be inherently imbalanced, although in many circumstances there will be a clear power imbalance. If a former employee can establish that their relationship with their former employer was inherently imbalanced, then the onus shifts onto the former employer to demonstrate that the agreement was fair.

- **Unconscionable bargaining.** This may arise when an employee's negotiations with their employer are abused. It may be a back-up option if there was no duress or if it can't be proven that the former employee's relationship with their former employer was one of inherent imbalance. Generally, it will be relevant where the former employee did not understand the implications of the deed of release and can demonstrate that there are unique factors to their circumstances which prevent the former employer relying on the document signed by the employee. Factors which an employee may use to establish unconscionable bargaining include mental disability, lack of education and language skills.[6]

The following are examples where there may be grounds to apply to a court for a deed of release to be set aside:

Sixty-five-year-old university lecturer 'Bob' was targeted for a redundancy but was reluctant to accept the offer. His head of department didn't mince words when she told him that either he could leave with a payout and a good reference, or he would be put through a performance management process which he would fail. She added that under those circumstances a good reference would be impossible, which would make it difficult for him at his age to obtain another position at the same level. He accepted the offer.

A ruthless HR manager threatened 'Anna', who complained about being bullied, with allegations of misconduct if she didn't accept the low settlement amount offered as an incentive for her to resign:

'You can accept the offer and leave, or you can return to work, and you may face an allegation of misconduct for making a false claim of bullying.'

The threat was a bluff and Anna had strong grounds for her allegation of bullying, but she was experiencing serious anxiety and depression after a long period of abuse at work. She wasn't well placed emotionally to challenge a misconduct allegation, even a phony one, so she reluctantly accepted the offer and resigned.

'Jan' made a formal complaint about her bullying but was struggling to participate fully in the investigation because of her associated ill health. She had been on stress leave for many months because of her bullying. The HR manager told Jan that the offer of a financial settlement was 'on the table' only until the end of the week. The offer was made on a Tuesday afternoon.

The deadline deprived Jan of a reasonable opportunity to carefully consider the implications for her family, career and financial circumstances. Also, she didn't have a reasonable opportunity to consult a lawyer, even though her deed of release stated that she had been advised by her employer to seek legal advice about the terms and conditions.

'Ryan' was told:

'If you don't accept the offer, you are going to find it impossible to get another job in this industry.'

This implied that the employer would not recommend Ryan to future employers in their industry and may actively take steps to publicly tarnish his reputation if he didn't agree to the terms of the proposed payout and resignation.

Former employees who apply to the court to have their deed of release set aside will need to be able to establish to the court's satisfaction that the employer placed excessive pressure on them to sign the document. As stated earlier, and demonstrated in the examples given, some employers go to extreme lengths to pressure unwanted employees to agree to resign with a payout and with legally-binding terms and conditions. But unethical behaviour of this type may be difficult for an employee to prove to the court, especially if there's no one to corroborate their claim.

Of the four case examples presented here to demonstrate duress in the payout process, only one occurred with witnesses — 'Anna's'. With her union representative, I accompanied Anna to the meeting with her HR manager to discuss Anna's payout. I was a silent witness only and played no role in the negotiations. Later I offered to be a witness for Anna if ever she decided to apply to the court to have her deed of release set aside. Anna said at the time and since that she was too traumatised by her bullying experience to re-immerse herself in the distressing process.

Information provided in this chapter is general and not legal advice. Bullied employees who've received a payout should be cautious about testing the terms of their deed of release based on anything they've read here. In some instances, however, there may be grounds for questioning the validity of a deed of release. But advice should be sought first from a lawyer before taking action.

IMPACT ON THE FALSELY ACCUSED

Falsely-accused employees can be victims too. An important issue rarely acknowledged publicly is the adverse impact on an employee mistakenly or falsely accused of bullying when their accuser appears to be 'rewarded' with a payout by the employer or workers' compensation insurer.

In Chapter 5 Impact on Targets, a long list of psychological, physical, work and social impacts on employees who've been targeted for bullying was provided. Workers who've been wrongly accused of bullying a co-worker but are exonerated after an investigation can be impacted similarly. The impacts can be exacerbated when an employer appears to reward an accuser by offering them a financial incentive to resign to void their complaint and prevent further claims.

While researching for this book I discovered an incident where a team leader wrongly accused his manager of bullying, but the manager was cleared by the employer of any wrongdoing. The accuser, however, was transferred by the employer to a position in another department accompanied by a better salary package than the wrongly-accused manager. The employer's decision to move the accuser away from the manager was to avoid likely ongoing tension between the two.

From the employer's perspective, a payout or transfer may be a solution to the problem, but a wrongly-accused employee may view the situation differently. The following is an example:

'Jack'

An allegation of bullying had been made against Jack by a subordinate, not directly to the employer but through a workers' compensation claim. The aggrieved employee had submitted a claim but had not informed her employer or Jack about alleged bullying or her intention to claim workers' compensation. The claim was for financial compensation for time off work and medical expenses for psychological injury.

Jack and others from his unit were interviewed by the employer who concluded that Jack was innocent of wrongdoing. The claimant was adamant that she wanted no contact with the employer or Jack, so her version of events could not be tested via the employer's investigation.

An agent for the employer's workers' compensation insurer interviewed the claimant and Jack separately. Jack was informed afterwards by his employer that the claim had been unsuccessful, and Jack felt vindicated. But the claimant requested a review of the decision and after a conciliation meeting with the insurer, the claimant was granted a payout and other benefits, including reimbursement of medical expenses and an offer to return to work. The claimant accepted the financial compensation but resigned from her job shortly after.

Jack said he felt the claimant had been 'working the system'. According to Jack, the claimant had indicated to several of her colleagues that she had wanted to retire because she was worn down by prolonged serious health and family problems. Bullying by Jack had never been raised as one of the reasons.

Jack's manager explained that providing the claimant with compensation on the condition that she not take her claim further, was about preventing the matter from escalating. By requesting a review of the initial decision, the claimant had clearly shown a preparedness to take the matter further. The manager assured Jack that the decision had nothing to do with a change in judgement about his culpability. Jack felt, however, that the claimant was being rewarded for unethical behaviour.

Jack believed that his exoneration from the accusation of bullying was tainted by the decision to pay off his accuser and he was worried that when word got back to his co-workers about the outcome, it may be seen by them as evidence of his wrongdoing. There were rumours in the office to this effect, but Jack was instructed by his manager not to discuss the matter with his co-workers.

At the time, Jack thought about resigning, but was talked out of it by his wife and colleagues. Now retired, Jack still speaks about this incident as the only blemish on his 40-year career.

SUMMARY

- The focus of this chapter is on the deceitful and intimidating attempts made by employers using a secret payout to conceal bullying, primarily for reputation protection and to avoid litigation.
- Commonly secret payouts are referred to as 'commercial settlements', 'financial settlements' or in casual conversation as 'go-away money' and 'hush money'.
- *Wikipedia* defines 'hush money' as 'a form of bribery in which one person or party offers another an attractive sum of money or other enticement, in exchange for remaining silent about some illegal, stigmatic, or shameful behaviour, action or other fact about the person or party who has made the offer'.
- Often employers make ridiculously low payout offers even when they've been advised by their lawyers that should a case go through the judicial system, the damages awarded would be much higher.
- A deed of release can only be legally signed under a party's free will. Any type of coercion is considered duress if it allows one person to take advantage of another and may render the deed of release invalid. A former employee should seek advice from a lawyer before taking action on their deed of release.
- In most instances it will benefit an employee to have a union representative or lawyer to assist them with negotiations for a payout.
- A payout or any other benefit given to an employee who has falsely accused a co-worker of bullying may be interpreted by the accused as rewarding the accuser for bad behaviour.

13

DON'T TRUST HR!

HR is part of the problem, not the solution

There are serious flaws with the advice given to bullied workers to seek help from their human resources department. HR is not there to help you, but to protect the company from you.[1]

ROLE OF HR

HR is an integral part of an organisation's management structure. Previously HR was referred to as 'the personnel department' or 'personnel'. Historically, its basic role has been to maximise the productivity of an organisation by getting the best from its workforce — its human resources. Responsibility areas include:

- creating and managing policies
- compliance with legal obligations
- job design
- staff recruitment and training
- compensation and benefits
- performance management
- organisational development
- health and safety

- staff conduct and discipline
- managerial relations
- labour relations
- organisational culture and environment.

In big corporations the HR department can be large and employ many staff, while in smaller organisations the HR function may be handled by just one person — the manager or proprietor of a business. In some small organisations HR tasks are contracted out. In small not-for-profits the function might be performed by the manager, treasurer, another member or sub-committee of the board.

Professor Ray Bright from Australian Catholic University raises the changing role of HR. Initially focused on recruitment, pay and conditions, the role of HR has evolved to become more intimately aligned with a company's business objectives.[2] He says that while this is seen generally as a good thing, a 'glaring problem' not addressed within the new role is employee complaints procedures. Many writers in the fields of workplace bullying, sexual harassment and management agree.

Professor Bright argues:

> *Despite all the rhetoric, businesses want to minimise complaints. Complaints are seen as time-consuming and non-core business. They are irritants that need to be managed. The trouble is many complaints relate to the poor behaviour of managers towards juniors, including bullying and sexual harassment. Who is charged to investigate the allegations against management? Management.*
>
> *Generally, the HR department is all about helping the business achieve its objectives. Against this background, we should not be surprised when whistle-blowers are ignored, silenced or punished and where wrongdoing by managers is downplayed or*

'managed away' through moving or even promoting the alleged miscreants. Too often it boils down to a cold-hearted analysis of whether the accused or the accuser is more valuable (to the company) to solving core problems.

MUCH MALIGNED

In the literature on workplace bullying and sexual harassment, HR is the most maligned unit in an organisation. This is because of HR's problem with balancing what's best for the employer with what's best for the employee. For some HR workers it's clear cut — their first loyalty is to their employer. But for those with dual allegiances it can pose a serious ethical dilemma in instances involving bullying. A difficulty for employees who consult HR about their bullying is knowing which category their HR contact is in.

In Chapter 1 Bullying Is Serious, it was revealed that reporting of workplace bullying by news media is almost a daily occurrence somewhere in Australia. Recent reporting has also included a spate of high-profile sexual harassment claims. The reporting trend commenced in the US, but quickly spread to Australia with claims against prominent personalities in the performing arts, politics and corporate sectors.

Lyn Goodyear, CEO of the Australian Human Resources Institute, said that in many cases victims of sexual harassment had reported their complaints to HR initially, but they were not treated seriously and no action was taken.[3]

An article appearing in the *New York Times* points to the complicated role of HR in harassment cases. The authors say that the recent spate of complaints has included many reports by complainants of 'being ignored, stymied or retaliated against' by HR units. HR was portrayed in the article as being part of the problem rather than part of the solution.[4]

According to the article, investigating allegations of harassment against a top executive or valued staff member can be perilous for the careers of HR officials. Therefore, when faced with such a risk, HR officers are more inclined to suppress allegations than get to the bottom of them.

The article maintains that women's reluctance to report their harassment to human resource departments prompts some employers to boast that the absence of complaints is evidence of a respectful workplace. However, in many instances not reporting is more about employees' fear of retaliation or a belief it will be a waste of time.

Some employers with appalling records of bullying brag the loudest about having clean records and are nauseatingly insincere in citing clichéd company values such as integrity, openness and respect. The well-worn responses from dodgy employers when challenged is to spruik that 'worker safety is their highest priority' and they 'take their bullying and harassment policy very seriously'. Whenever I hear these hackneyed phrases from company representatives, the needle on my inbuilt BS meter lurches into the red. Almost always they're hiding something.

Cynthia Shapiro, author of *Corporate Confidential: 50 Secrets Your Company Doesn't Want You To Know — And What To Do About Them*, cautions about complaining to HR departments.[5] She says that 'HR is not there to help you, but to protect the company from you'. She says HR officers are taught to smile and provide reassurance to an employee who presents with a grievance. However, according to Shapiro, unbeknown to the employee, help from HR is always conditional on the employee's concerns not running counter to the interests of the company. Shapiro says there are many HR departments that operate under orders to shut down an employee with a grievance to protect the company from the potential damage that a lawsuit might inflict.

In an article titled 'Employee Complaint Investigations: What Human Resources Won't Tell You', organisational psychologist Shelley Baker agrees and cautions employees with a grievance to treat their relationship with HR officials professionally rather than as a friendship. She says that an HR official may come across as natural, polite, professional, trustworthy and even on the side of the employee. But when the matter escalates to a claim against the employer, that same nice HR official will be helping the company defend against the claim.[6]

Dr Gary Namie and Dr Ruth Namie, founders of the US Workplace Bullying Institute and authors of *The Bully at Work* and *The Bully-Free Workplace*, are clearly on side with this analysis. The first piece of advice on their list of things to do after being bullied at work is 'don't trust HR'. They warn that HR is 'a biased truth seeker' when investigating bullying because its first loyalty is to the company.[7]

Australian human rights lawyer Kathryn-Magnolia Feeley and author of *Workplace Bullying Lawyers' Guide — How to get more compen$ation for your client*, says that HR worldwide routinely denies that workplace bullying is part of their organisational culture. Their bullying awareness programs are only there to create an impression that they're doing something. But all they really achieve is to make the victim feel more powerless and let the perpetrator get away with bullying.[8]

In an article about sexual harassment in the *Saturday Age Good Weekend* magazine, journalist and ABC broadcaster Virginia Trioli quotes Victorian QC and senior employment barrister Fran O'Brien who believes that going to HR with troubles at work is a waste of time.[9] O'Brien describes HR's sexual harassment policies as 'popsicle policies' because 'they're all icy and sweet and they look good, but they have nothing underneath; the personnel departments really don't understand what's involved'.

When an investigation into claims of bullying against a manager is unavoidable, it's common for the manager to be treated more considerately by HR and, if the claim is substantiated, the penalties, if any, are often lenient. For example, they might be taken aside by their manager for a 'quiet word' and at worst given a light slap on the wrist.

In contrast, a less-valued lower-level staff member might receive an official documented warning in the serious 'three-strikes-and-you're-out' category. Sometimes this can include being put on a final warning immediately, a demotion, transfer or dismissal.

Depending on the size of the organisation, managers will likely have more dealings with their HR department than lower-level employees. As a result, they may have close working relationships and even personal friendships with HR colleagues. This can put a claimant at a disadvantage when there's an official grievance about a manager. The following is an example:

'Jill'

Jill was a lower-level staff member who made a bullying complaint against her supervisor. Shortly after submitting her complaint, Jill observed the HR manager with whom the claim was lodged sitting on the edge of the alleged bully's desk engaged in a highly jovial conversation with the accused.

There was no way of Jill knowing what the two were talking about but, understandably, she was highly anxious and jumped to the conclusion that they were laughing about her bullying complaint. Although she thought she had a strong case, Jill began worrying if her claim would get a fair go.

Her fears were borne out in the biased and tactless way that the HR manager handled the investigation resulting in an unfavourable outcome for Jill. She discovered some time later that the HR manager and the alleged bully were good friends in and outside of work.

Advice about contacting HR for information and support assumes that HR staff are trustworthy and have the health and safety of employees as a priority. Experience suggests, however, that integrity is in short supply in some HR departments.

A major problem is that HR staff aren't always properly equipped for the job such as having relevant qualifications, training or experience, especially with best-practice employee complaints and investigation processes. As a result, they struggle when confronted with grievances about bullying, especially when the alleged behaviour is subtle or sly, making it difficult to establish the truth.

Australian Human Resources Institute CEO Lyn Goodyear advocates for better standards for human resources professionals, certifying bodies to set standards, training in understanding the law and how it applies to workplaces, and bringing an open objective mind to an investigation. She also recommends that when confronted with demands by senior executives to put allegiance to them over the organisation, human resources officers need to exercise the full range of their professional skills which includes the capacity to be persuasive and, when required, to be brave.[10]

It's far easier said than done, however, for HR staff nowhere near the top of the management hierarchy to be 'persuasive' and 'brave' in dealing with a bullying or sexual harassment complaint against a senior manager or highly-valued employee. It can be job-ending and even career-ending for them.

Professor Bright says that if organisations were serious about the welfare of employees, they would establish genuinely independent oversight of the complaints process and publish appropriately anonymised performance statistics outlining the number and nature of complaints, those upheld and the penalties imposed. But Professor Bright questions whether currently there is any genuine appetite to address this problem.[11]

I agree, and finish this chapter with the same caution that I gave at the start — don't trust HR.

———

SUMMARY

- HR is not a neutral body, an ally of or personal counselling service for employees.
- HR's normal role, among other things, is to head off trouble caused by a potential or actual complaint about bullying.
- HR will often be on management's side in defending against threats to the organisation, including complaints about bullying.
- While the initial response to the employee with an enquiry or complaint about bullying by an HR officer may be deceptively friendly and empathetic, an employee should not see an HR officer automatically as a friend or confidant.
- HR isn't obliged to warn employees that any information shared may be used against them if the matter escalates. This may include information about personal problems away from work and medical history.
- Employees wanting to discuss their bullying should consider seeking advice from outside the company such as from a lawyer, a trade union or another professional or person who has an informed appreciation of the problem.

14

BEFORE COMPLAINING

Vast forces are mobilised against those who complain

Complaining about bullying is risky. In this chapter the hazards are highlighted.

REPORTING IS RARE

Most workplace bullying isn't formally reported. Targeted employees either put up with it or resign. The reasons include they:

- don't recognise that they're being bullied
- are in denial — 'this can't be happening to me'
- think that receiving a certain amount of bad treatment at work is normal
- have a greater threshold for abuse than others
- experience bullying that's carried out slyly without witnesses
- are subjected to bullying at the so-called milder end of the scale, that is incivility, which is not seen as serious
- hope that things will eventually get better without the need for action
- believe that reporting will be a waste of time and make things worse

- don't want to risk dismissal or other retaliation
- are biding their time before resigning or retiring
- don't want to be stigmatised as a victim of bullying
- don't want to be seen by workmates as a 'dobber'
- are reluctant to stigmatise a co-worker as a bully
- don't know how to make a complaint or where to seek help.

SIEGE MENTALITY

Organisations with cultures of bullying and cover-up approach complaints routinely with a siege mentality. This means their starting position is to assume that a complaint, whether justified or not, is an attack on the organisation which potentially will damage it and those in charge. Consequently, rather than see a complaint as a possible employee health and safety issue, the complaint and complainant are seen as the problem. In these types of organisations a complainant may be viewed as:

- a troublemaker and liability to the organisation
- misinterpreting reasonable management actions for bullying
- misinterpreting a clash of personalities/difference of opinion for bullying
- using a complaint to distract from and cover up their own poor work performance or misconduct
- a difficult person to get on with
- affected by non-work-related personal problems which have spilt into the workplace
- having a grudge against the alleged bully or organisation.

In most instances, reporting bullying is a last resort for workers and by the time they get around to making a complaint they're at or almost at the end of their tether. When an employer adopts a siege mentality and ignores a legitimate concern about bullying, they're overlooking the ongoing serious risk to the worker's health and safety.

Making matters worse is when the employer fails to take action on a complaint and the bully sees it as an unspoken endorsement of their behaviour. Buoyed by the employer's response, it's not unusual for a bully to escalate their mistreatment of a target, including in more creative and devious ways if they suspect they could be under greater scrutiny than before. It can also be an opportunity to recruit minions to the bullying effort (mobbing) which can shield the bully from unwanted scrutiny. As indicated earlier, a major reason given by targets for not reporting their bullying is fear of retribution from the bully.

JUST A DIFFERENCE OF OPINION

A common response by employers to a bullying complaint is to misinterpret it as a personality conflict and recommend mediation. Some employers, on the other hand, intentionally disguise bullying as a lesser problem by downgrading it to a clash of personalities.

The confidentiality requirements for mediation reduce the adverse impact on the organisation because it limits knowledge of the problem to fewer people. Also, mediation is a cheaper option for an employer than a long, drawn-out investigation, particularly when it involves the employment of external investigators and ongoing legal advice. Even though mediation isn't an effective strategy to address workplace bullying, it creates an impression or rather an illusion that the employer has taken positive steps to resolve the problem. This can be a useful addition to the employer's defence if the matter escalates later to industrial or legal action initiated by the victim.

Workplace bullying, however, isn't about personality differences; bullying is defined as prolonged and frequent mistreatment. It can arise from an initial conflict between co-workers, but attempting to address the problem as a conflict will fail when the situation has escalated to repeated victimisation, intimidation or terrorisation. In these circumstances, the time for mediation as an effective problem-solving strategy has long passed.

BULLY-MANAGERS PROTECTED

Earlier the idea was raised that bullies are often seen as a 'protected species'. In general, problems between managers and lower-level employees are resolved in favour of managers. This is because managers have greater power over subordinates and decision-making. Also, employers are more inclined to support managers over lower-level employees given they have a bigger investment in a manager. This is why they pay them more and give them extra benefits. Additionally, managers have wider relationships in the organisation than lower-level employees, including with HR. They have greater access, including informal access, to bosses, including the big boss. They may meet regularly at work and socialise outside of work providing plenty of opportunities to speak candidly about work-related issues. They have opportunities to discuss problems they're having with employees which can include denigrating staff they don't like.

Managers can be held in high regard by their employer because of their special skills, previous good performance, long service and loyalty. This makes it difficult for a lower-level employee to take on a manager successfully in any situation and win, and especially when alleging that they're a bully.

RETRIBUTION

Irrespective of the legitimacy and outcome of their complaint, employees can suffer damage to their reputation and standing in the organisation, and be ostracised by co-workers, especially by the bully and their allies. It's not uncommon for employers to penalise complaining employees. This may include the use of exclusionary and isolation tactics, withdrawal of privileges, a reduction in or inconvenient changes to working hours, increasing or reducing responsibilities, allocating more demanding or less satisfying job tasks, transfer, overlooking for promotion, demotion, redundancy or dismissal.

WELL-INTENTIONED EMPLOYERS

Although my main emphasis has been on forewarning targets of bullying about devious employers, many employers are keen to do the right thing by their staff and are justifiably proud of their record in maintaining respectful workplaces. But workplace bullying is impossible to eliminate entirely, even in a respectful workplace. When it does happen, usually it's complicated and difficult to resolve. Employers committed to doing the right thing can struggle when confronted with bullying when they:

- lack a good enough understanding of the problem or prevention strategies
- don't have clearly stated policies and procedures on workplace bullying, or
- if they have policies, often they're just statements of good intentions and have little impact in practice
- are untrained and inexperienced in complaints and investigation processes
- are confronted by powerful oppositional forces in the organisation, such as an 'old boys club'.

DESIRED OUTCOMES

Before preparing a formal complaint to an employer, it's important for an employee to be clear about what they want to achieve. For example, is it to:

- stop the bullying?
- achieve a sense of justice?
- regain lost dignity and self-esteem?
- bring closure to the matter?
- punish the bullies, management and/or the employer?
- cause inconvenience or hurt to a disliked co-worker, including getting rid of them?

Given the many pitfalls associated with making a formal complaint, it will be helpful for an employee to consult an informed impartial person able to provide feedback on the employee's reasons for making the complaint. Ideally, it should be someone outside the organisation such as a trade union official or workplace health and safety regulator.

IRRESPONSIBLE COMPLAINTS

Making a formal complaint to an organisation about bullying is a very serious thing to do with wide-ranging implications for all concerned — the complainants, the alleged bully or bullies, managers and the organisation — irrespective of whether there are valid grounds for the complaint or not.

Just as an employer has a responsibility to provide a healthy and safe workplace for employees, workers have a responsibility for the care of co-workers and their employing organisation. A complainant, therefore, has an obligation to ensure that their claim is genuine and competently presented given the likely adverse impact on the reputation, career and health of those accused, regardless of whether they're at fault or not. The following is an example of an irresponsible complaint handled poorly by the employer.

'Rod'

Rod was a middle manager in a large national supermarket chain. One of his staff members, 'Rona', was having difficulty meeting important deadlines, including failing to have a major report ready on time for the CEO to present to the board. Rona was given plenty of notice and a reduced workload so she could get the job done. She assured Rod that the deadline was achievable and at no time did she indicate she was struggling to complete the report until a few days before it was due. Of course, the CEO wasn't pleased and directed Rod to 'fix the problem'.

Rod spoke to Rona and offered to provide additional help including allocating an additional part-time staff member to reduce her workload. Rona had already used up her allocated sick leave, so Rod offered her additional paid leave if she needed time off. Without notice, however, Rona stopped coming to work. Her father rang Rod and abused him for bullying his daughter.

Shortly after, Rod was contacted by the company's compliance department whose role included investigating allegations of bullying, sexual harassment and discrimination. Rod's HR contact advised him not to worry as the meeting was just routine. Rod had kept HR in the loop about Rona, and his performance improvement plan had been approved by HR.

One of the two representatives from compliance introduced the meeting with:

'Rona...has made a formal complaint in which she alleges that you have breached the company's occupational health and safety policy in relation to bullying. The complaint is serious and if substantiated will result in disciplinary action.'

Rod said that he felt they had prejudged him before hearing his side of the story. The complaint was read in full to Rod who disputed its accuracy.

Fortunately, Rod had kept documented records of all communication with Rona about her performance with copies forwarded to HR. The records indicated that he had adopted a very positive and supportive approach with her. He had even agreed to her request for her workstation to be shifted away from an air-conditioning duct to a location of her choice which included re-routing of electrical and computer cabling and lighting.

After examining the records, the compliance representatives changed their tune and said they accepted Rod's version of events and ended the meeting. There was no apology given to Rod or further communication about the matter.

Rona was transferred to another department, but within a month she had made a bullying complaint against her new manager, alleging she had overheard him using strong language which she found offensive. The target of the manager's one-word outburst ('Shit') was his unreliable computer and he wasn't a serial offender, attested to by his co-workers. Nevertheless, he was still hauled before compliance and, like Rod, was exonerated quickly.

Rod said that he had moved on, but five years later he was still annoyed about his mistreatment by Rona, the compliance department and HR.

It's important that intending complainants:

- not misinterpret reasonable management actions for bullying
- make every effort to understand fully their occupational health and safety authority's definition of bullying and their organisation's code of conduct policy
- seek external expert advice about the validity of their concerns about bullying
- not make false allegations to punish or disadvantage a co-worker or the employer
- not submit a poorly presented written complaint
- consider the pros and cons of making a formal complaint.

WHEN COMPLAINING IS A BIG RISK

According to WorkSafe Victoria, OHS law requires employers to consult with, so far as is reasonably practical, employees who are, or who are likely to be, directly affected by a health and safety matter such as bullying.[1] But in some organisations consulting with or complaining about bullying is itself a major health and safety risk.

Already mentioned is a range of risks for employees who decide to report their bullying internally. Highlighted in this section are the occasions when reporting bullying may be perilous. This includes when the alleged bully:

- is the managing director/owner, CEO, board chairperson or board member, senior executive or a close friend or relative of high-ranking people in the organisation
- is seen as indispensable to the organisation because of their special expertise
- is closely identified with the brand or reputation of the organisation
- has strong links with major supporters of the organisation, for example, donors, government and community leaders
- is popular among co-workers and management
- has given long and loyal service to the organisation
- the organisation has a strong culture of bullying and cover-up
- the employer generally views employees as liabilities rather than assets
- the employer believes that 'cracking the whip' is an effective way to get employees to work hard
- the complainant has not kept detailed records of their alleged bullying
- there is no one to corroborate the complainant's version of events
- the complainant has a poor work performance and/or conduct record and is seen by the employer as dispensable
- the complainant is new and yet to establish solid relationships in or their value to the organisation.

Before making a complaint, employees should undertake a thorough assessment of the personal risks. An exception is when there's immediate danger to their health and safety involving physical violence, threats of physical violence and stalking, which require prompt action such as informing an employer and/or the police.

SPEAK TO THE BULLY?

Usually, an employer or investigator will want to know what attempts the complainant has made to manage or resolve the problem themselves. Normally a formal written complaint should outline what positive steps the employee has taken in this regard. Failing to make a genuine attempt to resolve the problem before making a complaint may not reflect well on the employee, especially if obvious solutions have been overlooked.

Approaching a co-worker to resolve an issue may be reasonable when the problem is relatively minor with amicable and rational discussion between the parties possible. But if the problem is the alleged bully's prolonged and frequent abuse of the target, then it won't be a viable option. Common sense suggests that raising concerns with a person who inflicts harm on others may not be a risk-free exercise. This issue is covered in more detail in Chapter 20 Toughing It Out, in the section 'Standing up to a bully'.

CONSULTING A GP

It's important for an employee considering making a formal complaint to ensure that they're in good enough mental and physical shape to engage in what could be a nasty and prolonged battle with their employer. A complainant who is still reeling from their initial bullying ordeal and suffering high levels of anxiety and depression could falter during the rigours of an investigation.

A ruthless employer will capitalise on the vulnerability of a complainant, not only by focusing on the flaws with their written complaint, but also on the psychological frailties impacting on their ability to follow through with the complaint. It's not unusual for an employer's investigator to question a complainant like a lawyer might interrogate a hostile witness in court. In a case in which I was involved as a support person at the request of the complainant and her union representative, the complainant broke down under the investigator's aggressive interrogation, was unable to continue with her complaint and resigned a few weeks later.

A GP who has an appreciation of an employee's current state of mental and physical health should have an opinion on whether they would be able to cope with the rigours of a bullying complaint and investigation. Of course, this is dependent on the GP also having an appreciation of the organisational dynamics and demands on and risks for the complainant of an investigation. An uninformed GP, for example, may suggest options such as confronting the bully, consulting HR or taking legal action without fully appreciating the serious risks associated with each of these options. Therefore, an employee should assess the GP's capacity to provide informed guidance in this area before taking action on their advice.

CONSULTING CO-WORKERS

Employees should be cautious about discussing with co-workers their intentions to make a formal complaint. Loyalties between co-workers can be ambiguous and quite different from the allegiances that exist among close friends outside of work. For example, it's not unusual for management to rely on informants from the front line to keep them in touch with potential problems and issues, including who the troublemakers are. Informants are rewarded in various ways, from simply having their loyalty acknowledged to being given priority for promotion, the prized jobs or projects and easier workloads.

Co-workers, despite previous friendships with the bullied employee, may turn against them after they start talking about being bullied and their intention to make a formal complaint. In the first instance, co-workers may not agree with the employee's perception that they're being bullied. Even if they agree that the employee has a legitimate grievance, they may believe that nothing positive will be gained from reporting it. They may see a complaint as unnecessarily stirring up trouble. They're also likely to feel that a close association with the complainant may carry personal risks such as falling out of favour with the alleged bully, their supporters and the employer.

In the last chapter I emphasised that HR is not an independent body, so caution should be exercised before seeking its counsel on matters to do with bullying. Remember the quotation at the start of the last chapter — 'HR is not there to help you, but to protect the company from you'.[2] Sometimes it can be better to get independent expert advice from a union, workplace health and safety authority or lawyer prior to discussing the matter with HR.

WITNESSES

Following on from the last section, observers of the target's bullying will likely be reluctant to risk becoming a target of bullying themselves or jeopardise their standing with an employer by agreeing to be a witness for a complaint, even if initially they agreed to do so. When the potential risks become clearer, it's common for co-workers to reconsider their offer to be a witness. In some instances, they may feel under pressure from the alleged bully or management not to get involved.

Without witnesses, a bullying complaint will be an uphill battle. More about this appears in Chapter 15 Preparing a Complaint.

ADVICE FROM FAMILY AND FRIENDS

Family and friends may struggle to provide sound advice because of their lack of awareness of the big picture. As a result, their advice may be overly simplistic with little appreciation of the personalities involved, the nature of the organisation or the possible range of consequences for an employee who reports their bullying.

Loyalty by family members and friends may obscure their recognition that the employee could be misinterpreting their situation and they're not being bullied at all. In telling their story to others, it's common for employees to present a biased version of events including leaving out important information, such as about their own poor behaviour or performance. This issue was covered in Chapter 7 Why Bullying Happens in the section 'Am I the problem?'. As a result, it may mean that loved ones and friends offer advice that's incompatible with the actual circumstances.

For a range of reasons, it may be difficult for family members and friends to be objective and encourage informal, amicable and less-risky solutions. The following is an example:

'Peta'

Peta was bullied by her supervisor in a large regional health service. Her GP had prescribed medication for Peta's anxiety and depression and she took a couple of months sick leave. When she returned to work, her bullying continued and she seriously considered resigning.

However, Peta's boyfriend pressured her into standing up to the bully. His advice was to bring the bullying into the open, which resulted in Peta publicly accusing the alleged bully at a staff meeting. This resulted in the alleged bully making an official complaint to management against Peta for harassment, which was upheld after an investigation, and Peta was given an official warning by her employer.

The outraged boyfriend then told Peta that she mustn't 'take this lying down' and she should lodge a formal complaint. With her boyfriend's help, Peta put together a brief but not well-presented written complaint and submitted it to HR. It was aggressively worded on her boyfriend's advice and threatened to go to the Fair Work Commission or take legal action if the employer ignored the complaint. Peta provided no witnesses to corroborate her version of events, so it was just her word against the accused's.

After an investigation, Peta's allegations were found unsubstantiated by her employer who accused Peta of mischief-making bordering on misconduct. She was cautioned that this type of behaviour would not be tolerated again. The boyfriend told Peta that she needed to take legal action against her employer, but by that time Peta had had enough and resigned.

Peta's boyfriend had been badly bullied at work some years previously which resulted in his dismissal. He revealed to Peta that he regretted not fighting back at the time. Peta felt that it explained why he was so persistent in pressuring her to be assertive with her bullying complaint.

AN EXTERNAL COMPLAINT

Much of the information in this chapter also applies to making a formal complaint about bullying to an external organisation such as a workplace health and safety authority. Employees should read the advice provided on the relevant authorities' websites and/or make direct contact with a representative before proceeding with a complaint. In the first instance, it's important that employees establish whether there appear to be strong grounds for a complaint.

ANONYMOUS COMPLAINT

It's common for bullied employees to make an anonymous complaint to an external health and safety authority. But employees should weigh up whether their anonymity can be maintained once the authority follows up their complaint. Often it's not difficult for an employer who's been reported anonymously for bullying to figure out which employee made the complaint. Workplace health and safety investigators report that almost always when they visit a worksite to follow up an anonymous report of bullying, the employer wants to know who made the complaint. Investigators don't reveal this information to the employer, but often it's not hard for the employer to work out.

NO GOING BACK

Once an employee makes a complaint about bullying, their relationships at work will likely change forever. Irrespective of whether the allegations are proven or not, the alleged bully may never forgive or trust their accuser again and could seek revenge. Allies of the alleged bully will likely become the enemy of the complainant as soon as bullying allegations are made. They, too, may seek revenge. Co-workers may be reluctant to associate with the complainant fearing they may be perceived by the bully and their allies to be colluding with the complainant.

Generally, employers see a bullying complaint and a complainant as a nuisance regardless of whether there are valid grounds or not. Investigating a complaint can be costly for an employer in relation to time and money. It can be disruptive to production and services and affect profitability. It can damage an organisation's reputation or brand. A bullying allegation can damage the standing and possibly the career of the manager/s on whose watch the bullying occurred as well as the manager who appointed the bully to a position of responsibility.

RISKS OF NOT REPORTING

The aim of this chapter isn't to discourage workers from reporting their bullying. Rather, it's to highlight that the process is complicated and risky, and to help those intending to make a complaint, or even an enquiry, to be better prepared.

When bullying involves physical violence, threatened physical violence or stalking, workplace health and safety authorities recommend it should be reported to the employer or police immediately. Not taking prompt action may pose a serious immediate risk to the bullied employee's health and safety.

———

SUMMARY

- Most workplace bullying isn't formally reported; employees put up with it or resign.
- Some employers are more concerned about the inconvenience, costs and damage to their reputation from bullying rather than the risks to employees' health and safety.
- Commonly employers mistake bullying for a personality conflict and recommend mediation. Other employers intentionally disguise bullying as a lesser problem such as a clash of personalities.
- Attempts to address bullying as a conflict when the situation has escalated to repeated victimisation, intimidation and terrorisation will fail.
- Bullies who are managers have extra protection because of their greater influence.
- It's not uncommon for employers to penalise complaining employees.
- Employers committed to doing the right thing may struggle to deal with with bullying because they lack an understanding of the problem.
- Employees considering a complaint need to be clear about what they want to achieve.
- A complainant has a responsibility to ensure their claim is genuine and well presented.
- Before making a complaint, employees should undertake an assessment of the personal risks.
- Once an employee complains about their bullying, relationships at work will change forever.
- Employees should be cautious about discussing with co-workers their intentions to make a formal complaint.
- Co-workers may be reluctant to be a witness for fear of becoming a target of bullying themselves.

- It may be difficult for uninformed and loyal family members and friends to be objective and encourage targets to pursue amicable, less-risky solutions.
- Not reporting some forms of bullying promptly may pose a serious immediate threat to an employee's health and safety.

15

PREPARING A COMPLAINT

Employees shouldn't accuse a co-worker of bullying when it's not bullying

A formal complaint about bullying is serious, so a complainant needs to get it right. Complaints or applications to external authorities such as workplace health and safety regulators and the Fair Work Commission should follow their guidelines. General guidelines for making a complaint to an employer are presented in this chapter.

By this stage it is assumed that the intending complainant:

- is clear about what bullying is according to workplace health and safety law, and what it isn't
- has carefully considered the issues presented in the last chapter
- has thought about all other options to resolve the problem
- has consulted an informed independent person about their intentions to complain, such as a union official, workplace health and safety authority or lawyer
- has checked with their GP or other health care professional that they're physically and mentally able to cope with the rigours of a complaints process.

DETAILED RECORD

An employee will need to have kept a detailed record of the bullying behaviours they wish to complain about. By themselves, general statements such as 'he's got it in for me', 'she's always criticising me', 'he speaks to my workmates, but ignores me' simply won't do. These are the types of casual remarks that might be made during an informal whinge to a family member or friend. They need to be formalised for an official complaint.

A formal complaint about mistreatment at work is very serious and must be treated as such by all parties. An employee who's got a grievance about workplace bullying expects it to be taken seriously by their employer. Similarly, an employee is mutually obliged to take the preparation of their complaint seriously.

An employer may prescribe a specific process for making a formal complaint as part of their policy on bullying. More likely, however, is that employers won't have a formal complaints process, even when they've got a policy on bullying. This applies particularly to smaller employers. As highlighted earlier, some employers' policies are just for show. Such employers may not anticipate ever having to deal with a bullying complaint or, if they do, may not want to help an employee to prepare theirs. It's much easier to pick holes in or dismiss a complaint when it's poorly presented.

All complaints about bullying, regardless of their standard of presentation, should be thoroughly investigated by an employer.

DEFINITION OF BULLYING

The definition of bullying has been emphasised throughout this book, mainly because bullying is widely misinterpreted as 'a decision that's gone against me', 'something I don't like' or 'something I don't want to do', but which doesn't necessarily fit the definition of bullying.[1]

Allegations of bullying must be consistent with a definition provided by Australian authorities mandated to deal with the problem, as follows:

> *An employee is bullied at work when a person or group of people act repeatedly and unreasonably towards them or a group of workers and the behaviour creates a risk to health and safety. It includes victimising, intimidating, humiliating or threatening.*[2]

Also, if an employee doesn't receive a satisfactory response from their employer, they might decide to pursue the matter further with an external body such as their State's workplace health and safety authority, the Fair Work Commission or through the legal system. Each will assess the validity of the employee's grievance using the same definition.

Employees will quickly become unpopular at work if they mistakenly accuse a colleague of bullying when clearly, according to the official definition, it's not bullying. I spoke to employees who'd been falsely or mistakenly accused of bullying and who had to endure the ordeal of an official investigation. For most it was a highly traumatic experience. See the example of 'Rod' in the previous chapter.

DON'T USE THE 'B' WORDS

As explained at the beginning of this book, the term 'bullying' has been used in the title and text to engage readers and enhance readability through using familiar language. A formal complaint about bullying, however, requires a different approach involving different language.

In the Introduction it was emphasised that 'bullying' and 'bully' are emotionally-charged and offensive terms which make everyone's hackles rise, especially when they're the target of allegations. It also applies to their supporters or others who are likely to be impacted such as managers and employers. An employee making an internal enquiry about their possible mistreatment at work should avoid using the 'b' word. This also applies when making a formal complaint.[3] It can invoke angry, highly-defensive and even retaliatory responses from those affected. An employee may find themselves treated with suspicion, be isolated by co-workers and subjected to retaliation at the very mention of the 'b' word, even after what they thought was just an initial informal enquiry with their employer.

Terms such as 'informal' and 'off the record' don't really apply to enquiries by employees to managers, employers or HR departments. The very mention of bullying is a warning of a pending problem which managers and employers need to be on alert at one end of the scale and, at the other, to initiate a strategy to prevent it from worsening to protect the worker, the organisation or both.

Also, mistakenly describing behaviour as bullying will damage a complainant's credibility. Starting aggressively from the outset might seem like a good idea for a bullied employee who's had enough and decided to fight back. While the accuser may be convinced that the accused is guilty as charged, in the interests of natural justice the accusations need to be tested via an investigation so, in the first instance, allegations should be expressed tactfully. This won't necessarily protect an employee entirely from negative responses from those involved, but it may reduce the types of extreme responses described above.

Some examples citing specific bullying behaviours include:

- 'Carl' makes an excessive number of requests for me to do work outside my position description.
- 'Liz' frequently makes unwarranted criticisms about my work.
- 'Rob' regularly belittles my ideas and opinions in the presence of my colleagues.
- 'Dennis' rarely provides me with enough time to complete my work.

- 'Paul' continually ridicules my religious beliefs.
- 'Louise' regularly directs abusive language at me.

Each of the above examples is a statement of the type of bullying involved in the complaint. Each must be accompanied by detailed accounts of every incident. Remember that according to the definition of workplace bullying, an employee is bullied when a person or group of people act repeatedly and unreasonably towards them and the behaviour creates a risk to their health and safety. In other words, there needs to be a pattern of unreasonable behaviour over time. More is said about this in the upcoming section 'Complaint structure and contents'.

In most instances, mistreatment at the most serious end of the scale, such as violence, threatened violence or stalking, the rules of tactfulness don't apply and, according to workplace health and safety authorities, an employer or the police will need to be contacted promptly.

EXPECT A VIGOROUS DEFENCE

It's crucial that a complainant presents a strong case with solid evidence because those with something to lose if the case is proven will defend against it vigorously. For example, the accused or their employer will likely use one or more of the following responses:

- say that the alleged behaviour never happened
- agree that it did happen, but assert that it was reasonable management practice
- claim that they're disappointed/insulted/hurt by the allegations
- allege the claimant is trying to distract from their own poor work performance
- accuse the claimant of seeking revenge after receiving constructive criticism
- contend the claimant is over-sensitive because of personal problems/ill health

- accuse the claimant of being a difficult personality and unpopular among staff
- produce every piece of negative information from the claimant's personnel file that might help undermine their allegations
- in some instances, adjust documented files retrospectively to include actual incidents that were unrecorded at the time, but which reflect poorly on the claimant
- in some instances, create false documented records to damage the claimant's credibility
- provide witnesses who are prepared to provide a different version of events, including lying.

It's not unusual for someone facing accusations of bullying to present their version of events more convincingly than a complainant can present their case. Most bullying is perpetrated by managers on subordinates, so it's common for the accused to be better educated, more experienced and better informed about organisational policies and health and safety law. They may also have greater access to expert advice. This was covered in the previous chapter under 'Bully-managers protected'.

Claimants, therefore, need to ensure that they've provided a very strong case which can't readily be dismissed, especially if they work in an organisation adept at covering up an entrenched culture of bullying. In the previous chapter, concerns were raised about the risks to employees who complain about their bullying in these types of organisations.

PATTERN OF BEHAVIOURS

The aim of collating incidents in a formal complaint is to establish that there's been a pattern of unreasonable behaviour. Although a bully can control things to a certain extent, they won't be able to avoid engaging in a pattern of bullying behaviour over a period of weeks or months. Recording the events will likely reveal this pattern.[4]

A pattern of unreasonable behaviour doesn't necessarily mean repetition of the same specific behaviour. A range of different unreasonable behaviours may be used by the perpetrator/s on the target over a period. Collectively, however, they will amount to an overall pattern of unreasonable behaviour which creates a risk to the target's health and safety. See the example of 'Dan' at the start of Chapter 4 Bullying Behaviours.

COMPLAINT STRUCTURE AND CONTENTS

There's a range of ways that employees present their claims, from short handwritten documents with little structure to a style that is more structured, detailed and word-processed. Given that an employee expects their claims to be taken seriously, the format, content and quality of their presentation should set the scene for their concerns to be investigated properly. A short, scribbled note, for example, is unlikely to be taken seriously by employers, workplace health and safety regulators or anyone else party to the complaint.

For serial bullies and those devious employers keen to cover up their organisation's bullying problem, a poorly presented complaint will play into their hands. Alternatively, employers genuinely concerned about their employees' health and safety will follow up all complaints, irrespective of how they're presented. Workers who have difficulties with language, literacy, illness or ability are examples of those who may struggle with the presentation of a complaint and require assistance.

The template for presenting a complaint provided by WorkSafe New Zealand is very helpful.[5] WorkSafe NZ acknowledges the contribution of material from Fair Work Australia. The following is based on WorkSafe NZ's guidelines:

Incident 1 (Repeat as required)

When did it happen?
Time:
Date:

Where it occurred:

Those present:

What was said, who said what, who did what:

Why do you think it is bullying?
It is unreasonable because:

It is repeated because:

It's endangered my health and safety because:

(Attach relevant evidence, such as reports from a medical practitioner, psychiatrist/psychologist, counsellor)

List those who witnessed this incident:

How this incident made me feel:

How this incident has affected my work:

Explain any prior actions you have taken to address the problem:

What you want to happen as a result of this complaint:

Give this complaint to the appropriate person in the organisation.

USING WITNESSES

Common sense suggests that using witnesses who have a strong allegiance to the alleged bully may not be a good idea. In some instances, however, there may be an argument for using hostile witnesses; after all, they were present and know what happened. But it's risky, and the complainant will need to highlight to an investigator their likely lack of impartiality.

Even if witnesses lie about what they saw and/or heard, an astute investigator might use a roundabout way to get the truth from them. On the other hand, a less astute investigator might easily be taken in by a hostile witness who's a good liar or charmer. Overall, there are probably more risks than advantages in using hostile witnesses for a bullying complaint.

Discussed earlier was that sometimes witnesses are reluctant to get involved because they fear being bullied too, and in many instances their fears are well justified. It can be argued there's an ethical obligation for a bullied employee to ask witnesses for permission before naming them in a formal complaint. Listing them as witnesses can imply to the accused and the employer that they're on side with the complainant, which may not be the case; in fact, they may be strongly opposed to the complaint.

Usually, a claimant's case will be weaker without witnesses, but there are questions about whether putting a co-worker in the firing line as a witness without their permission is the right thing to do. It's a difficult one that individual claimants will have to decide based on individual circumstances.

ADVICE ON PRESENTATION

The standard of presentation will have an important bearing on the outcome of a claim. The facts rarely speak for themselves; they need to be explained clearly and in detail. In this section suggestions are provided on preparing a well-presented claim.

1. Aim for a high-standard presentation.
2. Rushing will likely result in mistakes and omissions.
3. Seek help with spelling, punctuation, grammar, language and writing if these are areas of difficulty.
4. Reach a compromise between writing too much and not enough.
5. Avoid over-emotional language, except for the section on how it made the claimant feel but, even then, refrain from an excessive outpouring of emotions.
6. Chapter 5 Impact on Targets can serve as a checklist for claimants about how they've been affected.
7. The temptation to attach meaning or motivation to the perpetrator's behaviour should generally be avoided; just stick to the facts through an outline of what happened.
8. Supporting information should be attached, such as copies of emails and other correspondence or notifications, transcripts of text messages, medical and/or counsellor reports, job description, etc.
9. Have a break from the document for a few days after completion, then go back and review it.
10. Ask an informed independent person to cast a critical eye over a final draft.

Even a well-prepared complaint might not ensure a positive outcome for a complainant. Sham internal investigations are not uncommon whereby dodgy employers decide from the outset to find an employee's allegations unsubstantiated. Even if an investigator finds that there are grounds for the employee's claims, the employer is under no legal obligation to accept them; the employer has the final say.

It can be hard, therefore, to predict with certainty how a complaint about bullying will be treated by an employer. Rather than assume the worst, however, a complainant should be positive, do their best with the documented complaint, but be prepared for things not to go smoothly. In particular, the accused may put up a strong defence, possibly with lies, so the complainant should be ready.

It should also be kept in mind that if a bullied employee is not happy with the response by their employer to a complaint, they can decide to pursue the matter further with a higher authority within the industrial or legal systems. The original complaint may be used to support an employee's case. If the original complaint was poorly presented, however, it may disadvantage the employee, especially if the employer uses it to discredit the complainant as part of their defence.

SUMMARY

- Detailed records of bullying incidents are required in a complaint to show that there's been a pattern of mistreatment.
- Employees will be unpopular if they accuse a colleague of bullying when it's not bullying.
- Allegations of bullying must be consistent with the definition provided in workplace health and safety regulations.
- Using the word 'bullying' in enquiries and formal complaints may invoke angry, highly-defensive and even retaliatory responses from those affected.
- The rules of tactfulness don't apply when reporting bullying at the most serious end of the scale, that is, for violence, threatened violence or stalking.
- A complainant's case must be strong because the accused will vigorously defend against it.
- Witnesses play a crucial role in a complaint about bullying, but they will be reluctant to get involved because they fear being bullied as well.
- Even a well-prepared complaint might not ensure a positive outcome for a complainant, especially when dodgy employers keen to conceal their bullying problem decide from the outset to find the complaint unsubstantiated.
- A complainant should be positive, do their best with the documented complaint, but be prepared for difficulty.

16

HAVING AN ADVOCATE

Advocates are vital when the processes are dodgy

An employee making an internal complaint about bullying may benefit from an advocate.

People can advocate on their own behalf, but in this instance, reference is being made to a person who puts a case on someone else's behalf. The term is commonly used when someone or a group represents or fights for the rights of others. Those supported by advocates can include just one individual or entity or a group of people. Often advocacy is undertaken on behalf of others when they're not well-placed to speak or act on their own behalf such as those experiencing disadvantage or illness, or who lack the required knowledge or confidence.

In the field of workplace bullying, some advocates charge fees, for example a lawyer; others are employed specifically to do advocacy, for example a trade union officer; they can be a professional worker whose job role includes an advocacy component, for example, a social worker, counsellor or medical practitioner; some advocates are volunteers, for example, a co-worker or informed person from the community; and sometimes family members and friends take on an advocacy role.

With workplace bullying, an advocate should be more than a passive support person such as one who accompanies a co-worker to a grievance or disciplinary meeting as an observer but doesn't have a speaking role. An advocate has an active and skilled role that is best undertaken by someone who's familiar with the issues and has strong negotiation abilities. A good advocate shouldn't be a pushover.

Ensuring that an employee is treated fairly is an important role of an advocate even when the eventual outcome is unlikely to favour the employee. For example, if an employee is guilty of serious misconduct at work, disciplinary action or dismissal may be inevitable, but the role of an advocate will be to ensure that proper, fair and just processes are followed.

Because of their greater knowledge, skills and experience, some employees are better equipped than others to advocate on their own behalf. For example, a well-educated and experienced senior manager who's well informed about the culture of their organisation, health and safety regulations, their rights, options and where to obtain support, might be able to speak or negotiate on their own behalf.

On the other hand, being targeted for bullying can be highly distressing. Consequent anxiety and depression will almost certainly impair an employee's ability to cope with the rigours of a complaints and investigation process, irrespective of their position or abilities. An advocate can play an import role in helping a distressed employee through their ordeal.

LEGAL ADVOCACY

In matters to do with workplace bullying, generally employers rely on lawyers more than employees do. Employers are highly anxious about the possibility of legal claims by employees for compensation for personal injury, including the bad publicity that might ensue. Some employers don't hesitate to involve lawyers early after a complaint about bullying has been received, not just for advice but sometimes as an intimidatory tactic against a complainant. Employers may even pre-empt a formal complaint and consult their lawyer when an employee makes an initial enquiry about bullying. When an employee threatens or implies legal action, the likelihood is greater the employer will respond by involving their lawyer. The following is an example:

'Sally'

Sally was accused by her supervisor of falsifying her time sheets at the supermarket where she worked. She responded to HR that the accusation was 'defamation'. What she really meant to say was that she was disappointed that the accusation had been made against her because it was false and a slur on her character.

Rather than seek clarification about what Sally meant by her comment, the nervous HR manager jumped to the conclusion that she was contemplating litigation for defamation. As a result, he arranged the first meeting to discuss the matter with Sally in the office of the company's lawyer. The experience was highly intimidating for Sally who attended the meeting by herself.

Although Sally was eventually cleared of any wrongdoing, the process was made more complicated and stressful for her by the addition of a legal theme. It also provoked the employer into adopting a defensive position whereby Sally was treated as an adversary.

In a biased investigation, the company's assertive approach towards Sally seemed motivated more by removing the threat of litigation than discovering the truth. Fortunately for Sally, the evidence against her was weak, but the pathway to clearing her name was bumpier than it needed to be.

If an employer is unreceptive, uncooperative or even hostile to a bullying complaint, it's reasonable to assume that the process is going to be demanding for a complainant. In such situations, a complainant might be advantaged by the support and protection of a lawyer. In highly volatile circumstances, lawyer-to-employer or lawyer-to-lawyer communication can be safer and more effective for a complainant than the complainant communicating directly with a hostile other side. Often a lawyer can filter out some of the nastiness that otherwise would be directed at the complainant by the alleged bully and/or their employer.

Founders of the US Workplace Bullying Institute Dr Gary and Dr Ruth Namie believe that an employee who intends to formally complain about their bullying at work will have a low chance of success without a lawyer as an advocate.[1] There's a saying that a person who represents themselves in court 'has a fool for a client'. The same may apply to complainants representing themselves in an internal bullying investigation.

Ongoing legal representation might cost an employee thousands of dollars, but an initial consultation could be an investment worth considering.

A word of caution, however. There's a saying 'when your only tool is a hammer, every problem will start to look like a nail', sometimes referred to as 'the law of the instrument'.[2] In other words, an employee who seeks advice from a lawyer about bullying may be led down a legal and adversarial pathway with their employer, but it may not be the only or best solution.

In some instances, it may be the best option and what the employee wants, but in other instances, involving a lawyer prematurely may set a confrontational tone and pre-empt exploration with the employer of alternative, more amicable and less costly options. For example, it may preclude the pursuit of mediation if the problem is really about a difference of opinion between co-workers and not workplace bullying. It's important to keep in mind that many reports of bullying by employees are not bullying at all, but rather a misinterpretation of legitimate management decision-making. This issue was outlined in Chapter 3 What Isn't Bullying. The following is a response from an employer about a recent experience he had with an employee and their lawyer.

'Employer W'

I'm struggling to think of an example where a bullying allegation has been raised that involves a lawyer where the accuser really wants a resolution so they can continue in their job, but rather they're wanting to resign with a payout. However, I acknowledge that in some instances resigning with a payout may be the only resolution they can see at the time, and they may be pushed in this direction by a lawyer.

Lawyers need fees to exist and I doubt whether many would say a case is weak and refuse to take it, especially if they know that most employers will settle to make it go away and for an amount that will cover the lawyer's fee. The alternative is that the situation hangs over everyone's heads for possibly many months and so diverts people's attention from other aspects of their work.

My recent experience with mediation with an employee and their lawyer left me angry as the lawyer deliberately, in my view, distorted facts to suit his case. I knew that actions taken by us to try to resolve the matter with the employee were genuine and with the best of intentions, but they were twisted by the lawyer to suit his story.

TRADE UNION ADVOCACY

Trade unions are not commercial enterprises and, therefore, not reliant on consultation fees like lawyers are. The union representatives I've had dealings with are stretched to the limit and, unlike lawyers, are not on the lookout for extra work. They may still recommend specific industrial action to an employee, including adopting a confrontational approach with their employer. But in the first instance, however, the union's priority is to protect the employee and their job by resolving problems quickly and amicably.

Having a union representative present in meetings with employers can even things up as well as act as a buffer against a hostile other side. Trade union officials can be particularly supportive of employees during bullying investigations. Investigators who aren't impartial, for example, a manager from HR, lawyer or an outside consultant hired by the employer, can be aggressive in their communication with claimants. Instead of genuinely trying to test the allegations and establish the truth, a biased investigator may try to discredit the claimant and their allegations.

Generally, an experienced union official will know when dodgy employers or investigators are up to no good. They can challenge a particular line of questioning, call for a break in a meeting when the employee is struggling, or can request a postponement if the employee breaks down under the pressure of interrogation. If the employee is distressed, which is most likely, they may not be able to do any of these things for themselves. Investigators are less inclined to bully or manipulate an employee when their methods are being scrutinised by a union representative.

It can be particularly helpful for a trade union official to represent an employee at a meeting with the employer and/or their representative when ill health prevents the employee from attending in person or participating fully. Sometimes it can be in the interests of emotionally vulnerable employees to keep them away from meetings when employers are predisposed to uncivil behaviour.

Workers employed in organisations with a culture of bullying may do well to consider joining their union without delay. The following example reinforces this advice.

'Roger'

Callous HR manager Roger, when confronted with a bullying complaint, misconduct allegations or performance concerns about an employee, would breathe a sigh of relief when informed that the employee wasn't a union member. This information was shared with me by a former colleague of Roger who said Roger's nickname in HR was 'The Hangman'. Despite his senior position and high salary, Roger had no qualifications or training relevant to his position as HR manager.

Lack of trade union representation allowed Roger free rein to handle issues with employees efficiently and effectively in his company's best interests, but not always in the best interests of employees. His management approach was contrary to the noble values that his company touted — honesty, respect, transparency and quality. Roger was underhanded and insincere, vulgar and disrespectful, sly and secretive, shoddy and incompetent — a nasty all-rounder.

To intimidate employees who'd submitted a formal complaint about their bullying, Roger routinely conducted meetings with them in the boardroom of the company's city-based lawyer. Picture Roger and the lawyer on one side of the giant boardroom table and the hapless employee sitting alone on the other side. Roger carried out forced redundancies without notice and often insensitively where, for example, the distressed targets were given minimal time to exit their workplace and were marched from the building by Roger in the company of a uniformed security guard.

He regularly colluded with department managers to get rid of unwanted staff using managing-out strategies including false allegations of misconduct, sham investigations and bogus performance improvement plans. Many employees were done over by Roger and his faithful and equally callous band of HR minions.

A union representative who'd had many dealings with Roger over many years described him in highly colourful language that I decided not to include here.

PROBLEMS WITH ADVOCACY

Be aware that while having an advocate such as a lawyer or union official can be helpful, it won't be of much benefit if they're incompetent or overworked. If they've got a big caseload, they won't have enough time to devote proper attention to support an employee.

If they're burnt out they'll be mentally weary, cynical and lack enthusiasm for and commitment to their work. Their negativity and lethargy may discourage an already demoralised claimant. They'll be a pushover for the other side. The same applies if they're incompetent.

Unfortunately, workers don't usually get to choose which union officer or lawyer will represent them. Also, the union or legal firm may switch representatives based on their other priorities, sometimes with minimal notice. This can be to the employee's disadvantage, especially if it's on the day of or close to an important meeting such as financial settlement negotiations when the replacement has had insufficient briefing or time to prepare. The following is an example:

'Dan'

Dan, a warehouse labourer, made allegations of bullying against three of his co-workers. Aspects of Dan's bullying were used as an example in Chapter 4 Bullying Behaviours.

After a biased internal investigation by the company's HR manager, Dan's allegations were found unsubstantiated. A difficulty for Dan's claim was that the three accused colluded to deny the allegations and there were no other witnesses. Therefore, it was just Dan's word against theirs.

After reading Dan's detailed allegations it would be difficult not to conclude that his bullying claim was genuine. The company may have secretly agreed because it offered Dan a commercial settlement to resign subject to signing a legally-binding non-disclosure statement and an agreement not to make a further claim for compensation from the company.

By this time Dan had engaged a lawyer to represent him. On the day of the meeting to discuss the financial settlement, without notice the lawyer failed to show up leaving Dan by himself to negotiate with the company's HR manager and lawyer. Dan could have asked for a postponement of the meeting, but he was too anxious to ask and his employer didn't offer it as an option.

Dan was no match for the cunning of the HR manager and company lawyer. He accepted their first offer which was two months' pay. With the support of his lawyer, Dan should have been able to negotiate a much bigger settlement.

Lawyers can assess quickly whether an employee has a strong legal case for compensation. They can estimate the potential amount of court-awarded compensation and can see through an employer's shady attempts to get off lightly with an excessively low first offer.

Dan's lawyer never explained to him why he had failed to attend the meeting and, quite rightly, didn't invoice Dan.

POOR ADVOCACY

The following are indicators of poor advocacy:

- failing to show up for important meetings
- being unprepared for meetings
- substituting unprepared advocates for meetings because of competing work priorities
- failing to return phone calls
- not sending important letters/emails or produce important reports on time, or not at all
- lacking negotiation skills
- being inappropriately passive in meetings and negotiations
- using unwarranted aggressiveness at meetings
- opting for the easiest or quickest solutions, but not necessarily the best ones for the employee
- telling the employee that they're busy and stressed and don't have the time to do everything.

Usually concerns about the competency of an advocate won't become apparent until their representation is under way. It's important that an employee communicates with their advocate any concerns about their advocacy or any other aspects of the arrangement sooner rather than later. An employee who's suffering from anxiety and depression from their bullying ordeal will likely have difficulty doing this. They may have to get someone else to communicate their concerns to their advocate. A capable family member, friend, counsellor or GP may be suitable for this task.

———

SUMMARY

- An advocate is a person who puts a case on someone else's behalf, commonly representing or fighting for their rights.
- Ensuring that an employee is treated fairly is an important role of an advocate even though the eventual outcome may not favour the employee.
- An advocate can play an important role in helping a distressed employee through an ordeal.
- A lawyer can filter out some of the nastiness that otherwise would be directed at the complainant by the alleged bully and/or their employer.
- Although ongoing legal representation is costly, an initial consultation with a lawyer could be a good investment.
- Meetings with employers about bullying can be highly threatening for employees, but with a union representative or lawyer present it can even things up and act as a buffer against a hostile other side.

17

IN-HOUSE INVESTIGATION

Employers should follow up formal complaints, informal reports, enquiries and suspicions about bullying

Often internal investigations of complaints about workplace bullying are conducted ineptly, dubiously or both. This chapter outlines how investigations should be carried out as well as the most common shortfalls.

Formal complaints, informal reports, enquiries and suspicions should always be treated seriously by employers, with in-house processes in place to deal competently and fairly with them. Even if formal complaints haven't been received, when employers suspect bullying, it should be followed up. It's an organisational hotspot and intervening early can prevent it from getting out of control.

Despite some employers using crude and sometimes dodgy methods of investigation, best-practice principles and processes do exist. WorkSafe New Zealand's information about workplace bullying is among the most helpful that I've seen.[1] It's based on Fair Work Australia's information, but goes further. WorkSafe NZ says it's important that employees know what to expect when they make a complaint.

Like many government regulatory authorities, however, it focuses on aspirations and ideals that stop well short of providing important practical information. Knowing what to expect, for example, should include a warning about inadequate and/or dubious investigation practices or that reporting bullying is risky and, in some instances, could be job- or career-ending for a complainant.

As recommended in the last chapter, before making a formal complaint about their bullying, employees should consult their union, a workplace health and safety authority or a lawyer. Unless there are compelling reasons to do so, generally it's not suggested that every potential complainant or their employer should engage a lawyer to represent them as the first step. This does not preclude consulting a lawyer for advice. In some situations, however, hiring a lawyer may impede the possibility of resolving matters more amicably.

But the point being made here is that employees intending to complain formally shouldn't undertake the perilous journey alone without expert guidance and support. It's common for employers to seek advice from lawyers and senior executives when faced with a bullying complaint, so when complainants go it alone, they run the risk of being 'outgunned' by the other side.

FAIR AND JUST INVESTIGATION

WorkSafe NZ provides principles to consider when dealing with allegations of bullying based in part on natural justice, which is about a duty to act fairly. They cover all parties to a complaint.

PRINCIPLES AND WHAT THEY MEAN

Treat all matters seriously
Take all complaints and reports seriously. Assess all reports on their merits and facts.
Ensure the people (internal or external) who deal with the complaint are trained to do a fair and thorough investigation, and use the principles of natural justice.

Act promptly

Reports should be dealt with quickly, courteously, fairly and within established timelines.

Ensure non-victimisation

It's important that anyone who raises an issue of bullying is not victimised for doing so. Whoever the complaint is made against and any witnesses should also be protected from victimisation.

Support all parties

Once a complaint has been made, both parties should be told what support is available, for example, employee assistance programmes or peer support systems.

Treat all parties involved with sensitivity, respect and courtesy.

Anyone involved is entitled to have a support person present at interviews or meetings, for example, a union representative, lawyer, co-worker or friend.

Be neutral

Impartiality towards everyone during the process is critical.

Where possible the person in charge of the investigation or resolution process should not have been directly involved in the incidents and must avoid any personal or professional bias.

Communicate the process and outcome

All parties need to be told what to expect during the process, how long it will take, the reasons for any delays and what will happen at the end. Give them clear reasons for any actions that are taken or not taken.

ASPIRATIONAL, NOT ACTUAL

Many investigations don't reflect the best ideals as outlined above. When employers are presented with a complaint about bullying, there appear to be five main response categories with some overlap. They are as follows:

- **A sincere well-handled investigation** — strong and genuine culture of respect, integrity and transparency; good understanding of workplace bullying prevention accompanied by clearly-stated policies and processes; management, internal and external consultants are well-trained and competent in employee investigations.

- **A sincere but poorly handled investigation** — genuine culture of respect, integrity and transparency but inadequate understanding of workplace bullying prevention; policies and processes on workplace bullying in place, but limited in-depth appreciation of what they mean or how to apply them; management and external consultants lack training and competency in employee investigation and blunder through various if not all phases of the process.

- **A sham investigation** — used to achieve a predetermined conclusion under the guise of legitimacy; can be used to conceal bullying or as a covert strategy to manage out unwanted staff; failure to observe impartiality; disparity in treatment of complainant and the accused; strategic delays throughout the process to unsettle complainant; ignoring investigator's findings if contrary to the employer's preferred outcome; explanation of findings not provided to complainant or accused.

- **A failure to investigate** — no genuine action taken on complaint; premature judgement of employee's grievance as groundless; rash or lazy assessment of the complainant's concern as a clash of personalities, with the parties asked to resolve the problem themselves or to participate in employer-initiated mediation; strategic downgrading of a serious bullying complaint to a clash of personalities to conceal the problem; no policies on bullying in place, or there are, but only for show.

- **A commercial settlement** — a response by an employer to prevent a potentially serious industrial problem from escalating to costly litigation and public humiliation/brand damage; sometimes referred to as 'go-away money' or 'hush money'; can be part of the process or conclusion to any of the above categories; may be a response to a request for compensation from an employee, union representative or lawyer; subject to legally-binding non-disclosure agreement and exclusion from further compensation; can be signed under duress by highly distressed employees desperate to end their ordeal; plays into the hands of callous employers eager to bring the matter to a conclusion quickly and more cheaply than court-awarded compensation for serious psychological injury; often accompanied by an ultimatum to accept the offer immediately or miss out with the threat of return to a miserable work life. Based on the experiences of the employees I consulted, including recipients of commercial settlements, it's about as dodgy an arrangement as you can get, despite attempts by employers to masquerade it as win-win.

INITIAL STAGE

The initial stage of a complaint may include the following steps:

- The employer's policy may stipulate that an employee intending to lodge a complaint must notify their supervisor or manager except when the manager or supervisor is the subject of the complaint, in which case the employee should go to the next senior manager or HR.
- Generally, the complainant should follow the employer's format for making a written complaint, but if there isn't one, the example included in Chapter 15 Preparing a Complaint can be used which makes provision for listing of specific allegations, dates, times, witnesses, etc.
- if required, employees should be assisted to complete their

written complaint by a willing, able and impartial person who could be a supervisor or manager, but not if they are connected in any way with the complaint or the accused. If this support is not available, an independent person such as a union representative, lawyer or other capable person may be suitable.

RECEIVING A COMPLAINT

The investigation process is usually initiated after a complaint is received. The following is based on WorkSafe NZ's advice to employers:

Inform the subject of the complaint as soon as possible after it is received, including:

- the details of the complaint and who made it
- the investigation process and their rights, including to have a support person present
- the requirement for confidentiality and non-victimisation
- the possible consequences
- expectation of behaviour during the investigation
- take reasonable steps to protect the complainant from reprisals
- ensure privacy is maintained
- organise an investigation process
- if there are safety concerns, organise security measures such as an escort to/from work for the affected party/parties
- as an interim measure during the investigation, ensure the safety of the complainant and the accused including suspension on pay, extended sick or special leave, reassignment of the complainant or accused
- provide guidance to the complainant and/or the accused on how to respond to one another if they need to remain in day-to-day contact during the investigation.

It's common for employers to overlook all or most of these important recommendations. The following are examples:

The chairman of the small not-for-profit board informed 'Kim', the manager, that she'd been reported for bullying but, incredulously, refused to provide her with any details. Kim was given a final warning without a formal investigation and, under threat of immediate dismissal, was told not to speak about the matter to anyone. She resigned shortly after.

Park ranger 'Tom' was asked to attend a meeting with his supervisor. He wasn't told beforehand that the purpose of the meeting was to discuss bullying accusations that had been made against him by a co-worker. It deprived him of the opportunity to prepare for the meeting or to have his trade union representative present.

Local government administration officer 'Jenny' spoke to her manager about being bullied. The manager said that he couldn't do anything unless Jenny lodged a formal complaint. This was contrary to his employer's policy which prescribed early intervention wherever possible prior to a formal complaint.

Sales manager 'Robyn' was accused of bullying by one of her co-workers. She was told by her manager that the allegations were very serious and she was facing disciplinary action if they were proven. Robyn was eventually cleared of any wrongdoing, but the investigation didn't commence for two months because it was the Christmas sales period. Then it was postponed for another two weeks when the investigator was away on annual leave. The experience left Robyn with a legacy of serious anxiety and depression necessitating a period of extended sick leave and medication for anxiety and depression.

'Jeff', an assistant warehouse manager in a national retail chain, made an informal enquiry to the HR manager about bullying by his supervisor. Jeff asked that his enquiry be kept off the record. But Jeff wasn't informed by the HR manager at the time that all matters to do with bullying had to be recorded and investigated. Jeff's supervisor was informed about Jeff's enquiry. An investigation was conducted and concluded that there were insufficient grounds for Jeff's bullying 'allegations'. Jeff said that he wouldn't have gone to HR had he known that his enquiry would be treated as an official complaint.

'Jodi', who worked for a large manufacturing company, made a formal bullying complaint about her supervisor. Two other staff, friends of the supervisor, cornered Jodi in the car park before work and verbally abused her. When Jodi reported the intimidation to her manager he responded, 'What do you expect when you shit on your workmates? You're just going to have to cop it.'

'Tony', a forklift driver in a timber yard, reported three of his co-workers for bullying him. Immediately they were informed they escalated Tony's bullying which included deflating his car tyres, smearing his forklift's seat with grease, and adopting an intimidating manner whenever they were nearby. When Tony reported his co-workers' behaviour to his supervisor he was told to 'be a man' and confront them. Tony was frightened by the aggressive trio and was unable to follow his manager's advice. He withdrew his complaint and resigned shortly after.

'Laura' was offered a commercial settlement amounting to a year's salary and a good reference if she would resign which would void her bullying allegations against the HR manager. Laura had been on extended leave for six months suffering anxiety and depression, which the company's consultant

psychiatrist had assessed as being caused directly by her mistreatment by the HR manager. The financial arrangement was subject to a legally-binding non-disclosure agreement and an undertaking not to pursue compensation from the company in the future. There was no investigation of her allegations.

THE INVESTIGATOR

Ideally the investigation should be undertaken by an independent, unbiased, preferably external, and experienced professional. An investigator should be an impartial fact-gatherer as they examine the evidence presented by the complainant, responses from the alleged bully and witnesses to establish whether there are grounds for the allegations. Where possible the person in charge of the process should not have had direct involvement in the areas of complaint or a personal interest in the outcome of the investigation.

The terms 'independent' and 'impartial', however, are used loosely with in-house investigations. For example, it's not uncommon for a so-called independent investigator to be:

- the manager on whose watch the alleged bullying occurred and/or who appointed the alleged bully to a position of responsibility
- someone who has a close working relationship/friendship with either the complainant or the alleged bully
- a manager investigating another manager who believes that managers should stick together
- someone whose main role is to protect the interests of the organisation, for example, the managing director, CEO, a board member, the HR manager/HR officer, the company lawyer or their appointee
- an external consultant who relies on the organisation for part

of their income and who may feel pressured to produce the outcome preferred by the employer.

NO PUNISHMENT?

For an employee whose allegations of bullying have been substantiated, it may appear that there have been no consequences for the offender. In some instances, this may be the case, but in others the consequences, including penalties, are simply not apparent.

In her article *What HR Won't Tell You About Employee Investigations*, organisational psychologist Shelley Baker says that if the allegations are substantiated, a complainant may be told only that the matter has been 'handled appropriately'.[2] On the one hand, this could mean that nothing has been done and the matter has been conveniently swept under the carpet after a sham investigation or there's been no investigation at all. On the other hand, it may mean that action has been taken but the details are confidential. Examples include:

- a disciplinary entry in the offender's personnel file, such as a warning
- a reduced performance rating
- a reduction in pay level
- denial of promotion
- withholding of a bonus
- remedial training
- pressure to resign or retire early, sometimes with a commercial settlement as an inducement
- non-renewal of contract.

Other actions may be more obvious such as a demotion, transfer to another department, branch or region. Sometimes an employer may respond more leniently to an offender when they've given good service to the organisation. They can be transferred to another department without loss of standing or salary and, in some instances fewer or no staff under their supervision. Alternatively, a new position can be created for them such as project manager where they largely work alone.

Sometimes these options are used when an employer fears that demoting or dismissing an offender could result in industrial, legal or public relations fallout. It's not unusual for employees who are dismissed for misconduct to claim wrongful dismissal on the grounds of bullying, sexual harassment or racial discrimination. Another strategy used by employers is not to renew the contracts of offenders. It may mean waiting a year or two, but the legal risks for the employer are reduced. The downside of this option is that the bully remains in the workplace with the associated risks for employees and employers.

NOT THE BIG END OF TOWN

A major limitation of most of the information on employee investigations is that it seems to target larger employers. The advice offered assumes that if they don't already have the knowledge and expertise to conduct a competent investigation, they have the potential, motivation and financial resources to gain it.

However, most employers are small businesses or not-for-profits where the limited HR functions are carried out by the owner, manager, a volunteer committee in the case of not-for-profits, or outsourced. Many of the wider HR concerns and responsibilities, such as staff conduct policies, bullying complaints and in-house investigations, simply aren't a priority because of limited time and/or lack of knowledge and financial resources.

In some instances, the alleged bully may be the only other staff member and could be the manager, proprietor, or a committee member. They may be family or a personal friend of the person in charge. Nepotism and cliques are commonplace in smaller organisations, especially family businesses and small not-for-profits, which can make it difficult and sometimes impossible for a bullied employee to get anywhere with an in-house complaint.

Irrespective of their size and limited resources, however, small employers aren't off the hook; they still have legal obligations to adhere to workplace health and safety laws with penalties for breaches.

SUMMARY

- Formal complaints, informal reports, enquiries and suspicions about bullying should be investigated by employers.
- Most government regulatory authorities focus on aspirations and ideals rather than on the practical realities.
- Before a formal complaint about bullying, employees should consult their union, a workplace health and safety authority or a lawyer.
- Few complainants have access to an investigation process which ticks all the right boxes.
- Ideally, investigations should be undertaken by an independent, unbiased, preferably external, and experienced professional.
- The terms 'independent' and 'impartial' are used loosely with in-house investigations.
- After allegations of bullying have been substantiated, the consequences for an offender may not be apparent.
- Staff conduct policies, bullying complaints and in-house investigations simply aren't a priority for many small employers because of limited time, lack of knowledge and financial constraints.

18

COUNSELLING

The distress and humiliation of bullying may be relieved by personal counselling

Being targeted for bullying can be a dreadful experience. Earlier, serious psychological, physical, and work and social consequences for victims of workplace bullying were listed. Counselling may help.

For some, the psychological, work, social and financial fallout from their bullying experience are more than they can bear. But it's not only the bullying itself that's a bad experience. If an employee decides to complain to their employer or report their bullying to workplace health and safety authorities or the police, apply for workers' compensation or take legal action, in many instances it will be a distressing experience as well. An investigation into alleged bullying can be a continuation of the complainant's bullying. Also, it's not unusual for the accused to be mistreated during an investigation and the example of 'Rod' who was wrongly accused of bullying was presented in Chapter 14.

This book began with the sad story of 'Jane' who was brutally bullied by her employer. Jane was left with an ongoing legacy of anxiety, depression and post-trauma stress. She commenced by attending counselling weekly, then fortnightly and now monthly. She believes that she wouldn't be able to cope without regular counselling.

WHAT IS COUNSELLING?

Counselling is a general term to describe the process of talking about and working through personal problems with a professional counsellor. The counsellor helps to clarify the issues, increase self-awareness, explore possible options, establish goals and develop a plan to achieve them.

Counselling is different from an informal chat about the problem that a person might have with their family, friends or co-workers. Counselling is a structured meeting facilitated by someone with special training in counselling. Counselling may take the form of a one-off session, a few appointments or regular meetings with a counsellor over months and, in some instances, years depending on the seriousness of the problem and the client's capacity to pay.

Counselling sessions are confined to a set period of time, most often between 45 minutes and an hour. Sometimes counselling can occur in a group, such as with family members or with other people struggling with the same problem.

Counselling provides confidential support which means that everything discussed with the counsellor is between the client and the counsellor only. An exception is when a counsellor is legally required to report something to authorities they've been told by the client that is a risk to the client's well-being or the welfare of others.

People who provide counselling use different labels to describe what they do. It's common to add the type of counselling to the name, such as grief counselling, marriage counselling, relationship counselling, sexual assault counselling, addiction counselling, consumer counselling, financial counselling and rehabilitation counselling.

Some counsellors refer to what they do as therapy and call themselves a family therapist, sex therapist, psychotherapist and behavioural therapist.

Psychologists who provide specialist counselling attach the area of specialty to their title, such as counselling psychologist, clinical psychologist, child psychologist, developmental psychologist, educational psychologist and sports psychologist.

There aren't too many counsellors who can legitimately claim to specialise in workplace bullying, although most are still able to assist an employee with the emotional fallout from their mistreatment at work. Some counsellors claim to specialise in mediation, but mediation isn't an appropriate response to an employee who's been regularly targeted for bullying. Highlighted in Chapter 3 What Isn't Bullying were the findings of research which suggested that mediation is often misused and overused as a strategy to address the problem of bullying and can exacerbate the situation when an imbalance of power already exists.

COUNSELLING APPROACHES

Counsellors borrow from a range of psychological approaches, but selecting a counsellor based on their qualifications or theoretical approach will be beyond most people. However, Professor Michael J. Lambert in his introduction and historical overview of psychotherapy and behaviour change in Bergin and Garfield's classic book on the topic, suggests that no one counselling type can claim superiority over another.[1] While counsellors may favour particular approaches, they use variations and modifications and usually select what they feel is best for the client and their circumstances.

According to Professor Lambert, the success of counselling is largely dependent on the client and therapist. This relates mainly to the capacity of the counsellor and client to develop a productive and trusting working relationship, the professional skills of the counsellor and the preparedness of the client to co-operate fully in the counselling process. Although Professor Lambert doesn't comment on it, the client's capacity to pay the counsellor's fee is a crucial factor. Many people would benefit from ongoing counselling, but simply can't afford to pay fees upwards of $100 per session. See the upcoming section 'Counsellors' fees'.

WHO ARE COUNSELLORS?

Counsellors should be trained, impartial and competent professionals with whom clients can develop a therapeutic relationship. In addition to their counselling qualifications, they often have backgrounds and qualifications in a range of human service work such as psychology, social work, medicine, psychiatric nursing and occupational therapy. This provides them with practical grounding for their counselling work. A professional counsellor is not the same as a psychiatrist. A psychiatrist is a medical doctor who has extra training specialising in mental health. A psychiatrist may offer counselling and can prescribe medications to help manage the symptoms of mental illnesses.

In Australia the relevant professional associations for counsellors are the Australian Counselling Association (ACA), the Psychotherapy and Counselling Federation of Australia (PACFA) and the Australian Psychological Society (APS).

Not all counsellors, however, are professionally qualified and, as strange as it may seem, there's no law in Australia that requires a person who provides counselling to have either qualifications or experience or be registered with a professional association. This means almost anyone can call themselves counsellors or psychotherapists and charge fees. Employees who've been targeted for bullying at work should proceed with caution in seeking support from these individuals.

CHOOSING A COUNSELLOR

Ideally, the best way to find a suitable counsellor is through a personal recommendation. As with all professions, there are good counsellors and not-so-good ones. Because it's difficult to tell the difference initially, an employee seeking counselling may have to rely on others for advice, such as a GP or someone they know who may be familiar with the work of a particular counsellor. A person may need to contact more than one counsellor to find one that's suitable.

It will be helpful to know if the counsellor has a conflict of interest regarding the employee's company or organisation, such as doing contract work for them currently or in the past. Some employers retain employee assistance counsellors to offer support to their workers. There may be issues about impartiality and confidentiality when the counsellor is paid by the employer. Potential problems might include the counsellor taking the employer's side or feeding back information to the employer on the employee's progress. Using an independent counsellor should avoid these problems.

If a potential counsellor is reluctant to respond to enquiries or makes an enquirer feel uncomfortable, then perhaps it's best to think twice about engaging them. A good counsellor will be able to handle most questions from a prospective client without becoming defensive or rude. The last thing a bullied employee needs is to be mistreated further during an enquiry about counselling.

COUNSELLORS' FEES

Counsellors' fees vary. Some counsellors, such as those who work in universities or community health centres, may be free or charge lower fees. Others may charge up to $150 or more per hour. The price charged by counsellors has no bearing on the quality of the service provided. Some counsellors offer a reduced fee to people experiencing financial difficulties.

Some counsellors may be eligible for a Medicare rebate, which means that the costs of a limited number of counselling sessions will be covered by Medicare, or clients may have to pay a small gap fee. To receive a Medicare rebate, a person must get their GP to put them on a mental health care plan. The GP will assess whether the person is eligible.

Medicare doesn't provide rebates for all counsellors. Employees seeking counselling will need to check with a potential counsellor about their eligibility. If an employee has private health insurance, they may be eligible for a partial rebate depending on their policy.

SUMMARY

- Counselling is different from informal support offered by family, friends and co-workers; it's more structured and takes the form of a one-off session, a few appointments or regular meetings.
- Counsellors use a range of approaches, but there's no strong evidence that one approach is superior to another.
- Employees who've been targeted for bullying at work should proceed with caution in seeking support from these individuals.
- Caution should be taken with seeking counselling from an individual who doesn't have relevant qualifications that provide them with eligibility for membership of a professional association.
- The best way to find a counsellor is through a personal recommendation, from either a GP or someone who is familiar with their work.
- The prices charged by counsellors have no bearing on the quality of the service they provide. In other words, if they charge more than others, it doesn't mean that they're better than the others.
- Some counsellors are eligible for a Medicare rebate, which means that the costs of counselling sessions may be covered by Medicare, or clients may have to pay a small gap fee.

19

TAKING LEGAL ACTION

Litigation is a slippery slope extending a bullied worker's distress

If an employee decides to take legal action against their employer for compensation for personal injury, their experience with the employer's insurance company will likely be tough.

One example is the case of manager 'Lena' who had a five-year legal battle with her employer's workers' compensation agency. Lena alleged that she was bullied by her manager and suffered a psychological injury as a consequence. The workers' compensation agency spent hundreds of thousands of dollars denying the employer's liability for Lena's claim. There were many hearings at courts or tribunals. Lena incurred hundreds of thousands of dollars in legal costs. After five years of trying to wear her down, the insurance company abandoned the case and had to pay Lena's compensation claim and her legal costs. But she was left with an enduring legacy of poor mental health — much worse than was caused by her original bullying.

Although news media report frequently on workplace bullying in Australia, less common is reporting of litigation for compensation for personal injury caused by bullying. This is because most action on bullying by employees rarely gets this far, and when it does it's settled confidentially out of court.

As indicated previously, workplace bullying is largely a covert event because of the shifty way that it's carried out and the great lengths many employers go to cover it up. Contributing to the veil of secrecy is the fact that most bullying isn't reported formally, either to employers or to workplace health and safety regulators; those who've been targeted either put up with it or resign.

Already highlighted is the wide range of devious strategies that unscrupulous employers use to deter or quash complaints. They include outright denial, casting aspersions on the credibility of the complainant, and making the accuser's life at work difficult to pressure them to withdraw their complaint or resign, which voids their complaint.

Bullied employees who explore the possibility of legal action against an employer discover that it will likely be a slippery slope which, in the first instance, extends and exacerbates the distress of their bullying, possibly over years as in Lena's case. There's no guarantee of a successful outcome, and even if they do win, once they pay their lawyer's fee, barrister's fee and the costs of reports from experts such as psychiatrist and physician, and sometimes a private investigator, often there's not much money left over to justify the experience, at least not financially.

Generally, damages awarded by the courts for a debilitating psychological injury are not as high as for an incapacitating physical injury and certainly nowhere near enough to set up an employee financially for life as some of them initially fantasise about. When settled out of court, as most cases are, the amount is usually lower than would be awarded by the court. If an employee loses their case, they can be liable for the other side's costs in addition to their law firm's legal outlays, known as disbursements, which can total many thousands of dollars.

It's difficult to argue against the pursuit of vindication, self-respect and dignity. Founders of the US Workplace Bullying Institute Dr Gary Namie and Dr Ruth Namie maintain that fighting back aids a bullied employee's need for fairness and being able to move on with their dignity intact.[1] They caution, however, about the likely costs to an employee's health, the toll 'vicious defensive employers' can impose with help from their lawyers, and economic losses.

According to Dr Jan Harper, author of *Mobbed: What to Do When They Really Are Out to Get You*, the risks for employees of fighting back at any stage of the bullying process are far too high.[2] Dr Harper was awarded financial damages for personal injury caused by bullying, but she said that her payout was small compensation for the loss of her career as an anthropologist at a university and the adverse impact on her health. An excerpt from Dr Harper's reflections on her experiences is included in Chapter 20 Toughing It Out.

In their book *The Bully at Work*, the Namies express similar views to those of Dr Harper:

> *The justice you seek to reverse the unfairness experienced in your bullying workplace can rarely be achieved in a courtroom. We know targets who have won more than $1 million in a settlement and still were not satisfied. The bully still had his job and was telling lies years after the lawsuit.*[3]

The Namies add that filing a lawsuit will lead to predictable retaliation from an employer, tremendous financial expense, and the risk of exacerbating the emotional damage caused by bullying. Lawyers are expensive; they read documents slowly and charge for everything, including short phone calls to and from their clients. Many victims of bullying report that in the courtroom anxieties are triggered and repeat the worst feelings experienced during the original bullying, which puts them at serious risk of being re-traumatised. Cross-examination by unsympathetic defence lawyers can re-immerse victims in the distress and humiliation that they felt during their bullying.

In this chapter some of the issues for employees considering legal action against their employer have been presented. The information does not constitute legal advice. Legal information provided here has been summarised from documentation written by qualified legal practitioners. For more detailed information specific to an individual's circumstances, a lawyer should be consulted.

NO WIN, NO FEE

A no-win-no-fee arrangement, also called a conditional costs agreement, is used generally where a client is unable to pay for legal services, and where a lawyer believes there's a realistic chance of winning the case.[4]

Successful claimants will have to pay their lawyer up to half the amount awarded by the court. There are also other costs, disbursements and fees that they will still have to pay, whether they win or not. These additional costs can take their legal expenses to over half. The costs charged in a no-win-no-fee arrangement can be higher than those charged in a standard costs agreement. This is because the lawyer is risking that they won't be paid for their services if the case isn't successful.

SEDUCTIVE ADVERTISING

Nowadays many legal firms strongly market their personal injury litigation services which are usually made more attractive by the availability of no-win-no-fee arrangements. Legal firms' personal injury advertising aims to encourage or induce a person to:

1. Make a claim for compensation damages under an Act or law for a personal injury; or
2. Use the services of the practitioner or a named law practice in connection with the making of a claim.[5]

Advertising slogans can be seductive for despairing employees hoping for financial compensation, justice and/or retribution through legal action. A sample of marketing slogans from Australian law firms includes:

- We believe you are worth fighting for
- Our best accident lawyer will ensure you get maximum compensation
- Workers' compensation is your right
- We help you with your claim, ease your fears, allowing you to heal yourself and get your life back on track
- The payout you deserve
- No injured person should be denied access to justice because of their financial situation
- We win cases like yours
- We're about one thing: Winning. The fee will be fair and the service will be outstanding
- Get the compensation you deserve
- Tough case, we're together
- We fight for fair.

After reading the list of enticing slogans, it would be understandable for claimants to think that winning their legal case is a foregone conclusion. For readers' enlightenment, however, I've listed some common marketing slogans repeated from the list above in bold type, followed by a sobering editorial comment.

- **Workers' compensation is your right**, *yes, but only if you've got a watertight case.*
- **The payout you deserve**, *but after legal costs you'll get only a fraction of what you deserve.*
- **We win cases like yours**, *even though at this stage we know nothing about your situation, so really we have no idea if we can win your case or not.*
- **We help you with your claim, ease your fears, allowing you to heal yourself and get your life back on track**, *but in the first instance, the lawyers of your employer's insurance*

company will use every technique to discredit your version of events which, given your current fragile state of mind, will break your spirit and add to your PTSD's range of highly distressing flashbacks.

- **Get the compensation you deserve**, *but after meeting you and assessing your chances we may decide that you deserve nothing.*
- **Tough case, we're together**, *but we're more together with less risky full-fee-paying clients.*

It doesn't automatically follow that an enquiry about litigation will result afterwards in actual litigation. Irrespective of their tantalising marketing slogans, lawyers experienced in personal injury litigation will assess quickly whether a potential client has a valid claim. But they need to lure them into their office first to check out the possibilities. They will also assess the eligibility of a case for a no-win-no-fee arrangement, which is the probability of the case settling at an amount enough to pay the lawyer's fees and disbursements.

A problem may arise, however, when a bullying victim is exposed to a legal firm's seductive advertising and, before speaking to a lawyer, assumes that they've got a strong case. After suffering the humiliation and distress of being bullied at work, maybe over years, despairing employees may be heartened by the renewed hope offered by a potential legal solution. Although their newfound optimism might be shattered at a first meeting with a lawyer, there could be problems beforehand if they've already threatened their employer with legal action. The very mention to employers of litigation for damages for psychological damage caused by bullying may set in motion the 'vicious defensive' process referred to earlier by Ruth and Gary Namie.[6]

LITIGATION LOANS

Some lawyers suggest that potential clients unable to afford legal costs enter into a litigation loan agreement. This is a commercial loan from a credit provider that covers the cost outlays while a case is in progress, and which must be repaid with interest once the matter is finalised. The advantage for claimants is that they can pay legal fees as their case progresses and settle with the lender at the conclusion of the case. The advantage for lawyers is that their financial risks from a no-win-no-fee arrangement are reduced. As with a no-win-no-fee agreement, a loan company must be satisfied that the case in question has a high probability of settling at an amount enough to repay their loan.

Associate Professor of Law at the University of New South Wales Michael Legg highlights that currently the major risk for consumers of entering into a litigation loan agreement is that in Australia, licensing and capital adequacy regulations are lacking. In the first instance, this means that anyone or any entity can fund litigation. Second, without capital adequacy requirements, there's no protection for complainants (or defendants) ensuring that the funder has enough resources to be able to pay the legal fees.[7]

Additionally, because of the lack of regulations governing litigation lending, loan companies can charge exorbitant interest rates, sometimes as high as 60 per cent. Because the loan is not repaid until after a case is settled, it incurs compound interest which is interest calculated on the initial principal and also on the accumulated interest of previous periods of the loan. Ever-increasing debt to the loan company may pressure claimants to settle their case quickly, including for less than it's worth.

Also, if they win, they may end up with little or no money left over from their settlement after paying their lawyer's fees, disbursements and the loan. They may even face the possibility of going into debt.

Before entering into a litigation loan agreement, potential claimants should obtain independent legal and financial advice. In the first instance, the section on litigation funding in *'No-win-no fee' costs agreements* by the Queensland Legal Services Commission is a must-read.[8]

CLASS ACTION

Class actions are most common where the allegations involve multiple people who've been injured by the same defendant in the same way. Instead of each damaged person bringing their own lawsuit, the class action allows all the claims of all class members to be resolved in a single proceeding through the efforts of the representative plaintiff(s) and appointed class counsel.

A class action can be commenced where:

- seven or more people have claims against the same person/s
- the claims are in respect of, or arise out of, the same, similar or related circumstances
- the claims involve at least one substantial common issue of law or fact.

Generally, the courts are flexible with their interpretation of these requirements. Despite the apparent simplicity of the above criteria, however, it's important not to underestimate the complexity involved in constructing a class action properly. The amounts claimed in class actions are often large, legal costs are similarly large, the average duration of class actions is around two years, and adverse publicity may be generated for the respondents involved.[9]

Of the 513 class actions in Australia between 1992, when the Federal class action regime commenced, and 2017, the most prominent class actions included claims by investors, other than shareholders, and claims by shareholders and consumer protection issues. The average number of class actions filed annually in Australia between 2012 and 2017 was 36.[10]

FINDING A SUITABLE LAWYER

Advice provided in this section has been sourced from the Law Institute of Victoria.[11]

There is a range of ways to choose a lawyer:

1. Get a referral from a lawyer
If an employee has used a lawyer before and is happy with the service provided, but their lawyer doesn't practise in personal injury caused by bullying, they can be asked for a referral to someone who does, and preferably obtain two or three names.

2. Ask friends or acquaintances
If an employee has never dealt with a lawyer before, they can ask someone who has. It's important to know if they were satisfied with their lawyer. Particularly if not, why not? A personal recommendation is usually a good way to help make a choice.

3. Other professional people
People who an employee has contact with, such as a trade union, counsellor, doctor or accountant, may know a lawyer.

4. States' Law Institutes/Legal Services Commission referral services
These organisations can put employees in touch with a lawyer. With an official referral letter from the institutes/commissions, participating law firms will see clients for a consultation of up to the first 30 minutes, free of charge. This inquiry interview can be used to determine with the lawyer whether the case may be valid, what the available options are, and receive an estimate of costs to proceed with the matter. Even if an employee is not clear whether there is a legal case, they can still take advantage of this service.

There's no guarantee that a suitable lawyer will be found at the first attempt. But it's important to locate a lawyer the client feels comfortable with and whose advice can be taken with confidence.

Attempts to identify a suitable lawyer for advice and/or litigation may be difficult. Wading through the advertisements on the Internet is confusing. For example, the quantity of no-win-no-fee legal firms is overwhelming. Many claim that they're better than the rest. Some imply that the others have questionable ethics because they conceal or gloss over hidden costs. Yet others maintain that no-win-no-fee is not a good option because lawyers undervalue no-win-no-fee clients in favour of full-fee-paying clients and, consequently, provide the former with a substandard service.

A client will likely make a large investment of time and money in resolving a legal problem, so careful choice of a lawyer is important.

BEING WELL PREPARED

Some parts of this section, mainly the dot point items, have been adapted from information provided by the Law Institute of Victoria.[12]

It's important to give a lawyer a clear picture of what the problem is and what outcome is wanted. Prior to a first meeting, it's important to collate as many facts and documents related to the case as possible so they can be presented to the lawyer for assessment. The more information available the better, as it will help the lawyer provide accurate and prompt advice. For example, prior to a first meeting, potential clients should:

- Prepare questions for the lawyer.
- Write down expected outcomes.
- If helpful, organise for a support person to attend the first meeting.
- If necessary, arrange for an interpreter to be available.
- Write down events that have constituted mistreatment at work,

including time, dates, witnesses, emotional impact at the time, the impact on work performance and health, action taken to address the problem and outcomes.

Use the first meeting to obtain as much information as possible. Important things to know include:

- Does the lawyer have experience with your kind of problem?
- Can the lawyer give an estimate of the likely time involved?
- Can the lawyer begin work immediately?
- What options exist to deal with your legal matter?
- What steps are involved in solving the problem?
- How much time is each step likely to take?
- What are the chances of success, and would it be better to try to negotiate a settlement?
- Is there anything that can be done to reduce the time the lawyer has to spend on the case, and so reduce costs?
- Can the lawyer give an early estimate of what the total legal costs might be, including disbursements, and how they will be calculated?
- When will a final estimate of costs be provided?
- When are costs paid?
- Is no-win-no-fee an option, if this hasn't already been established?*
- Does the lawyer keep clients regularly informed of all developments in cases as they happen?*
- Will the lawyer be the assigned primary contact person?*
- What is the best way to communicate with the lawyer once legal proceedings commence?*
- What is the maximum response time for the lawyer replying to telephone or email queries from clients?*
- What is the likelihood of the case being transferred to a different lawyer in the practice?*
- What impact might this have on the outcome of the case?*

- Is there eligibility for legal aid? (Not all lawyers take legal aid cases.)

* Additional items by the author

At the first and subsequent meetings with a lawyer, take notes of what is said for personal records. The notes can be typed later and sent to the lawyer for confirmation of their accuracy.

The lawyer should be informed of any concerns about the employee's imminent personal safety at work.

Most problems between lawyers and clients stem from a lack of communication. If problems arise, the client should speak with or write to the lawyer.

Potential clients should not be put off immediately by a seemingly cold-hearted lawyer. A non-empathetic lawyer may present some difficulties for an employee distressed by their bullying experience. But the main prerequisite for a good lawyer, however, is their capacity to provide a client with accurate information, sound advice and strong representation. They're not a personal counsellor who's been trained in empathy. While a lawyer's capacity for compassion will likely be an asset, having it is more about their personality. It's their ability to represent the client competently which is the most important.

A personal counsellor may help a bullied employee through their experience, including coping with the legal process.

SUCCESSFUL LITIGATION

Taking legal action for damages is a complicated process which carries many risks for a bullied employee — emotionally and financially. Reliving their experience through the legal process is likely to trigger the return of distressing psychological symptoms of mistreatment thus prolonging and exacerbating the trauma.

For most potential litigants, thoughts about receiving substantial financial compensation for psychological injuries caused by their bullying are fanciful. More likely they will be left wondering whether litigation was worth the trouble. For those who've been seriously re-traumatised by their litigation experience, the answer may be obvious.

Employees considering taking legal action for injury compensation may benefit from reading *Workplace Bullying Lawyers' Guide — How to get more compen$ation for your client* by Australian human rights lawyer Kathryn-Magnolia Feeley.[13] It's not only relevant for lawyers, but for everyone dealing with workplace bullying. It provides much more detailed information than the general information included here, especially about the medical information required for litigation, legal arguments, Australian legislation and policy, templates and case studies. According to Feeley, the book is liberally sprinkled with case law so that when defence lawyers try to object, they can be 'clouted with authority' from case law.

Feeley says the starting point for achieving success in litigating cases of injury caused by workplace bullying is proving:

- the injury was caused by the workplace
- the nature of the actual injury.

This involves investigating the workplace in question and verifying the actual injuries with medical, psychiatrists' and psychologists' reports. Once an employee has evidence that a workplace is dangerous and that injuries were the result of their workplace, then they're ready to proceed with litigation.

Common law requires that information on an application containing a statement of offences must at least identify the essential factual ingredients of the actual offence. Therefore, evidence needs to include a detailed events chart which records the injury-causing workplace events in logical order to demonstrate an emerging pattern of unacceptable behaviour.

It's essential that applicants take the chart seriously and complete it daily. For bullying to be considered by the court, it must be continual and systematic. Refer to the sample chart in the section 'Complaint structure and content' in Chapter 15 Preparing A Complaint.

Feely says that most aspects of workplace bullying can be insidious, and the bully's defence lawyers may try to make the applicant appear to have 'litigation neurosis', 'paranoid personality traits' or 'irrational and emotional thinking'. One of these will form the basis of their argument. Psychiatrists for the defence will aim to prove mild depression to trivialise the applicant's claim for damages due to workplace injuries. Therefore, an events chart that records every bullying action is crucial evidence to show that the applicant has been subjected to a pattern of bullying behaviour rather than a misinterpretation of events, a personality disorder or mental health condition.

Employees considering taking legal action on their bullying should consult a lawyer who will be able to provide advice based on the employee's individual circumstances.

SUMMARY

- A no-win-no-fee arrangement, also called a conditional costs agreement, is used generally where a client is unable to pay for legal services, and where a lawyer believes there's a realistic chance of winning the case.
- Lawyers' slick media marketing techniques may lead to premature conclusions by an employee that they've got an open and shut case. There could be problems if employees, romanticising about successful litigation prior to a consultation with a lawyer, threaten their employer with legal action.
- A litigation loan agreement is a commercial loan from a credit provider that covers the cost outlays while a case is in progress, and which must be repaid with interest once the matter is finalised. There are pitfalls with this approach to funding legal costs.
- Class actions involve a group of people who've been injured by the same defendant in the same way and where bringing a lawsuit allows all the claims of all members to be resolved in a single proceeding.
- Ways to locate a suitable lawyer include a referral from a lawyer known to the employee but who doesn't specialise in employment or personal injury law, friends and acquaintances, other professional people, and States' Law Institutes/Legal Services Commission referral services.

20

TOUGHING IT OUT

It's hard to leave a job you love

If you're the target of a workplace bully, your greatest safety may be to find another job[1] Workplace bullying can cause mental and physical health problems, destroy careers, break up families, ruin work friendships, create massive financial difficulties and lead to problems with physical health and emotional issues.

In this chapter the pros and cons of targets remaining in a bullying work environment are presented, especially when leaving doesn't appear to be a practical option. There don't appear to be many pros, especially in an organisation which has a strong culture of bullying. But, in some instances, there are ways to reduce the risks. Also examined is the option of cutting losses, resigning and starting afresh.

In earlier chapters it was revealed that most employees who've been targeted for bullying either tough it out, resign or do both, that is stay temporarily and leave as soon as they can. Only a small proportion of employees attempt to resolve their bullying with a formal complaint. Most believe it will be a waste of time and result in retaliation from the bully and/or their employer.

It's important that employees learn what workplace bullying is and what it isn't and not rush to report bullying or resign from their jobs before exhausting all possibilities to work things out.

There are many books dedicated to managing stress at work — coping with toxic workplaces, noxious managers, difficult co-workers, working with narcissists, borderline personalities, sociopaths, psychopaths, assholes, jerks, weasels and snakes. In the Helpful Reading section, a small selection is included.

REASONS TO STAY

Canadian author Katherine Williams, author of *Workplace Bullying: A Survival Guide*, says that the safest way for targets of bullying to proceed is to find another job as quickly as possible.[2] However, while the inclination for many employees might be to escape the distress and humiliation of their bullying without delay, resigning isn't always an easy option for them. The following are some of the reasons:

- current financial commitments may be reliant on their present level of income
- there are no other local job opportunities requiring their specialised skills
- their limited qualifications, experience and skills may restrict opportunities to obtain other work
- alternative employment opportunities may be limited generally
- relocating to another region or State for employment involving shifting/selling home, changing children's schools, moving away from close friends and community may be costly and result in massive social upheaval
- they may be close to retirement restricting their desire and/or ability to change jobs
- they've worked hard to advance their career and may be reluctant to consider a lesser job

- loss of self-esteem, confidence and trust from the trauma of their bullying may lead them to believe that they're not capable of getting another job
- a belief that they're indispensable to their job, company or field of work
- feeling that if they've done nothing wrong, they shouldn't have to leave
- denial of the seriousness of their situation and failure to recognise the damage to their mental and physical health
- inability to obtain a good job reference because of their bullying circumstances
- fear that future employers may see them as 'damaged goods' and be reluctant to risk giving them a job
- despite their mistreatment, some areas of the job may remain satisfying such as:

  – fulfilling nature of the actual work tasks
  – strong relationships with co-workers, patients, clients and customers
  – attractive salary and benefits such as a company car
  – recognition for achievement at work and more widely
  – promotion opportunities
  – job security
  – convenient location
  – pleasant physical surroundings.

Although the satisfying aspects of a job can provide motivation to put up with or manage bullying, a serial bully could be determined to destroy every positive feature of their target's work life, sometimes with the support of management. It's not uncommon for the best job an employee has ever had to become the worst job because of bullying. Sometimes the perceived advantages of staying are outweighed by the drawbacks, particularly when the impact of ongoing bullying on an employee's health is extreme.

STANDING UP TO A BULLY

In a US Bullying Institute study, respondents who'd been targets of bullying recommended standing up to the bully.[3] Their advice includes:

- Don't take any kind of crap from anybody.
- Fight back from the beginning.
- Don't back down.
- Challenge the bully and stand up for your own beliefs.

Advice about standing up to the bully appears to assume that the bully may be reasonable or a coward and will back off. It's difficult to endorse the above advice because of the *unknowns* and *unpredictables* which could make a bullied employee's circumstances far worse, such as:

- the targeted employee's capacity to effectively challenge their bully
- the possibility of a bully responding aggressively when challenged
- the state of health of the bullied employee and their ability to cope with a worsening of their bullying if the bully intensifies their mistreatment when challenged
- if the employee's bullying is condoned or directed by management as an insidious managing-out strategy
- whether there are multiple bullies ganging up on the employee (mobbing)
- if standing up to the bully will result in accusations of incompetence, insubordination, discipline or even dismissal.

It's a fallacy that serial bullies always back down when challenged. In the first instance, an employee may not be capable of effectively challenging their bully. Bullying saps the confidence and self-esteem of targets, affects their capacity to function day-to-day, and may result in the onset of a range of temporary or longer-term mental health problems such as anxiety and depression. More about the health and social consequences for targets of bullying appeared in Chapter 5 Impact on Targets.

It may be difficult, therefore, for an affected employee to summon up or even feign bravado to confront their bully. In some instances, a bully may back down or ease up when confronted, but they're just as likely to escalate their bullying, especially if encouraged and supported by accomplices, including management.

Various authors maintain that taking a stand against a bully can restore a bullied employee's self-respect and lost dignity and satisfy their need for justice and, in some instances, this may be true. However, Noa Davenport and her colleagues, authors of *Mobbing: Emotional Abuse in the American Workplace*, say that when management is involved in an employee's bullying, attempts to resolve the problem by any reasonable means are simply a waste of time.[4]

Several authors have suggested that if a bully is at the serious end of anti-social personality disorder, there's not much hope of successfully challenging them.[5,6,7] See Chapter 10 Bullying And Personality for more about this issue.

COPING STRATEGIES

There is a range of books which include suggestions about how employees can manage bullying at work. In this section, brief excerpts for readers' consideration are included from a small sample. More are included in the Chapter References and Helpful Reading sections.

Is complaining pointless?

The reflections of Dr Jan Harper, anthropologist, target of workplace mobbing and author of *Mobbed! What to Do When They Really Are Out to Get You*, are a good place to start.[8] Dr Harper writes:

Most of what we complain about at work is really pointless. Most of the so-called grave injustices and abuses we suffer are really better off ignored. Had I endured the small injustices, I would never have endured the great ones. If I had laughed off the bad behaviours, I would never have suffered the atrocities. Had I left my ego at home when I went to work, I never would have had it slaughtered by the people I worked with and trusted.

It doesn't mean I deserved it. It doesn't mean that they were right to do it. And it doesn't mean that it is okay by any means. What it means is that I walked straight into a den of wolves and offered up my jugular, when I should just have kept my mouth shut and observed them.

What I've learnt is that in so many cases, mobbing turns into a wildfire of torment because the person who has been targeted has let their mind run in an endless loop of wrongs they think need to be righted, cannot control their emotional moods and rage, and they have put their egos ahead of their interests — which is completely disempowering. We need to learn to control how and what we think, how and what we feel, what we say and how we say it.

It also means weighing our options, not based on idealism, but on reality. And the reality is that pursuing justice is usually a lonely pursuit and one that offers little reward. We need justice in the world and we need idealists, but don't put your career on the line for your ideals (nor sell your ideals for your career). There are other ways to fight for fairness. But when it comes to the injustice in our own worlds, far too many mobbing targets find themselves blinded and buried in their pursuit for justice. And once blinded and buried, we cannot effectively achieve any meaningful victory over injustice.

Coping with 'assholes'

Professor Robert Sutton, in his best-selling book *The No Asshole Rule* advocates that targets of bullying at work should alter their mindset about what's happening to them.[9] He advises:

- Avoid self-blame for having become a target. Bullying is about the bully and not the target. The target's self-worth is not linked to how they are treated by the bully.
- Detach emotionally from the bully's abusive tirades; it's about the bully and not the target.
- Develop learned optimism which is about seeing bullying as a temporary situation. Eventually, the target or the bully will move on, up or out.
- While hoping for the best, targets should expect the worst. Targets should lower their expectations of the bully and the workplace in general.
- Look for small victories rather than large-scale changes. Maintaining the power to control small aspects of their circumstances at work can have a major impact on their well-being as well as reducing their sense of hopelessness and helplessness.
- Targets can use a variety of ways to limit their exposure to bullies. Communicating via written memos and emails can prevent going face-to-face with demeaning, humiliating tirades from bullies.
- Find and build some vital pockets of support at work among kind, decent people. Targets need to discover that the entire organisation is not filled with insensitive people.

N.I.C.E.

Ronald Shapiro and Mark Jankowski, US civil rights lawyers and authors of *Bullies, Tyrants and Impossible People*, say they developed the N.I.C.E. system to deal with people who are difficult, angry, irrational, emotional, demanding, close-minded, tyrannical, illogical, rude and who, as a result, can create a personal encounter that is dreaded, feared, hated, upsetting, intimidating, challenging, distasteful, disgusting, offensive, stomach-churning, or all of the above.[10]

The authors say that many of us would rather avoid all contact rather than face one of these types. But they add that we can't just put our heads in the sand and hope that the problem will go away. According to the authors, N.I.C.E. is a systematic approach for dealing with all of life's difficult people without becoming one of them. They claim that it's simple, proven, and applicable to virtually any type of difficult person or situation. They add, however, that the acronym N.I.C.E. doesn't imply that the user might be soft or a pushover. On the contrary, they say, it requires them to be focused, assertive and resourceful. An outline of the N.I.C.E. system is as follows:

N.I.C.E.

N — Neutralise your emotions. The more emotional you are, the less rational you will behave. The more your emotions are neutralised, the more you can be in control of a bullying encounter.

I — Identify your bully's type: (1) those people who make situations or circumstances difficult, (2) those people who believe that being unreasonable is effective, and (3) those people who have embedded personality characteristics or disorders that result in bullying behaviour.

C — Control the encounter. Once you know your enemy's type you can use effective techniques to determine the outcome of the encounter.

E — Explore options. Even after you shape the outcome, you may still be at an impasse with the bully. Examine alternatives that will not make the bully feel like they have lost power over you. One important option is ending the encounter without escalating the conflict. 'If you give me this stupid letter of reprimand, I'm calling my lawyer' is not a good way to de-escalate the situation. Save ultimatums for instances when the best deal is no deal at all.

Before attempting to apply the advice provided in the preceding extracts, I strongly recommend a more detailed examination of the authors' work. Included here are only brief summaries which, by themselves, might suggest that the advice is easily applied. But some of the advice such as detaching emotionally, controlling meetings with bullies, identifying a bully's personality type, and reducing face-to-face contact with them is more easily said than done.

Self-help books or advice on the Internet should not be the only sources of guidance for employees' problem-solving on workplace bullying. In some instances, the advice given may be totally unsuited to the employee's individual circumstances. Sometimes the authors have education, intelligence, insights, experience, motivation, confidence and abilities that far exceed those of many of us, so it can be misleading when they imply that their advice suits everyone.

Advice from books, including this one, and the Internet should always be combined with guidance from informed people familiar with an employee's individual circumstances such as a GP, counsellor, trade union representative or lawyer.

RESIGNING

In his book, *The Asshole Survival Guide*, best-selling author Professor Robert Sutton commences his chapter Make a Clean Getaway with 'I believe in quitting.'[11] He disputes the idea that *quitters are losers and losers are quitters.* Sometimes it may be difficult if not impossible for an employee to remain in their job such as when:

- all attempts to resolve the problem through reasonable means have failed

- bullying is having or could have a serious impact on the employee's mental and physical health
- the situation is affecting adversely the employee's life away from work
- there are no policies and processes in place to protect workers from bullying
- it's clear that the targeted employee is at the top of a serial bully's hit list
- bullying is being used deviously by management to force an employee's resignation
- the workplace is so toxic that no one is immune from bullying or being a bully.

It's important that bullied employees have considered all reasonable avenues to resolve the problem prior to resigning.

FINDING ANOTHER JOB

While coaching on job-seeking is beyond the scope of this book, I've included some considerations for employees who decide to leave their job because of bullying. As a rule, it's better to apply for another job while still employed. Unfortunately, sometimes there can be a stigma associated with being unemployed which implies that the job applicant somehow is to blame for their unemployment which, of course, is not always the case. The Covid-19 pandemic, for example, resulted in many employees losing their jobs when their employers' businesses became unviable. But even then, some prospective employers may be suspicious about the reasons why an employee was chosen over others to be let go.

There seems to be general acceptance in the employment field that securing employment is usually more complicated when an employee has left their last job 'under a cloud'. Prospective employers usually ask applicants why they want to change jobs or why they left. It may be challenging to respond to these questions when the truthful answer is:

- I was sacked.
- I was bullied.
- I hated my job.
- I hated my boss.
- I didn't get on with a co-worker.
- My job has severely affected my health.

It's important that a job applicant be prepared to answer the challenging questions and in a way that reflects positively on them. This issue is covered in the remainder of this chapter.

PROBLEMS WITH LYING

It can be a challenge for these workers who have left their jobs 'under a cloud' to find the right thing to say to prospective employers. Lying is risky because of the possibility of being found out, which will usually end any prospects of being offered a job by that employer. Employers usually require references from an applicant's last job. If a reference yields little more than an employee's start and finish dates with no indication of their positive value to the organisation, an employer may conclude that something is fishy about the applicant's reasons for changing jobs.

Depending on the nature of the job, employers may be thorough with their assessment of job applicants. Background checks could include investigation of the applicant through informal industry networks as well as the content of applicants' social media connections such as Facebook, Twitter and LinkedIn. If an applicant leaves a gap in their employment record to conceal circumstances that they believe might jeopardise the outcome of their job application, an astute employer may pick this up and ask the applicant questions about it or make private enquiries.

When a lie is discovered after an applicant has been given the job, an employer may dismiss the employee if misrepresentations in the job application about essential qualifications, training and experience would have prevented the applicant from getting the job in the first place. At the very least, the lie will taint the employer's trust of and respect for the employee even if eventually they turn out to be a good performer.

BEING TRUTHFUL

Telling the truth may be problematic, too. Usually, prospective employers shy away from applicants who they think might be a risk. For example, if an applicant reveals that they want to leave their current job because of a personality clash with their manager or another co-worker, a prospective employer may be reluctant to offer them a job if they think the applicant could be a source of conflict in the workplace.

Despite greater acceptance of mental health as a legitimate illness, if an applicant admits to having depression, for example, it may scare off some prospective employers. It's common for employees who've been bullied at work to have extended periods of sick leave because of the associated stress. An employer may be reluctant to offer an applicant a job if they fear poor attendance is a possibility. There's a good argument that an employee facing mental health or other problems would be best not to work for an employer unable to show empathy and support. But if job choices are limited, considerate employers may be in short supply.

An applicant may reveal that they want to leave their current position because they're being bullied. If the prospective employer has little or no appreciation of bullying as a workplace problem, they may think poorly of the employee for allowing themselves to be bullied or for being over-sensitive. It's not unusual for people who haven't been bullied, especially senior managers, to think that only weak people put up with their bullying and bullies are easy to deal with. Of course, neither assumption is correct.

If an applicant reveals that they were sacked from their last job, it could put them out of contention immediately, even though there may have been extenuating circumstances.

A stance taken by some job candidates is to be totally open about why they want to leave their current job or left their last job. I once offered a position to a job applicant who revealed in the interview that he'd been bullied in his last job, it had severely affected his health and after an extended period of sick leave he resigned. During the interview we devoted extra time trying to establish whether he was up to performing our job at the required standard. With a few doubts remaining, the interviewing panel decided to give him a go and, fortunately, we had no regrets. He was a very capable staff member and a great asset to the team.

In a less respectful and supportive work environment, however, and without an understanding supervisor it may have been more difficult for him to cope with some of the job's rigorous aspects. We were prepared to take the risk, but some employers wouldn't.

Whatever an applicant's reasons for leaving a job, and whether they want to reveal them to a prospective employer or not, they should give serious consideration to anticipating the inevitable difficult questions. It will provide them with the opportunity to consider and rehearse their answers and put themselves in the best possible light as an applicant.

BEING POSITIVE AT INTERVIEWS

Although negative experiences are likely to be the main cause of a bullied employee's decision to resign from their job, it's important that they explain positively the reasons for wanting to move on. Generally, employers want trouble-free staff who can do the job, are reliable and good at problem-solving. Therefore, focusing on the skills learnt in current and previous jobs, teamwork skills, and positive relationships with customers, clients, the community and other stakeholders is important. General principles for job application interviews in circumstances when the applicant has left their last job under difficult circumstances include:

- Don't lie; there's a good chance they'll find out the truth.
- Don't criticise the former/current employer or co-workers.
- Don't give long-winded answers.
- Don't be intentionally vague.
- Don't use the word 'bullying'.
- Don't play the victim.
- Be prepared emotionally, as far as is reasonably possible, for sensitive personal issues to be raised.
- Don't treat an interviewer as a counsellor and unload on them.
- Try not to cry; the interview may continue, and the interviewers may be supportive, but the application will most likely be finished.
- Try to anticipate the difficult questions and write the answers down, particularly ones that focus on bullying experiences, and rehearse saying them.
- Don't be evasive if bullying comes out in an interview, but keep answers short and move the conversation back to positive statements about opportunities the new job offers.
- Don't volunteer information about the negative health effects of bullying, but have an answer ready just in case.
- Don't present pessimistically; it will likely scare off the employer.
- Role play an interview with a capable friend asking the difficult questions and critiquing the answers.
- Don't use referees who will provide a poor or vague reference; alternatives include previous managers or colleagues who can attest to good work performance, commitment, reliability and capacity to work well with others. It's important to ask a potential referee 'Are you able to give me a *good* reference?'

SUMMARY

- If you're the target of a workplace bully, your greatest safety may be to find another job as quickly as possible. This advice assumes that all other positive options to resolve the problem have been tried.
- It's important that employees learn what workplace bullying is and what it isn't and not rush to report bullying or resign from their jobs prematurely.
- Sometimes it may be impossible for a bullied employee to remain in their job because of the serious impact on their health and well-being, including on their life away from work.
- There are all kinds of reasons why bullied employees are unable to resign to escape their bullying — the unavailability of alternative jobs, financial and family commitments, age, health, lack of qualifications and skills among them.
- It can be especially difficult for an employee to leave a job when they've worked hard to progress to their position and salary level.
- It's not easy to leave when a job is highly fulfilling due to the nature of the work and the strong positive relationships formed with co-workers, clients, patients, customers, and other stakeholders including the wider community.
- It can be particularly hard for some employees when leaving their job requires leaving their community.
- As a coping strategy, employees might benefit from reframing their bullying circumstances, which means attempting to see things differently, including changing expectations, detaching emotionally and controlling ego-driven responses to perceived injustices at work.
- Leaving a job under a cloud can mean a tricky job application process.

21

ADVICE FROM THE BULLIED

HR can't be trusted with workplace bullying

I met individually with more than 50 employees who'd been bullied at work and I asked them to speak candidly about their experiences.

Because the sample was small, it allowed greater informality with flexible interviews, limited fixed questions, and employees using their own words to explain their experiences and feelings. Importantly, it gave me the opportunity to ask them to clarify things they said which allowed me to gain a deeper understanding of their experiences.

I used introductions through my personal network to recruit people who were prepared to speak with me. Because typical sampling methods were not used, no claims are made about the representativeness of the sample or reliability of the findings. But the kinds of things people said to me are consistent with what the available research and other authors say on the topic. So, it gives me some confidence in using the findings for the purpose of this chapter and throughout the book.

Their work backgrounds were varied and included all levels of government, police and emergency services, nursing, business, church, education, labouring, social work, psychology, medicine, hospitality, retail, horticulture, youth work, trades, construction, trade union, workplace health and safety regulation, engineering, hospital administration, call-centre and volunteering.

Their stories were candid, insightful and raw. For some, the experience of sharing their story was clearly liberating and therapeutic. For others, I'm not so sure. I suspect that some were re-traumatised. All meetings contained debriefing time and for some I made follow-up telephone calls to see how they were going. The information they shared with me is included throughout this book in various forms.

Towards the end of our meeting they were asked, 'So, based on your experiences, what advice would you give to other workers employed in bullying workplaces?' Their responses are listed below.

I do not endorse all the advice that follows. It comes from individuals who've experienced particularly difficult and distressing work situations and it may not apply to everyone. If employees want to seek advice about their own situation, they should consult their union, lawyer, GP, counsellor or other informed person.

The following list has received only minor editing.

1. Lie low and think twice about involvement in controversial issues at work.
2. Keep your political views, religious beliefs and support for your football team to yourself.
3. Avoid disagreeing with the bully, especially in front of other staff.
4. Work hard, meet deadlines, don't be late, don't always be the first to leave, don't whinge and don't give them any ammunition to use against you.
5. Never whinge to a bully about things they might interpret as a personal criticism.
6. Don't send angry emails to a bully; it will rile them up and they'll use them against you.

7. Don't send personal emails or use the Internet for non-work purposes; if they're out to get you they might look for supporting evidence on your computer. Don't tell other people by email that you're being bullied at work.

8. Keep issues and problems about your personal life to yourself at work; it could be used against you later, especially if they want to discredit your bullying complaint by saying that you're nuts or over-sensitive because of your personal problems.

9. Never complain to your co-workers about a bully — they're not trustworthy even though they might agree with you to your face.

10. Only have conversations with the bully about work matters.

11. Don't be conned by the bully or HR when they seem friendlier than usual; they could be setting you up for a fall.

12. Work friends are work friends; they're not like personal friends, so hold back a little on the trust.

13. Be careful what you say on the office phone; your enemies might be eavesdropping.

14. Never go over a bully's head to their manager to complain before you know if they're mates.

15. Managers stick together, so don't trust them.

16. HR is not to be trusted where bullying is concerned.

17. If HR or your manager tells you that your comments about being bullied are 'off the record', don't believe them; they have to note what you say in your file and tell their boss, in case it all blows up later.

18. Don't make the mistake of being cocky because you think you're indispensable; everyone can be replaced.

19. Look after yourself by having regular mental health days off.

20. Don't hesitate to take time off when things get on top of you.

21. If you're a workaholic and your work life turns to shit and you've got nothing good outside of work to fall back on, you're in big trouble, so lead a balanced life.

22. Know what the bully likes and dislikes, what makes them

angry (which could be everything!) and even the time of day when they're at their worst.

23. Without making it obvious, try to keep out of their way.
24. The toilet's a good place to hide from the bully and get some relief; the cubicles are good for crying in and tissues are close by.
25. Get a communication grapevine going for when a bully's on the rampage.
26. Don't be a 'know-all' or 'blabbermouth'; it will be a bullseye on your chest for the bully.
27. If things are really bad, don't stay and tough it out; there's too much to lose health-wise.
28. Leave while you can still get a good reference.
29. I told my bully that I would leave if he would give me an excellent reference — and he took me up on my offer!
30. Leave before you become too damaged; once this happens you might as well wear a flashing sign on your forehead saying 'DAMAGED GOODS — DON'T EMPLOY ME'.
31. If you're too old to get another job, bide your time and learn to live with the problem for a bit longer if you can.
32. Be diplomatic with everything you say at work.
33. Don't be sarcastic with or make fun of the bully; it's like poking a venomous snake with a stick.
34. Never swear at the bully, unless it's your last day!
35. Don't burn your bridges by slagging off at everyone when you quit; your new boss might hear about it. You never know; you might want to come back one day, maybe after the bully has gone. Exit quietly on good terms.
36. If you've been on extended sick leave because of bullying, don't believe management when they say everyone's looking forward to your return, because everyone isn't.
37. Never lose your temper at work.
38. Winning an argument with the bully is like winning a battle but losing the war; they'll get you back later.
39. If you need to disagree with the bully, begin your sentence

with 'With respect'; 'With respect, I think you're a dickhead' — ha, no, I'm just kidding, but still use 'With respect' to introduce your opposing view.

40. If the bully is your manager and wants to meet with you, and you have a bad feeling about what might be going on, ask them what the purpose of the meeting is and if anyone else is going to be there; it could be an ambush meeting to do you over.

41. Find out about the relationships between everyone at work; you need to know who you can and can't trust.

42. Don't be a sook and take every criticism personally.

43. Sometimes it's better just to let things go rather than take offence.

44. Reporting my bullying to my manager was the worst thing I ever did; it all went pear-shaped for me after that; I felt like a leper at work; people stopped being friendly and were even hostile towards me.

45. They got rid of the bully after I reported her; I found out later that they had wanted to get rid of her for years and my report gave them the ammunition they needed.

46. Having a chat to a lawyer about your situation could be the best thing you ever do.

47. If you can afford it, get a lawyer to be your mouthpiece rather than cop aggression from management directly.

48. Lawyers charge like wounded bulls, but at least have one consultation.

49. Listen carefully to what your lawyer has to say, but don't follow their advice blindly. Weigh it up. They might recommend a course of action which is more about getting them extra work from you rather than what's best for you.

50. Make sure you have someone with you if you speak with management about your bullying; someone who agrees with your concerns would be best, but if not, to be there as a witness to what's said at the meeting; get them to take notes

because later management will lie about what was actually said. A union official would be best.

51. Don't make idle threats about taking legal action or getting a lawyer; if you're going down the legal track, keep it to yourself until you're ready to go ahead.

52. Join the union now.

53. My union guy wasn't much good, but he was better than having no one.

54. I wouldn't have survived without my union rep; she put in beyond the call of duty.

55. Don't believe all the bullshit about unions; mine was great.

56. I called my union rep 'Mr Muscle' because of the way he protected me from management.

57. My union rep was overworked; I had trouble contacting her and she was always stressed; she told me that she was being bullied at work, which wasn't reassuring. I felt she was using me as her counsellor.

58. Keep a diary and record all incidences of bullying — when it happened, the names of witnesses, but don't leave it on your desk for prying eyes.

59. Don't expect the people you work with to volunteer to be your witnesses if you report your bullying; they're shit-scared of being put on the bully's hit list or falling out of favour with management.

60. Let your GP know what's happening.

61. I took anti-depressants for 12 months which helped me cope.

62. Get a referral to a counsellor.

63. You won't make it without a counsellor.

64. Tell everyone to see my counsellor; she really understands bullying.

65. My first counsellor was hopeless; he knew nothing about workplace bullying and implied it was my fault.

66. My counsellor seemed more interested in my relationships with my mum and dad than on my immediate problem with bullying.

22

RESPECTFUL WORKPLACES

Bullying can be managed when respect prevails

Staff-conduct policies and occasional workshops alone won't prevent bullying. It requires a strong workplace culture that fosters respect and trust for employees. Respect is how to treat everyone, not just those you want to impress.[1]

Workplace bullying can't be eliminated easily, especially in larger workplaces, but it can be managed and minimised where respect prevails. The creation and preservation of such workplaces is a shared responsibility between employers and employees, but managers at all levels play a crucial role in setting and maintaining the culture through the behaviours they model and expect of employees.

An overview of organisation culture change is provided in this chapter, although particular methods or a step-by-step approach are beyond this book's scope. Organisational change is a specialised field with its own theory and methods. Also, because every organisation is different, no one approach is suitable for every work setting.

Keeping this in mind, a small sample of strategies that have been suggested or used by other writers in this field to create more respectful workplaces is included for readers' interest and inspiration.

While they might seem simple and logical, putting them into practice can require a major effort, particularly in workplaces where bullying behaviours are firmly embedded and there's strong resistance to change.

WHAT IS A RESPECTFUL WORKPLACE?

The World Health Organization defines a respectful workplace as one that:

> ...encourages trust, responsibility, accountability, mutual respect, open communication and embraces the dignity and diversity of individuals.[2]

According to the Australian Public Service, employees want a respectful workplace where:

- they know what's expected of them
- they're safe and treated fairly
- their contribution and skills are recognised and valued
- they can work in harmony with co-workers
- their work performance and careers are enhanced through training and support.[3]

Canadian workplace civility advocate and author Sharone Bar-David says that the pendulum is moving away from employees having to fend for themselves at work. Employers are having to take more responsibility for creating psychologically safe work environments that allow employees to perform at their best.[4]

US workplace incivility researcher and author Christine Porath says the attributes of positive and healthy workplace cultures include:

- inclusivity, where people feel empowered and supported, enabling them to speak up and contribute to their full potential

- adaptability and flexibility, where people welcome and seek to introduce change and innovation
- purpose-driven, where people understand their contribution and how their work contributes to the bigger picture
- trustful, where people are trusted and empowered to do good work
- wellness-oriented, where people's health, safety and well-being are a priority
- creativity, where innovation is enhanced through people's creative and proactive behaviours.[5]

BENEFITS FOR EMPLOYERS

The Body Shop founder, Dame Anita Roddick, once said:

The end result of kindness is that it draws people to you.

Organisations are becoming increasingly aware of the wide range of benefits of maintaining respectful workplaces. They include:

- attracting and retaining the best staff
- enhanced employee morale and job satisfaction
- improved teamwork
- lower absenteeism and turnover
- increased employee commitment and productivity
- employees better able to manage conflict and change
- greater appreciation of people's uniqueness and differences
- reduced employee grievances and associated costs
- greater resourcefulness, creativity and innovation.[6]

WORKER WELL-BEING

Melbourne-based HR consulting company HR Central highlights how employers can maximise workplace productivity through worker well-being.[7] It includes:

- providing job descriptions that are realistic, relevant and measurable
- engaging with their employees and carefully observing the work environment to identify areas which could be improved or problems that need to be resolved
- addressing the 'motivation killer' — toxic people, abrasive personalities, lack of organisational vision, poor communication systems and autocratic management styles
- making workers feel more comfortable by trusting them, their input and working styles
- helping workers relax to help their physical agility, clear their mind and improve their productivity which in turn can also lead them to be happier in their work
- monitoring large workloads through regular work-in-progress meetings to see who's doing what, who's away, who's overloaded and who has free time.

An organisation touted in the literature regularly as a good role model in this area is successful US business software company SAP SuccessFactors.[8,9] It acknowledges the crucial role of work in employees' overall well-being and to the company's success. It accepts that it can be challenging for some employers to make the well-being of workers a strategic and cultural priority. While many employers address well-being at a superficial level, only a few put into place a successful holistic well-being strategy that achieves genuine culture change.[10]

As part of its approach, SAP SuccessFactors has all employees, including its CEO, sign and abide by what the company calls rules of engagement. It maintains that the rules play a crucial role in letting employees know what's expected of them.[11]

Behind its rules of engagement is maximising company productivity and profits through getting the best from its workers, with a respectful work environment playing a central role in the process. But SAP SuccessFactors takes it a step further than many because it makes it clear to employees that their performance will be judged in part by how well they demonstrate the values in their daily work.

It's a far better approach than many organisations adopt, which is to have a list of single-word values or short catchphrases with minimal and sometimes no explanation about how they apply to behaviours at work. It's unrealistic to expect that staff, particularly leaders, will possess an innate appreciation of what the values mean, how they're applied, and how to respond to behaviour that contradicts them.

WHAT ARE VALUES?

An organisation's values are public statements targeting stakeholders and which aim to promote standards of behaviour based on its morals, ethics, principles and beliefs.

That's the theory, but it's a myth that an organisation's culture has very much to do with the values statement that appears in the annual report. Unless the organisation has worked very actively over time to live its values, the values statement is simply one of intent and doesn't describe the culture as it really is.[12]

Management consultant and author Carolyn Taylor says that values can be divided into two types — enriching values and selfish values.[13] Examples of enriching values are:

- integrity
- honesty
- teamwork
- safety
- innovation
- excellence
- loyalty
- caring
- courage
- respect

- growth
- environment.

The second type of values, according to Taylor, is never listed because they're individuals' self-serving values. Examples include:

- more money
- increased status
- greater independence
- more power
- looking good
- increased popularity
- more control
- conflict avoidance
- enhanced reputation
- manipulation of others
- secrecy
- winning at all costs.

Despite not always being in the interests of the majority, the second set of values can play a large part in, and in some instances dominate, an organisation's culture. For example, one of the organisations that I've included in this book as a model of a serial bully states layer upon layer of enriching values, including those indicating that respect for employees is a high priority. The values, however, are bogged down at the aspirational stage with little progress made since the organisation was outed publicly a few years ago for seriously mistreating employees. Bullying continues to be a part of daily work life for workers, with strong pockets of resistance from the 'old boys' who are reluctant to relinquish their power and status in the organisation. Rewriting its values statements and glossing up the presentation was a promising start, but there's much more to it than just clever words touting good intentions.

Many employers put considerable energy into creating an illusion of a respectful workplace; it's a simpler and cheaper option, but it's also a lazy and ineffective option. The smoke-and-mirrors approach aims to deceive employees, the public and other stakeholders into believing that the organisation is a good corporate citizen. These organisations believe naively that the act of stating noble sentiments or slogans in a few words acquired from a list on the Internet or a book such as Richard Bayan's *Words That Sell* is an end in itself.[14] But these types of values are little more than marketing spin. Sometimes the deception works, however, but often the ruse is exposed eventually through the organisation's bad behaviour. In Australia it's difficult to go past the major banks and some prominent church institutions as examples.

Many organisations have good intent but simply lack the ability to translate desired values into practice. It's unrealistic to expect that employees will understand and instinctively apply their organisation's stated values. Rarely would it be the case that employees can walk their employer's values talk without ongoing training and supervision.

POSITIVE CULTURE

The cornerstone of a respectful workplace is a positive organisational culture. It comprises values and behaviours that place a high importance on the well-being of workers and other stakeholders. For employees, a respectful workplace must be meaningful and supportive; it's more than providing fair wages, nice lunchrooms and flexible dress codes, although these things are important also.

Worker well-being and organisational well-being are synonymous. But some employers don't get it and believe that having a positive culture is somehow separate from or subordinate to the business of their organisation, such as meeting financial and service targets. A positive workplace culture, however, is integral to maximising the achievement of financial, service and all other targets. Additionally, a strong positive culture fostering a respectful workplace sets the scene for a greater and enduring commitment to the organisation by employees and other stakeholders.

ROLE OF LEADERSHIP

The greatest influence on employees' ability to align their behaviour with their employer's values and culture is strong ethical leadership. Managers play a crucial role in setting the culture through the behaviours they expect and model for employees. The following list, also included in an earlier chapter, is just a small sample:

- recruitment — hiring staff whose personal values are compatible with the values of the organisation
- clear expectations and communication — letting staff know what's expected of them
- skills development — providing staff with tools, resources and opportunities
- accountability — helping staff understand their accountability obligations
- mission, vision and values education — explaining what they mean for the organisation and staff
- team participation — involving employees in planning and decision-making
- performance feedback — providing positive feedback as well as constructive criticism
- appreciate barriers — understanding the obstacles to success
- stakeholder involvement — seeking input and advice from stakeholders
- monitoring — keeping a close watch on organisational health.

CIVIL WORKPLACES

Although relatively new as a topic of public interest and study, workplace civility has much to offer our understanding of respectful workplaces and how to achieve them. As indicated in Chapter 2 What

Is Bullying?, usually incivility is thought to be at the milder end of the bullying behaviour spectrum or not bullying at all, and most often flies under the radar as a serious organisational problem. The definition of workplace incivility is:

> *Seemingly inconsequential behaviours that are rude, disrespectful, discourteous or insensitive where the intent to harm is ambiguous or unclear and where manner and body language set the tone for how the words are interpreted.*[15]

The research on workplace incivility reveals that targets can experience the same serious psychological and physical effects as do targets of bullying behaviours thought to be at the more serious end of the scale, such as physical violence, threats of physical violence and stalking.[16]

Sharone Bar-David says leaders and HR departments observing incivility lack the terminology and framework to address the problem effectively.[17] Uncivil behaviours are characteristically ambiguous and seem inconsequential to employers not familiar with the serious consequences for employees and the organisation. Serial perpetrators, therefore, are especially dangerous because they have the potential to inflict serious damage on co-workers unchecked.

Christine Porath maintains that even small gestures of civility can play a significant role in creating and preserving respectful workplaces.[18] Examples include thanking people, listening attentively, asking questions humbly, sharing credit, smiling and acknowledging others.

THE 10-5 RULE

An example cited by Porath and other writers is the 10-5 Rule. Explained simply, it encourages staff whenever they're within 10 feet from a co-worker, customer, client or patient to make eye contact and smile warmly. When they're within 5 feet, a sincere greeting or friendly gesture of acknowledgement should accompany the eye contact and smile. Many organisations have their own versions of the practice and in metric Australia it might be called the 3-2 Rule or something similar.

The approach, however, appears more suited to smaller work environments than bigger ones. For example, a friendly nod, smile and 'hello' to everyone passing by is likely to become hard going in a large, bustling workplace with lots of passers-by. Also, acknowledging everyone may be distracting for an employee's important reflection, mental planning and head-clearing time when they're away from their workstation. This doesn't mean that 10-5 isn't workable; rather, common sense needs to be applied to its use. Most important is employees having an awareness of, respect for and acknowledgement of their colleagues and others present in their workplaces.

In a workplace where impersonal interaction is the norm, getting 10-5 going may be difficult initially. It's unlikely to work as a standalone strategy; rather it needs to be part of a multi-faceted approach to achieving civility at work. Initially, managers need to take the lead.

CODE OF CIVILITY

Porath also cites the example of Californian law firm Bryan Cave where she helped employees identify the workplace civility norms which they believed were important for a respectful workplace. In just over an hour, employees were able to generate and agree upon 10 norms. The firm accepted and bound them into a civility code which they display prominently in the foyer. It's as follows:

Bryan Cave's Code of Civility

We greet and acknowledge one another.
We say please and thank you.
We treat each other equally and with respect, no matter the conditions.
We acknowledge the impact of our behaviour on others.
We welcome feedback from each other.

We are approachable.
We are direct, sensitive and honest.
We acknowledge the contributions of others.
We respect one another's time commitments.
We address incivility.

Bryan Cave's Code of Civility is an encouraging start because it indicates that employees are motivated to achieve a respectful workplace. There's much more to it, however, than spending an hour brainstorming 10 basic principles to be framed for the office wall. In most instances, employees will have to be shown via training how to put the principles into practice within the unique context of their workplace — its mission, goals, values, culture, traditions, pressures and priorities. In small organisations located on one worksite this may be relatively straightforward, but in bigger organisations spread over multiple sites the process will be more complicated.

CREW

One approach to addressing this issue is CREW (Civility, Respect and Engagement in the Workplace). It's a training technique for workplace respect and civility that recognises the uniqueness of every worksite by adopting a personalised approach to achieving positive change. CREW was adopted by the US Veterans Health Administration in 2005.[19] It aims to improve workplace climate through more respectful and civil interaction between employees.

CREW's research found that respect and civility impact positively on a variety of factors important to administrators, clinical and non-clinical staff. They include higher overall job satisfaction, reduced staff turnover and absenteeism, fewer employee grievances, and better outcomes for clients, customers and patients.

CREW facilitators meet regularly with workgroups for around six months helping them to focus on creating a civil and respectful work environment. The facilitators aid discussion and problem-solving and conduct activities that aim to improve how participants relate to one another. There's no standard manual for CREW as every worksite is different, even within the same organisation.

MANAGEMENT BY WALKING AROUND

A personal favourite is Management by Walking Around (MBWA). It was popularised in the 1980s by management consultants Tom Peters and Robert Waterman in their book *In Search of Excellence: Lessons from America's Best-Run Companies*[20] and Tom Peters and Nancy Austin's book *A Passion for Excellence*.[21] MBWA refers to a style of business management which involves managers informally wandering around the workplace at random to check with employees, equipment, or on the status of ongoing work. The theory underpinning MBWA is that through unstructured interactive mingling with employees at work, managers will be better able to understand their issues, ideas and concerns, in turn allowing informed action to be taken on the findings.

The three main elements of MBWA are:

1. The manager must take the time to walk around the workplace. This encourages better relationships and open communication between managers and employees.
2. The manager must start conversations with employees. Interaction can be related to the employee's work and, as appropriate, the employee's personal issues.
3. The manager creates networks within the workplace. Through having direct lines of communication between managers and employees it enables early intervention with problems.

The three essential components of MBWA are:

- Managers must listen to their employees. They can't just wander around chatting aimlessly; the activity is purposeful, and managers must hear what their employees say, including picking up on the subtle or intentionally understated messages. Initially, employees may be reluctant to express their views openly.

- Managers must use discussion as an opportunity to communicate the company's vision and values and how they apply to the employee's day-to-day work.
- Managers must be willing to provide immediate help when required. The approach is accompanied by a sense of urgency and a preparedness by managers to solve problems quickly. Brush-off statements like 'I'll look into it' have no place in MBWA.

In *Management by Walking Around (MBWA) — The Essential Guide*, Anastasia Belyh outlines the pros and cons of MBWA and how best to take full advantage of the approach.[22]

Helping employees with personal problems

The third essential ingredient of MBWA relates to organisational problem-solving. In this context normally it refers to addressing problems with the business of the company such as productivity, process management, job roles, communication, safety, staff turnover, services, customer relations, and so on.

The informality of MBWA also allows managers to develop closer relationships with employees, enabling them over time to strike up conversations about all manner of things, including providing opportunities for employees to discuss their personal worries. Of course, it wouldn't work in a toxic work environment where trusting relationships don't exist between management and employees, and where employees fear that they may be compromised if they reveal information about their personal lives. Toxic workplaces were discussed in Chapter 7 Why Bullying Happens, and the issue of employees confiding in HR with their personal problems is discussed in Chapter 13 Don't Trust HR!

It's a mistake to believe that when people come to work they're able to keep their personal worries separate. People aren't machines, although some employers still ascribe to the antiquated view that staff are simply a commodity, a means to get the job done, rather than human beings with emotions and complex personal lives.

Employees with personal worries, such as with relationships, finances, children, health and grief will be distracted while at work. Their minds will wander, and it will prevent them from doing their best work. This doesn't just mean working at a slower rate or doing lesser-quality work. It's been estimated, for example, that 60–80 per cent of workplace accidents are caused by personal stress when workers are distracted.[23] In some jobs, such as those involving machinery, hazardous materials, surgical procedures and dispensing medicine, mistakes can pose a serious risk to workplace health and safety and, in some instances, cost lives. Of course, workers can also be distracted by work-related problems, which can result in mistake-making and risks to workplace health and safety.

Employers and managers have a responsibility to get the best from their employees. Cracking the whip, a saying that appears to have had its origins in slavery and working farm animals, aims to make those on the receiving end work harder by threatening or inflicting physical pain. The principle remains popular in some workplaces where employees are thought to be inherently lazy, a liability, and whose main motivation is their wage and keeping their job. Therefore, close supervision, intimidation, threats and punishment are seen as effective ways to make them work harder.

However, Dame Anita Roddick, founder of The Body Shop cosmetics retail chain, strongly advocated a different approach, summed up well in her pithy quotation:

We were searching for employees, but people turned up instead.

In a respectful workplace, employees are viewed as human beings inherently motivated to perform well, who enjoy their work, and whose quest for job satisfaction is more than just about financial remuneration. Getting the best from an inherently motivated workforce means keeping them inspired, enthused and letting them know that they're an asset to the organisation. It requires knowing and treating employees as human beings, which includes acknowledging their personal worries and offering support.

It may include encouraging them to feel safe speaking openly about their problems, showing empathy, and being non-judgemental. It can mean referring them to external supports such as their GP or counselling. Councils, community health services and other local service providers can advise on where to get support. Every municipal area has a directory of community services.

Helping an employee through a personal crisis may require some flexibility with their working hours, which can include changes to starting and finishing times, reducing working time, offering compassionate leave, paid or unpaid special leave, or a working-from-home arrangement when possible. Changing or reducing an employee's responsibilities temporarily or, in extreme cases, permanently may help.

If an employee is reluctant to speak about their personal problems, however, this should be respected. But if their declining performance is impacting on their work, their team and the organisation, it needs to be discussed from an organisational viewpoint, such as putting them on a performance improvement plan coinciding with an offer of personal support.

CHANGING THE CULTURE

In workplaces where bullying is a serious problem, changing the culture won't be easy, especially when an organisation's cultural vision, values, attributes, behaviours and resources are way out of alignment. In Chapter 1 Bullying Is Serious, examples were highlighted from the public service, policing, emergency services and health whose efforts to change their bullying cultures were failing.

The basic principles underpinning cultural change include:

- behaviours aligned with values are the most powerful determinant of real change
- leadership at all levels is critical to driving organisational change
- readiness, receptiveness and approaches to change will vary with each organisation
- change happens when people are engaged in conversation that stimulates new and more effective ways of working
- systemic and sustainable change, especially in complex organisations, occurs over years.[24]

Preserving an already respectful workplace can be difficult sometimes when faced with routine day-to-day challenges and stresses. But if a strong foundation of respect already exists, it can act as a beacon to help the organisation, or the part that's wavering, to get back on track.

According to Danish management consultant Torben Rick, however, in some instances changing an organisation's culture can be as hard as changing the personality of a human being or the culture of a country.[25] This is because an organisation's culture comprises a complex interconnection of factors that impact on the way the organisation operates, such as its values, goals, roles, processes, competencies, communications, practices, attitudes, and assumptions.

In an analysis of sexual harassment in organisations, that is why some men participate in sexually denigrating women, forensic anthropologist Xanthé Mallett highlights the complexity of organisational culture change. She says that it's not just an organisational problem, but a societal problem. With sexual harassment behaviour, therefore, efforts to break down gender stereotypes in the organisation itself must coincide with attempts to break down gender stereotypes in society more generally. Women need to be elevated to positions of power to reduce male domination in all aspects of life. To break the chain of passing on negative attitudes towards women, the undermining of women's and girls' autonomy and value must be challenged during boyhood.[26]

Bringing about major culture change to a chronically dysfunctional organisation can be a mammoth task and, in some instances impossible, particularly in the short term. It will require a long-term plan and the ability to recognise that change is needed, a strong commitment at all levels to pursue it, and the capacity and commitment to cover the time and costs involved.

BULLYING PREVENTION

People who mistreat others are a fact of life, so bullying behaviours will likely emerge in most workplaces, including normally respectful ones. Limiting the damage by keeping on top of the problem is the key.

For anti-bullying policies to work effectively, the employer must put a high value on the health and well-being of workers. To protect employees from bullying, strict behavioural guidelines and strong penalties for infringements are required. However, having policies without a strong commitment to implement them properly is simply a waste of time.

It's crucial that employers have:

- a strong commitment to creating a bullying-free workplace
- clearly stated up-to-date policies on workplace bullying
- penalties for breaches, including for managers and supervisors who know of or have witnessed bullying behaviour but have taken no action
- training on workplace bullying for all employees at the commencement of their employment and regularly afterwards

- complaints processes which protect bullied employees from reprisals
- investigations that are genuine, prompt, impartial and competently undertaken
- outcomes that are authentic and based on truth and justice rather than driven by manager self-protection, brand protection, or protecting the accused who are seen as greater assets to the organisation than their accusers
- a preparedness to discipline perpetrators including their removal in the most serious cases
- remedial training for perpetrators
- regular audits across the organisation to assess if bullying prevention policies are being applied consistently and effectively
- observing workloads and staffing levels to reduce excessive working hours/expectations
- monitoring unexplained decreases in production, workplace accidents, dynamics between workers, increases in complaints, changes in patterns of absenteeism, sick leave and staff turnover to ascertain if workplace bullying has played a role
- regular scheduled discussions about culture and workplace behaviour during staff supervision, at meetings of staff, management, the board and health and safety representatives
- feedback from workers about bullying when they resign or retire through exit interviews.

GOOD CORPORATE CITIZENS THE KEY

I place faith in Australian employers to champion the cause of workplace bullying prevention. But they need to be shown the way. My confidence stems from steadily increasing membership of the ranks of good corporate citizens, especially over the last 30 years.

Good corporate citizens are employers who have a strong and genuine commitment to 'do the right thing', which involves meeting their legal, ethical, economic, social and environmental responsibilities. It includes valuing and treating staff well, with all that it entails. Years ago, good corporate citizenship was defined narrowly as obeying laws and paying taxes. But now it's much more. A term used liberally in the corporate social responsibility literature is 'enlightened self-interest', which means that good corporate citizens recognise that for their organisations to prosper they must balance creatively the needs of all their stakeholders – employees, customers, suppliers, animals, the environment and particularly the needs of the communities in which they operate.

It's been disappointing in recent times that so many of our big businesses, not-for-profits and religious organisations have touted themselves brazenly as exemplary corporate citizens, but have been exposed as impostors. There's plenty of evidence, however, that they're not the majority.

Good corporate citizens require support if they're to develop more respectful workplaces where employees are kept safe from bullying and other forms of mistreatment. Governments need to provide extra resourcing to the organisations they mandate to regulate workplace bullying as well as other peak bodies to provide employers, their managers and employees with a wide range of online and other educational media, including teaching, training, storytelling and discussion about organisational values and respectful workplaces and their relationship to organisational success. Online information and training, however, aren't enough. Respect needs to be integral to teaching in our education system at every level.

SUMMARY

- Preventing bullying requires a strong workplace culture that fosters respect and trust for employees.
- A respectful workplace is a shared responsibility between employers and employees.
- Managers play a crucial role through the behaviours they model and expect of employees.
- Many organisations don't walk the talk with their values.
- An organisation's cultural vision, values, attributes, behaviours and resources must be in alignment.
- Organisational change is complex and needs to be broken down into parts and addressed incrementally.
- Employers must have a strong, genuine commitment to implementing their policies on bullying
- The growth of good corporate citizenship over the last 30 years will aid the cause of workplace bullying prevention, but assistance is required from governments and the bodies they mandate to deal with the problem.
- Respect needs to be integral to teaching in our education system at all levels.

23

FINALLY...

Respectful workplaces are the answer

This book started with ambitious intentions — to contribute to the reduction of bullying in Australian workplaces and to lessen its harmful impact on workers, their families, employers and the economy.

A major focus has been on the human costs of workplace bullying. The scene was set with the tragic story of 58-year-old 'Jane' who was mistreated brutally by her bullies and employer. So badly that she had serious psychological scarring and couldn't work again.

As is so often the case with bullying organisations, outwardly Jane's former employer was respectable and even virtuous. It went to great lengths to present itself publicly and proudly as the embodiment of the values it boasted, including honesty, transparency, respect and courage, accompanied by an overriding concern for the common good. It even produced a regular glossy newsletter telling employees and the community about how well its values were put into action.

Behind the misleading facade, however, was a poisonous organisational culture underpinned by an opposing set of nasty self-serving values — deceit rather than openness, treachery rather than honesty, contempt rather than respect, and cowardice rather than courage. When Jane left the organisation, she was broken psychologically, but there was no remorse shown or support offered by any of the main villains for the harm they had caused her. For the CEO, HR managers and their sycophants, Jane's exit was a routine day at the office — another annoying problem out of the way. Good riddance, Jane!

Chapter 10 Bullying and Personality reveals that the capacity to dissociate from callous behaviours, to feel no guilt, remorse or empathy, and to be able to do this regularly, are anti-social personality traits. In lay terms, people displaying these traits are often called psychopaths. Recently, corporate social responsibility researchers have referred to bullying organisations as 'psychopathic' because the attitudes and behaviours they display routinely are similar to the criteria used by psychiatrists to diagnose individuals with anti-social personality disorder.[1] Personality disorders are thought to be deeply ingrained in people's behaviour making such individuals difficult to treat. Further exploration of the theory of psychopathic organisations may shed more light on why it's so hard to change the culture in toxic organisations where bullying is endemic.

With millions of workers being bullied daily in Australia, it's clear there are many organisations like Jane's. It doesn't mean that they're all rotten to the core; in most workplaces the good people outnumber the corrupt ones but, as is so often the case, the influence of the villains dominates because of their greater influence as leaders. Long shadows can be cast by leaders in organisations, and in toxic organisations the shadows are exceptionally long and particularly dark.

Of course, not all employers mistreat their employees, but if current estimates on workplace bullying rates in Australia are any indication, far too many do. The lowest estimate that I found was around 10 per cent or 1.2 million workers and the highest 50 per cent or 6 million workers.[2,3] It's probably somewhere in between, but I lean towards higher rather than lower. Most bullying isn't reported, so estimates are likely to be understated. Whatever the estimate, however, it's far too many people suffering miserable and sometimes wretched work lives, struggling daily to come to work and whose pain spills into every other part of their lives.

A CATALYST FOR CHANGE?

In Chapter 1 Bullying Is Serious, evidence was presented that in Australia attempts to address workplace bullying are failing. In the absence of strong advocacy for bullying prevention, high-profile advocates, recent major studies, royal commissions, inquiries and news media backing a case for major change, governments, employers and others can ignore, downplay or dismiss the serious human and economic costs of the problem.

As a result, workplace bullying in Australia is viewed generally as being within acceptable limits, part of the routine rough-and-tumble of work life, and with the costs simply the price of doing business. This is persuasive and convenient reasoning for governments and employers reluctant to do anything further about the problem, as well as avoid the potentially high costs of doing more. It's a bleak outlook, to say the least, given what's been presented in this book about the seriousness of bullying in Australian workplaces.

With this in mind, it was a struggle to figure out how to end the book on a genuine optimistic note. Resolving the predicament was when, commencing in February 2021, the issue of sexual harassment dominated news headlines for many weeks. It gifted the cause of workplace bullying an unexpected, welcome shot in the arm.

Simmering discontent about years of unaddressed inequality, violence and injustice for women had come to a head. On Monday, 15 March, under the banner 'March 4 Justice', more than 100,000 women gathered peacefully in city and regional centres throughout Australia to protest about their frustration and, in many instances, their outrage. It was an impressive turn-up given their numbers were limited by Covid-19 regulations. A petition with more than 90,000 signatures called for greater accountability for sexist behaviours in Parliament.

The event was triggered in February 2021 by the exposure of a pervasive culture of disrespect and abuse towards women in Canberra's Parliament House, a problem that mirrored the experiences of women everywhere. The catalyst was an alleged rape two years earlier of a young woman staff member by a senior co-worker. Not long after the allegation was revealed by news media, there were further accusations against men in government of sexual harassment and assault — all strongly denied by those named. The Government was widely criticised for mishandling and covering up the 2019 allegation which, according to the victim, intensified her trauma and grief. Again, it embodied the experiences of many women unable to achieve redress for their sexual abuse. There were further strong criticisms of the Government's failure to respond to wider accusations of sexism and misogyny in parliamentary culture — a problem, critics said, extended across party lines.

Spurring on protesters was that the National Inquiry into Sexual Harassment in Australian Workplaces report, *Respect@Work*, had been released a year earlier, in March 2020, but none of the urgent recommendations had been actioned by Government. It became clear that some key ministers hadn't even read the report. In their defence, they claimed that they were distracted by having to deal with the fallout from Covid-19 in 2020. A valid excuse on face value, but maybe not within the historical context of reviews and inquiries being used by governments to create an impression that something is being done about a serious problem, when it's little more than a ploy to take heat out of the issue over time. As a result, unwanted recommendations can be discarded or reinterpreted so that government responses can be based conveniently on their capacity or desire to deliver.

Pressured by persistent news media scrutiny of the young woman's sexual assault allegation, and particularly its poor handling by the

Government, the Prime Minister called for an independent review into Parliament House culture. The review was to be headed by Australia's Human Rights Commission Sex Discrimination Commissioner, Kate Jenkins. Ironically, the ink was barely dry on her report *Respect@Work*, which covered many of the same issues that would likely be examined in the new review.

On a positive note, however, the new review would provide Commissioner Jenkins with another opportunity to sheet home her urgent recommendations from *Respect@Work*. And, potentially, on this occasion the recommendations, combined with those from the new review, would gain greater traction with a government under mounting pressure to fix its own toxic work culture. Backing the Commissioner this time would be even closer scrutiny by news media aided by much stronger community feeling about the issue.

In an interview on ABC's *Insiders* program on 7 March 2021, Commissioner Jenkins described the current moment optimistically as a critical turning point. She said:

> *...in my time working in this area and particularly looking in workplaces over 30 years, I've never seen any moment like this. We are hearing the reality and we're getting changes that — our review [of the toxic culture at Parliament House] is absolutely quite historic, but I think that's across the board. I think our community is changing, so we're at a turning point. That is my sense.*[4]

HOW WILL WORKPLACE BULLYING PREVENTION BENEFIT?

A critical turning point in the field of sexual harassment holds much promise for the cause of workplace bullying prevention. In the previous chapter, it's argued that the foundation for bullying prevention is a respectful workplace. The *Respect@Work* report recognises the links between workplace bullying and sexual harassment and recommends improvements to the co-ordination, consistency and clarity between the anti-discrimination, employment and work health and safety legislative schemes. Ultimately, this will lead to the creation of more respectful workplaces for all workers, including those impacted by bullying.

Underpinning the sexual harassment of women is the power difference between men and women that relates to women's unequal place in society involving an inequitable distribution of power, resources and opportunities.[5] Government bureaucracies are a classic example of where power is integral to their nature and functioning and where the power differential between employees is wide. This is particularly when men are over-represented in leadership positions, creating a dominant masculine workplace culture. It's no surprise, therefore, that most victims of sexual harassment are women, and most perpetrators are men.

At a very basic level, however, one of the things that workplace sexual harassment and workplace bullying have in common is that the actions of perpetrators is serious misconduct endangering targets' health and safety at work — especially their psychological health. In toxic workplaces, such as Parliament House, frequently sexual harassment and workplace bullying co-exist, with some victims subjected to both forms of abuse. Over the last couple of years there have been regular allegations of workplace bullying in Parliament House, with most claims made by women — at least the ones brought to public attention by news media.

In Chapter 5 Impact on Targets, there's a long list of negative psychological, physical and social outcomes for victims of workplace bullying, many of which are shared by victims of sexual harassment. See also '3.8 Impacts of sexual harassment in the workplace' in the *Respect@Work* report.[6]

NOT BLIND OPTIMISM

The achievement of these important changes, however, won't be quick or easy. In the previous chapter the complexity of changing organisational culture was emphasised, which one writer likened to the difficulty of changing the culture of a country or the personality of an individual.[7] Another highlighted that sexual harassment is not just an organisational problem; it's a societal problem.[8] Therefore, efforts to break down gender stereotypes in an organisation must coincide with attempts to break down gender stereotypes in society, which is a tall order.

Also, it's not possible to overlook the succession of government-initiated royal commissions and inquiries that haven't gone anywhere. It's easy to be cynical about their effectiveness as a pathway for positive social change when so many reports have collected more dust than seen sunlight. In the four weeks spanning March and April 2021, for example, we were confronted by a stark reminder when five Indigenous people died while in custody. Most of the recommendations from the 1991 Royal Commission into Aboriginal Deaths in Custody have never been acted on. Tragically, in the 30 years since, more than 450 Aboriginal and Torres Strait Islander people have died while in custody.[9]

It wasn't encouraging either when, early in April 2021, the Government finally succumbed to public pressure to respond to the Human Rights Commission's *Respect@Work* report but, without hesitation, commenced the customary practice of culling recommendations. One of the first to be discarded was that the legal onus should be on employers to eliminate sexual misconduct. Commissioner Jenkins called it a 'missed opportunity'.[10] Casting it aside was criticised as a bad look from a government still reeling from revelations about its own failures to eliminate such behaviour.[11]

REAL OPTIMISM

Despite the strong likelihood that the Government will reject more of *Respect@Work*'s recommendations, I remain optimistic that this time it's different and anticipate the current momentum to address sexual harassment and sexual assault will continue. Ultimately, this will lead to safer workplaces for more Australian workers. The emergence of passionate next-generation high-profile advocates working side by side with stalwart campaigners from the community and news media is encouraging. The passion and ongoing commitment of Commissioner Kate Jenkins will bolster their efforts.

During my long career working in the community, much of which has been with grass-roots groups, I've been heartened regularly by the quotation from American cultural anthropologist Margaret Mead (1901–1978):

> *Never doubt that a small group of thoughtful, committed*
> *citizens can change the world; indeed, it's the only thing that*
> *ever has.*

In my experience, the commitment and passion of ordinary community people to initiate major societal change is unsurpassed. Often governments take the credit, but usually it starts with the vision and dedication of people in the community.

In her closing comments from the *Respect@Work* report, Commissioner Jenkins said of change:

> *This will require transparency, accountability and leadership. It*
> *will also require a shift from the current reactive model, that*
> *requires complaints from individuals to a proactive model,*
> *which will require positive actions from employers.*[12]

Strong organisational leadership, proactivity, transparency and accountability are also essential for the prevention of workplace bullying. Many of the 55 recommendations from *Respect@Work* are applicable to workplace bullying, and especially the report's basic assumption that positive workplaces which foster respect and trust for employees is the key. While bullying can't be eliminated altogether, it can be minimised and well-managed where genuine concern for the health and well-being of all employees is a high priority.

————

Please note: My comments in this chapter relating to sexual harassment and assault are based on recent events only up until the end of March 2021.

REFERENCES

INTRODUCTION

1. House of Representatives Standing Committee on Education and Employment. *Workplace Bullying: We just want it to stop.* November 2012. (Accessed 2018 online.)
2. Relationships Australia. *March 2018: Bullying in schools.* (Accessed 2018 online.)
3. House of Representatives Standing Committee on Education and Employment. *Workplace Bullying: We just want it to stop.* November 2012. (Accessed 2018 online.)
4. Gary Namie and Ruth Namie (2009), *The Bully at Work: What You Can Do to Stop the Hurt and Reclaim Your Dignity on the Job.* Source Books, Naperville, Illinois.
5. Andrea Adams with Neil Crawford (1992), *Bullying at Work: How to Confront and Overcome It.* Virago Press, London.
6. Tim Field (2009), *Bully in Sight: How to predict, resist, challenge and combat workplace bullying — Overcoming the silence and denial by which abuse survives.* Success Unlimited, Great Britain.
7. Gary Namie and Ruth Namie (2009), *The Bully at Work: What You Can Do to Stop the Hurt and Reclaim Your Dignity on the Job.* Source Books, Naperville, Illinois.
8. Gary Namie and Ruth Namie (2011), *The Bully-Free Workplace — Stop Jerks, Weasels and Snakes from Killing Your Organization.* Wiley, New Jersey.
9. Gary Namie and Ruth Namie (2009), *The Bully at Work: What You Can Do to Stop the Hurt and Reclaim Your Dignity on the Job.* Source Books, Naperville, Illinois.
10. David Morrison, Chief of Army. Lieutenant General David Morrison message about unacceptable behaviour by Army members, quoting David Hurley, the former Governor of New South Wales. *YouTube*, 12 June 2013. (Accessed 2018 online.)

1. BULLYING IS SERIOUS

1. The Australian Government Productivity Commission. *Performance Benchmarking of Australian Business Regulation: Occupational Health & Safety.* 2010. (Accessed 2019 online.)

2. House of Representatives Standing Committee on Education and Employment. *Workplace Bullying: We just want it to stop*. November 2012. (Accessed 2019 online.)

3. Tessa Baily and Maureen Dollard, *Mental health at work and the corporate climate: implications for worker health and productivity*. Prepared for the Australian Government Productivity Commission. The Asia Pacific Centre for Work Health and Safety. University of South Australia. 2019. (Accessed 2019 online.)

4. Christopher Magee, Ross Gordon, Peter Caputi, Lindsay Oades, Samantha Reis, Laura Robinson (2014), *Workplace Bullying in Australia*. Macquarie University, Sydney, Australia. (Accessed 2019 online.)

5. Peter Ryan, How a club unwelcome to Indigenous players became a safe place. *Sydney Morning Herald*. 6 February 2021. (Accessed 2021 online.)

6. Gary Namie and Ruth Namie (2009), *The Bully at Work: What You Can Do to Stop the Hurt and Reclaim Your Dignity on the Job*. Source Books, Naperville, Illinois.

7. Anne O'Rourke and Sarah Kathryn Antioch, Workplace bullying laws in Australia: Placebo or panacea? *Common Law World Review*, Vol. 45 (1): 3–26, 2016. (Accessed 2019 online.)

8. Cara Waters, 'Not working': Ombudsman calls for overhaul of unfair dismissal rules. *Sydney Morning Herald*, 6 August 2019. (Accessed 2020 online.)

9. Geoff Gilfillan and Chris McGann, *Trends in union membership in Australia*, Parliament of Australia. 15 October 2018. (Accessed 2020 online.)

10. *Wikipedia*. Union Busting. (Accessed 2020 online.)

11. Brett Worthington and Stephanie Dalziel, Pauline Hanson defends her decision to blindside Coalition on union-busting bid, leaving Government reeling. *abc.net.au/news*, 29 November 2019. (Accessed 2020 online.)

12. AMA Queensland *Resident Health Check Survey 2016*, Prepared by the AMA Queensland Council of Doctors in Training. (Accessed 2019 online.)

13. Victorian Public Service Commission, *People Matter Survey, 2017*. (Accessed 2019 online.)

14. Australian Associated Press, Victorian Country Fire Authority members mistreated girl, 17, in 'sickening' hazing, the *Guardian*, 6 December 2017. (Accessed 2019 online.)

15. Clare Mathie, Ben Millington and Brooke Wylie, NSW Ambulance Service boss apologises to paramedics it 'completely failed' amid workplace bullying, *abc.net.au/news*, 25 June 2018. (Accessed 2019 online.)

16. Kate Aubusson, Cries for help: NSW public health workers bullied and harassed. *Sydney Morning Herald*, 31 October 2018. (Accessed 2019 online.)

17. Daniella White, Damning report shows troubling level of bullying, unease in ACT Health, *The Canberra Times*, 1 February 2019. (Accessed 2019 online.)

18. Gary Namie and Ruth Namie (2009) *The Bully at Work: What You Can Do to Stop the Hurt and Reclaim Your Dignity on the Job*. Source Books, Naperville, Illinois.

19. Anne O'Rourke and Sarah Kathryn Antioch, Workplace bullying laws in Australia: Placebo or panacea? (2016) *Common Law World Review* Vol.45 (1) 3-26). (Accessed 2020 online.)

20. Cara Waters, 'Not working': Ombudsman calls for overhaul of unfair dismissal rules. *Sydney Morning Herald*, 6 August 2019. (Accessed 2020 online.)
21. Geoff Gilfillan and Chris McGann, Trends in union membership in Australia, *Parliament of Australia*. 15 October 2018. (Accessed 2020 online.)
22. Wikipedia. *Union Busting*. (Accessed 2020 online.)
23. Brett Worthington and Stephanie Dalziel, Pauline Hanson defends her decision to blindside Coalition on union-busting bid, leaving Government reeling. *abc.net.au/news*, 29 November 2019. (Accessed 2020 online.)

2. WHAT IS BULLYING?

1. Australian Fair Work Ombudsman website. (Accessed 2018 online.)
2. Australian Human Rights Commission website. (Accessed 2018 online.)
3. Canadian Centre of Occupational Health and Safety website. (Accessed 2018 online.)
4. Employment New Zealand website. (Accessed 2018 online.)
5. Bullying UK website. (Accessed 2018 online.)
6. Gary Namie and Ruth Namie (2009), *The Bully at Work: What You Can Do to Stop the Hurt and Reclaim Your Dignity on the Job*. Source Books, Naperville, Illinois.
7. Fair Work Ombudsman website. (Accessed 2020 online.)
8. Australian Human Rights Commission website. (Accessed 2018 online.)
9. Australian Human Rights Commission website. (Accessed 2021 online.)
10. Australian Human Rights Commission website. (Accessed 2020 online.)
11. Noa Davenport, Ruth D. Schwartz and Gail Pursell Elliott (2005), *Mobbing: Emotional Abuse in the American Workplace*. Civil Society Publications, Ames, Iowa.
12. Janice Harper (2016), *Mobbed! What to Do When They Really Are Out to Get You*. Backdoor Press, Tacoma, Washington.
13. David Yamada, Distinguishing workplace bullying from bullying and mobbing. *Minding the Workplace in the New Workplace Institute*. 2015. (Accessed 2020 online.)
14. Christine Porath (2016), *Mastering Incivility — A Manifesto for the Workplace*. Grand Central Publishing, New York.
15. Sharone Bar-David (2015), *Trust Your Canary — Every Leader's Guide to Taming Workplace Incivility*. Fairleigh Press, Toronto, Canada.
16. www.healthdirect.gov.au/cyberbullying. (Accessed 2020 online.)
17. www.northeastern.edu/securenu/cyberbullying-in-the-workplace. (Accessed 2020 online.)
18. *Wikipedia, Gaslight* (1944 film). (Accessed 2020 online.)
19. Stephanie Sarkis (2019), *Gaslighting: How to recognise manipulative and emotionally abusive people...and break free*. Orion Spring, London.
20. Jasmine Crittenden, How to spot a gaslighter in your workplace, *HRM*, November 2017. (Accessed 2020 online.)
21. *Wikipedia*, Hazing. (Accessed 2020 online.)

22. *Wikipedia*, Hazing. (Accessed 2020 online.)
23. Australian Securities and Investment Commission (ASIC), *Whistleblowing*. (Accessed 2020 online.)
24. Paul Hayes, Changes to mandatory reporting obligations come into effect. *NEWSGP*, 2 March 2020. (Accessed 2020 online.)
25. Lucy Shannon, Fears mandatory reporting of doctors with mental health issues leading to suicides. *abc.net.au/news*, 4 December 2019. (Accessed 2020 online.)
26. Cate Swannell, Reducing risk of suicide in medical profession. *Medical Journal of Australia*, 30 September 2020. (Accessed 2020 online.)
27. Michael J. Myers (2017), *Why Physicians Die by Suicide.* Self-published, USA.
28. Mary A. Lewis (2016), *Mobbed Out of Existence — A Cautionary Tale of Bullying and Mobbing in the Workplace*. Self-published.
29. Kathryn-Magnolia Feeley (2012), *Workplace Bullying Lawyers' Guide — How to get more compen$ation for your client*. Strategic Book Publishing and Rights Co., Houston.
30. Gary Namie, *Workplace bullying is not incivility or mere disrespect*, workplacebullying.org/naming. (Accessed 2019 online.)
31. David Yamada, Distinguishing workplace bullying from bullying and mobbing. *Minding the Workplace in the New Workplace Institute*. (Accessed 2015 online.)
32. George Carlin, George Carlin on soft language, *YouTube*. (Accessed 2019 online.)

3. WHAT ISN'T BULLYING

1. WorkSafe Victoria website. (Accessed 2018 online.)
2. WorkSafe Victoria website. (Accessed 2018 online.)
3. Anne O'Rourke and Sarah Kathryn Antioch, Workplace bullying laws in Australia: Placebo or panacea? *Common Law World Review*, 2016, Vol. 45 (1): 3–26. (Accessed 2019 online.)
4. WorkSafe Victoria website. (Accessed 2018 online.)
5. Carlo Caponecchia and Anne Wyatt (2011), *Preventing Workplace Bullying — An evidence-based guide for managers and employees*. Routledge, London.
6. *FindLaw New Zealand*, Bullying at Work. (Accessed 2019 online.)
7. Bullying UK website. (Accessed 2018 online.)
8. Christopher Magee, Ross Gordon, Peter Caputi, Lindsay Oades, Samantha Reis, Laura Robinson (2014), *Workplace Bullying in Australia*. Macquarie University, Sydney, Australia. (Accessed 2019 online.)
9. Gary Namie and Ruth Namie (2009), *The Bully at Work: What You Can Do to Stop the Hurt and Reclaim Your Dignity on the Job*. Source Books, Naperville, Illinois.
10. Kathryn-Magnolia Feeley (2013), *Workplace Bullying Lawyers' Guide — How to get more compen$ation for your client.* Strategic Book Publishing and Rights Co., Houston.
11. Loraleigh Keashly and Branda Nowell (2010), Workplace bullying, conflict and conflict resolution. In S. Einarsen, H. Noel, D. Zapf and C. Cooper (Eds).

Bullying and harassment in the workplace: developments in theory, research and practice, 2nd Ed. Taylor and Francis, London.

12. Kathryn-Magnolia Feeley (2013), *Workplace Bullying Lawyers' Guide — How to get more compen$ation for your client.* Strategic Book Publishing and Rights Co., Houston.

13. John Murphy (1992), *Not Just a Job: A Study of the Needs at Work of Residential Child Care Workers in Melbourne, Australia.* Doctoral thesis, Monash University.

14. Kathryn-Magnolia Feeley (2013), *Workplace Bullying Lawyers' Guide — How to get more compen$ation for your client.* Strategic Book Publishing and Rights Co., Houston.

15. Kathryn-Magnolia Feeley (2013), *Workplace Bullying Lawyers' Guide — How to get more compen$ation for your client.* Strategic Book Publishing and Rights Co., Houston.

16. Gael O'Brien, Workplace bullying: More common and damaging than you think. *Business Ethics. The Magazine of Corporate Responsibility.* 2007. (Accessed 2019 online.)

17. Sharone Bar-David (2007), *Trust Your Canary — Every Leader's Guide to Taming Workplace Incivility.* Fairleigh Press, Toronto, Canada.

18. Charlotte Rayner, Helge Noel, Cary Cooper (2002), *Workplace Bullying: What we know, who is to blame and what can we do?* Taylor and Francis Ltd, London, England.

19. Caitlin Buon and Tony Buon, The 'bully' within. *Counselling at Work.* Summer 2007. (Accessed 2019 online.)

20. Australian Fair Work Commission website. (Accessed 2019 online.)

21. Australian Fair Work Ombudsman website. (Accessed 2019 online.)

22. WorkSafe Victoria website. (Accessed 2019 online.)

23. Merriam-Webster online dictionary. (Accessed 2019 online.)

24. *Wikipedia,* Reasonable Person. (Accessed 2019 online.)

25. John Ventura (2005), *Law for Dummies* (2nd Ed.). Wiley Publishing, Hoboken, New Jersey.

4. BULLYING BEHAVIOURS

1. Christine Porath (2016), *Mastering Incivility — A Manifesto for the Workplace.* Grand Central Publishing, New York.

2. Sharone Bar-David (2015), *Trust Your Canary — Every Leader's Guide to Taming Workplace Incivility.* Fairleigh Press, Toronto, Canada.

3. Sharone Bar-David (2015), *Trust Your Canary — Every Leader's Guide to Taming Workplace Incivility.* Fairleigh Press, Toronto, Canada.

5. IMPACT ON TARGETS

1. Helena Cooper-Thomas, Tim Bentley, Bevan Catley, Dianne Gardener, Michael O'Driscoll, Linda Trenberth, The Impact of Bullying on Observers and Targets. *New Zealand Journal of Human Resource Management*. Vol. 14(2) Workplace Bullying Special. 2014. (Accessed 2019 online.)
2. Mark Cross (2020), *Anxiety*. ABC Books under licence by HarperCollins Publishers Australia. Sydney.
3. *The Diagnostic and Statistical Manual of Mental Disorders*, 5th Ed. (2013), American Psychiatric Association.
4. Katherine Williams (2009), *Workplace Bullying: A Survival Guide*. Baico Publishing, Ontario.

6. COSTS FOR EMPLOYERS

1. House of Representatives Standing Committee on Education and Employment (2012a), *Workplace Bullying: 'We just want it to stop'*. Committee Report. Commonwealth of Australia. (Accessed 2018 online.)
2. Safe Work Australia (2012), *Submission 74 to the House of Representatives Standing Committee on Education and Employment Inquiry into Workplace Bullying*. (Accessed 2018 online.)
3. Safe Work Australia (2015), *The Australian Workplace Barometer Report on Psychosocial Safety Climate and Worker Health in Australia*. (Accessed 2019 online.)
4. American Psychological Association, *Stress in America: Paying with our health*. 2015. (Accessed 2020 online.)
5. Sharone Bar-David (2015), *Trust Your Canary — Every Leader's Guide to Taming Workplace Incivility*. Fairleigh Press, Toronto, Canada.
6. Christine Porath (2016), *Mastering Incivility — A Manifesto for the Workplace*. Grand Central Publishing, New York.
7. Christine Porath and Christine Pearson, The Price of Incivility, *Harvard Business Review*, January–February (2013). (Accessed 2020 online.)
8. *Choice*. Legal fees: how much should they cost? 1 August 2018. (Accessed 2019 online.)
9. Law Council of Australia, *Client Legal Privilege*, LCA website. (Accessed 2019 online.)

7. WHY BULLYING HAPPENS

1. Sharone Bar-David (2015), *Trust Your Canary — Every Leader's Guide to Taming Workplace Incivility*. Fairleigh Press, Toronto, Canada.
2. Gavin Dick and Charlotte Rayner, Negative Interpersonal Behaviour at Work: An Evidence Based Classification of Workplace Bullying. *International Journal of*

Psychology and Behavioural Sciences 2013, 3(4): 95–108. (Accessed 2020 online.)

3. Victor Sojo, Workplace bullies and corporate psychopaths. Interview by Sana Qadar, *All in the Mind, ABC Radio National.* Sunday, 9 February 2020. (Accessed 2020 online.)

4. Anne O'Rourke and Sarah Kathryn Antioch, Workplace bullying laws in Australia: Placebo or panacea? *Common Law World Review* 2016, Vol. 45 (1): 3–26. (Accessed 2019 online.)

5. Commonwealth of Australia, *Respect: Promoting a culture free from harassment and bullying in the* APS, 4th Ed., 2011. (Accessed 2019 online.)

6. Linnda Durré (2010), *Surviving the Toxic Workplace.* McGraw Hill, New York.

7. Gary Namie and Ruth Namie (2009), *The Bully at Work: What You Can Do to Stop the Hurt and Reclaim Your Dignity on the Job.* Source Books, Naperville, Illinois.

8. Caitlin Buon and Tony Buon, The 'bully' within. *Counselling at Work.* Summer 2007. (Accessed 2019 online.)

9. Sam Horn (2002), *Take the Bully by the Horns.* St Martin's Press, New York.

10. Gael O'Brien, Workplace bullying: More common and damaging than you think. *Business Ethics. The Magazine of Corporate Responsibility.* (Accessed 2007 online.)

11. Charlotte Rayner, Helge Noel, Cary Cooper (2002), *Workplace Bullying: What we know, who is to blame and what can we do?* Taylor and Francis Ltd, London, England.

12. Kathryn-Magnolia Feeley (2019), *Workplace Bullying Lawyers' Guide — How to get more compen$ation for your client.* Strategic Book Publishing and Rights Co., Houston.

13. Carlo Caponecchia and Anne Wyatt (2011), *Preventing Workplace Bullying — An evidence-based guide for managers and employees.* Routledge, London.

14. Roy H. Lubit (2008), *Coping with Toxic Managers, Subordinates...and other difficult people.* Pearson Education Inc. Upper Saddle River, New Jersey.

15. Sam Horn (2002), *Take the Bully by the Horns.* St Martin's Press, New York.

16. Loraleigh Keashly and Branda Nowell (2010). Workplace bullying, conflict and conflict resolution. In S. Einarsen, H. Noel, D. Zapf and C. Cooper (Eds). *Bullying and harassment in the workplace: developments in theory, research and practice*, 2nd Ed. 2010. CRC Press, New York.

8. MORALS AND OBEDIENCE

1. Caitlin Buon and Tony Buon, The 'bully' within. *Counselling at Work.* Summer 2007. (Accessed 2019 online.)

2. Sam Horn (2002), *Take the Bully by the Horns.* St Martin's Press, New York.

3. Australian Fair Work Commission. 2020. (Accessed 2020 online.)

4. Naomi Ellemers, Johanneke van der Toorn, Yavor Paunov and Thed van Leeuwen. The Psychology of Morality: A Review and Analysis of Empirical

Studies Published From 1940 Through 2017. *Personality and Social Psychology Review* 2019, vol. 23(4): 332–336. (Accessed 2020 online.)

5. Graham Vaughan and Michael Hogg (2011), *Social Psychology* (6th Ed.). Pearson Australia, NSW.

6. Scott Lilienfeld, Steven Lynn, Laura Namy and Nancy Woolf (2011), *Psychology — From Inquiry to Understanding* (2nd Ed.). Pearson, Boston.

7. *Inside History*, Nuremberg Trials. (Accessed 2020 online.)

8. Michael Berenbaum, Adolf Eichmann — German Military Official, *Encyclopaedia Britannica Inc.* (Accessed 2020 online.)

9. *Wikipedia*, Nuremberg Trials. (Accessed 2020 online.)

10. *Wikipedia*, Hannah Arendt. (Accessed 2020 online.)

11. Graham Vaughan and Michael Hogg (2011), *Social Psychology* (6th Ed.). Pearson Australia, NSW.

12. Saul McLeod, The Milgram Shock Experiment, *Simply Psychology*. 2017. (Accessed 2020 online.)

13. Thomas Blass (2005), *Milgram: The Man Who Shocked the World — The Life and Legacy of Stanley Milgram*. Perseus Books Group/Hachette Book Group, New York.

14. Thomas Blass (1998), The Roots of Milgram's Obedience Experiments and their Relevance to the Holocaust. *Analyse & Kritik* 20 (1): 46–53. 2020. (Accessed 2020 online.)

15. Scott Lilienfeld, Steven Lynn, Laura Namy and Nancy Woolf (2011), *Psychology — From Inquiry to Understanding* (2nd Ed.), Pearson, Boston.

16. Stuart Dowell. Beaten, starved and tortured: The horrifying story of Hitler's concentration camp for children. *The First News Poland.* 4 December 2018. (Accessed 2020 online.)

17. Philip Zimbardo (2007), *The Lucifer Effect: Understanding How Good People Turn Evil*. Rider, London.

18. Scott Lilienfeld, Steven Lynn, Laura Namy and Nancy Woolf (2011), *Psychology — From Inquiry to Understanding* (2nd Ed.). Pearson, Boston.

19. Saul McLeod, The Stanford Prison Experiment 1973, *Psychology Today.* (Accessed 2020 online.)

20. Philip Zimbardo (2007), *The Lucifer Effect: Understanding How Good People Turn Evil*. Rider, London.

21. Saul McLeod, The Stanford Prison Experiment 1973, *Psychology Today.* (Accessed 2020 online.)

22. Saul McLeod, The Stanford Prison Experiment 1973, *Psychology Today.* (Accessed 2020 online.)

23. Philip Zimbardo (2007), *The Lucifer Effect: Understanding How Good People Turn Evil*. Rider, London.

24. Committee on Armed Services United States Senate Report Inquiry into the Treatment of Detainees in US Custody 2008. *Prison Legal News.* (Accessed 2020 online.)

25. Lee Ross and Richard Nisbett (2011), *The Person and the Situation*. Pinter & Martin Ltd, London.

26. Naomi Ellemers, Johanneke van der Toorn, Yavor Paunov and Thed van Leeuwen. The Psychology of Morality: A Review and Analysis of Empirical Studies Published From 1940 Through 2017. *Personality and Social Psychology Review* 2019, vol. 23(4): 332–336. (Accessed 2020 online.)

27. Naomi Ellemers, Johanneke van der Toorn, Yavor Paunov and Thed van Leeuwen. The Psychology of Morality: A Review and Analysis of Empirical Studies Published From 1940 Through 2017. *Personality and Social Psychology Review* 2019, vol. 23(4): 332–336. (Accessed 2020 online.)

28. Naomi Ellemers, Johanneke van der Toorn, Yavor Paunov and Thed van Leeuwen. The Psychology of Morality: A Review and Analysis of Empirical Studies Published From 1940 Through 2017. *Personality and Social Psychology Review* 2019, vol. 23(4): 332–336. (Accessed 2020 online.)

29. Naomi Ellemers, Johanneke van der Toorn, Yavor Paunov and Thed van Leeuwen. The Psychology of Morality: A Review and Analysis of Empirical Studies Published From 1940 Through 2017. *Personality and Social Psychology Review* 2019, vol. 23(4): 332–336. (Accessed 2020 online.)

30. Emilie A. Caspar, Julia F. Christensen, Axel Cleeremans, Patrick Haggard. Coercion Changes the Sense of Agency in the Human Brain. *Open Access*. 18 February 2016. (2019). (Accessed 2020 online.)

31. Devi Akella, Workplace Bullying: Not a Manager's Right? *Journal of Workplace Rights*. January–March 2016, 1–10. Sage. (Accessed 2020 online.)

32. Dartmouth College. How do we make moral decisions? New study shows how your moral behaviour may change depending on the context. *ScienceDaily*. 18 April 2019. (Accessed 2020 online.)

33. Naomi Ellemers, Johanneke van der Toorn, Yavor Paunov and Thed van Leeuwen. The Psychology of Morality: A Review and Analysis of Empirical Studies Published From 1940 Through 2017. *Personality and Social Psychology Review* 2019, vol. 23(4): 332–336. (Accessed 2020 online.)

34. *Medical News Today*. Cognitive dissonance: What to know. (Accessed 2020 online.)

35. Jonathan Martin and Maggie Haberman. How Kristi Noem, Mt. Rushmore and Trump Fueled Speculation About Pence's Job. *New York Times*. 8 August 2020. (Accessed 2020 online.)

36. Martin Belam. Donald Trump denies asking how to add face to Mount Rushmore. *Guardian*. 10 August 2020. (Accessed 2020 online.)

37. Victoria Bekiempis. 70% of Republicans say election wasn't 'free and fair' despite no evidence of fraud — study. *Guardian*. 11 November 2020. (Accessed 2020 online.)

38. Jay Michaelson. The Mentality That Explains Trump's Dead-Enders. *The Daily Beast* 16 November 2020. (Accessed 2020 online.)

39. Scott Lilienfeld, Steven Lynn, Laura Namy and Nancy Woolf (2011), *Psychology — From Inquiry to Understanding* (2nd Ed.). Pearson, Boston.

9. DEHUMANISING AND DEMONISING

1. Janice Harper (2016), *Mobbed! What to Do When They Really Are Out to Get You*. Backdoor Press, Tacoma, Washington.
2. *Wikipedia*. Dehumanisation. (Accessed 2020 online.)
3. Merriam-Webster online dictionary. Demonising. (Accessed 2020 online.)
4. Christiana Spens. The Theatre of Cruelty: Dehumanization, Objectification & Abu Ghraib. Contemporary Voices: *St Andrews Journal of International Relations*. 5 (3) (2014). (Accessed 2020 online.)
5. Jeremy Scahill, The Assassination Complex, The Drone Papers, *theintercept.com*, Article No. 1 of 8. 15 October 2015. (Accessed 2020 online.)
6. Jeremy Scahill, The Assassination Complex, The Drone Papers, *theintercept.com*, Article No. 1 of 8. 15 October 2015. (Accessed 2020 online.)
7. Mabo and Native Title — The End of Terra Nullius, the Beginning of Native Title. *Australians Together*. Updated 25 January 2021. (Accessed 2021 online.)
8. Lorena Allam and Nick Evershed. The killing times: the massacres of Aboriginal people Australia must confront. Special report: Shootings, poisonings and children driven off cliffs — this is a record of state-sanctioned slaughter. *Guardian Australia*. 4 March 2019. (Accessed 2020 online.)
9. Mabo and Native Title — The End of Terra Nullius, the Beginning of Native Title. *Australians Together*. Updated 25 January 2021. (Accessed 2021 online.)
10. Michael E. Ruane, A brief history of the enduring phony science that perpetuates white supremacy. *Washington Post*. 1 May 2019. (Accessed 2020 online.)
11. Friedrich Tiedemann. On the brain of the Negro, compared with that of the European and the ourang-outang. 1837. *Proc. R. Soc. Lond*. 3:398–399. (Accessed 2020 online.)
12. Michael E. Ruane, A brief history of the enduring phony science that perpetuates white supremacy. *Washington Post*. 1 May 2019. (Accessed 2021 online.)
13. Andrew Webster, Adam Goodes: 'If people only remember me for my football, I've failed in life.' *The Age*, 30 July 2015. (Accessed 2020 online.)
14. Andrew McGarry. *Eddie McGuire's gaffes file — when the Magpies chief and Channel Nine star's mouth got him in trouble*. abc.net.news. 20 June 2016. (Accessed 2020 online.)
15. Andrew Webster, Adam Goodes: 'If people only remember me for my football, I've failed in life.' *The Age*, 30 July 2015. (Accessed 2020 online.)
16. Sam de Brito, Goodes: It's past racism, it's bullying. *The Age*, 29 July 2015. (Accessed 2020 online.)
17. Alan Austin, Andrew Bolt continues on about Adam Goodes. *Independent Australia*. 29 July 2019. (Accessed 2021 online.)
18. Michael Bradley. Goodes' war dance reveals our moral confusion. *abc.net.au/news*. 30 July 2015. (Accessed 2021 online.)
19. Peter Ryan, How a club unwelcome to Indigenous players became a safe place. *Sydney Morning Herald*. 6 February 2021. (Accessed 2021 online.)
20. Abc.net.au/news. Adam Goodes declines Australian Football Hall of Fame honour. 8 June 2021. (Accessed 2021 online.)

21. Ruby Hamad. Dehumanisation 101: The tactic that explains why we are turning our backs on asylum seekers. *Sydney Morning Herald*. 28 September 2016. (Accessed 2020 online.)
22. Janet Phillips, *Asylum seekers and refugees: what are the facts?* Parliamentary Library, Parliament of Australia. 2015. (Accessed 2020 online.)
23. Janet Phillips, *Asylum seekers and refugees: what are the facts?* Parliamentary Library, Parliament of Australia. 2015. (Accessed 2020 online.)

10. BULLYING AND PERSONALITY

1. Daniel Cervone and Lawrence Pervin (2015), *Personality: Theory and Research*, 13th Ed., Wiley. Hoboken, New Jersey.
2. Brian R. Little (2016), *Me Myself and Us — The Science of Personality and the Art of Well-being*. Public Affairs, New York.
3. Margaret R. Kohut (2008), *The Complete Guide to Understanding, Controlling, and Stopping Bullies at Work*. Atlantic Publishing Group, Florida.
4. *The Diagnostic and Statistical Manual of Mental Disorders* 5th Revision. 2013. American Psychiatric Association.
5. Jose de Leon, Is Psychiatry Scientific? A Letter to a 21st Century Psychiatry Resident, *Psychiatry Investigation*. September 2013. (Accessed 2020 online.)
6. Alan Cavaiola and Dr Neil Lavender (2000), *Toxic Co-Workers — How to Deal with Dysfunctional People on the Job*. New Harbinger Publications, Oakland, California.
7. Paul Babiak and Robert Hare (2006), *Snakes in Suits: When Psychopaths Go to Work*. HarperCollins, New York.
8. John Clarke (2002), *Working with Monsters: How to Protect Yourself from the Workplace Psychopath*. Random House Australia, Sydney.
9. John Clarke (2009), *The Pocket Psycho*. Random House Australia, Sydney.
10. Tim Field (2009), *The Bully in Sight — How to predict, resist, challenge and combat workplace bullying*. Success Unlimited, Great Britain.
11. Paul Babiak and Robert Hare (2006), *Snakes in Suits: When Psychopaths Go to Work*. HarperCollins, New York.
12. Paul Babiak and Robert Hare (2006), *Snakes in Suits: When Psychopaths Go to Work*. HarperCollins, New York.
13. John Clarke (2002), *Working with Monsters: How to Protect Yourself from the Workplace Psychopath*. Random House Australia, Sydney.
14. John Clarke (2009), *The Pocket Psycho*. Random House Australia, Sydney.
15. Hilary Freeman, Psycho bosses on the loose, *Guardian*, 10 March 2001. (Accessed 2019 online.)
16. Adrian Furnham (2014), *50 psychology ideas you really need to know*. Quercus Editions, London.
17. Tim Field (2009) *The Bully in Sight – How to predict, resist, challenge and combat workplace bullying*. Success Unlimited, Great Britain.
18. John Clarke (2002), *Working with Monsters: How to Protect Yourself from the Workplace Psychopath*. Random House Australia, Sydney.

19. Robert Sutton (2017), *The Asshole Survival Guide – How to Deal With People Who Treat You Like Dirt.* Penguin Random House, United Kingdom.
20. Katherine Crowley and Kathi Elster (2006), *Working with You Is Killing Me: Freeing Yourself from Emotional Traps at Work.* Business Plus Hachette Book Group, New York.
21. Alan Cavaiola and Dr Neil Lavender (2000), *Toxic Co-Workers – How to Deal with Dysfunctional People on the Job.* New Harbinger Publications, Oakland, California.
22. Roy H. Lubit (2008), *Coping with Toxic Managers, Subordinates…and other difficult people.* Pearson Education Inc. Upper Saddle River, New Jersey.

11. EMPLOYERS' DIRTY TACTICS

1. Gary Namie and Ruth Namie (2009), *The Bully at Work: What You Can Do to Stop the Hurt and Reclaim Your Dignity on the Job.* Source Books, Naperville, Illinois.
2. *Crikey.com*, The tax office, 'hired assassins' and how to gag dissent. 5 February 2013. (Accessed 2018 online.)
3. *edelman.com*, 2018 Edelman Trust Barometer 2018. (Accessed 2019 online.)

12. SECRET PAYOUTS

1. *Wikipedia.* Hush Money. (Accessed 2019 online.)
2. Don Watson (2003), *Death Sentence — The Decay of Public Language.* Random House, Milsons Point, New South Wales.
3. Gary Namie, Workplace bullying is not incivility or mere respect, *workplacebully-ing.org/naming.* (Accessed 2019 online.)
4. John Britton (2008), Legal Services Commissioner Ethical Considerations for the Personal Injury Law Practitioner. *Lexis Nexis Queensland Personal Injury Law Conference: Recent Developments and Current Trends.* 14 November 2008. (Accessed 2018 online.)
5. Simon Longstaff (2017), *Everyday Ethics.* Ventura Press, Edgecliff, New South Wales.
6. *McDonald Murholme Employment Online.* What can I do if I was forced to sign a deed of release upon termination of employment? (Accessed 2020 online.)

13. DON'T TRUST HR!

1. Cynthia Shapiro (2005), *Corporate Confidential: 50 Secrets Your Company Doesn't Want You To Know — And What To Do About Them.* St Martin's Press, New York.
2. Jim Bright, Evolution of HR has left staff welfare behind. *The Age*, Saturday, 22 August 2020. (Accessed 2020 online.)

3. Lyn Goodyear, Staff must feel safe when taking harassment allegations to human resources, *The Age*, Wednesday, 9 January 2018. (Accessed 2019 online.)
4. Noam Scheiber and Julie Cresswell, Sexual Harassment Cases Show the Ineffectiveness of Going to H.R. *New York Times*, 12 December 2017. (Accessed 2019 online.)
5. Cynthia Shapiro (2005), *Corporate Confidential: 50 Secrets Your Company Doesn't Want You To Know — And What To Do About Them*. St Martin's Press, New York.
6. Shelley Baker, Employee Complaint Investigations: What Human Resources Won't Tell You, *toughnickel.com*. 27 July 2018. (Accessed 2019 online.)
7. Gary Namie and Ruth Namie (2019), *The Bully at Work: What You Can Do to Stop the Hurt and Reclaim Your Dignity on the Job*. Source Books, Naperville, Illinois.
8. Kathryn-Magnolia Feeley (2013), *Workplace Bullying Lawyers' Guide — How to get more compen$ation for your client*. Strategic Book Publishing and Rights Co., Houston.
9. Virginia Trioli, Secret Women's Business, *The Age Good Weekend*, 9 November 2019.
10. Lyn Goodyear, Staff must feel safe when taking harassment allegations to human resources, *The Age*, Wednesday, 9 January 2018. (Accessed 2019 online.)
11. Jim Bright, Evolution of HR has left staff welfare behind. *The Age*, Saturday, 22 August 2020. (Accessed 2020 online.)

14. BEFORE COMPLAINING

1. WorkSafe Victoria website, *Your guide to workplace bullying — prevention and response*. (Accessed 2019 online.)
2. Cynthia Shapiro (2005), *Corporate Confidential: 50 Secrets Your Company Doesn't Want You To Know — And What To Do About Them*. St Martin's Press, New York.

15. PREPARING A COMPLAINT

1. Rachael Wells, Most workplace bullying claims fall short, *Sydney Morning Herald*, 24 July 2011. (Accessed 2018 online.)
2. The Australian Fair Work Ombudsman website. (Accessed 2018 online.)
3. WorkSafe New Zealand website. (Accessed 2018 online.)
4. Frank Darby and Andrew Scott-Howman (2016), *Workplace Bullying*. Thomson Reuters, Wellington, New Zealand.
5. WorkSafe New Zealand website. (Accessed 2018 online.)

16. HAVING AN ADVOCATE

1. Gary Namie and Ruth Namie (2019), *The Bully at Work: What You Can Do to Stop the Hurt and Reclaim Your Dignity on the Job.* Source Books, Naperville, Illinois.
2. *Wikipedia.* Law of the Instrument. (Accessed 2020 online.)

17. IN-HOUSE INVESTIGATION

1. WorkSafe New Zealand website. (Accessed 2018 online.)
2. Shelley Baker, Employee Complaint Investigations: What Human Resources Won't Tell You, *toughnickel.com*, 27 July 2018. (Accessed 2019 online.)

18. COUNSELLING

1. Michael J. Lambert, *Bergin and Garfield's Handbook of Psychotherapy and Behavior Change*, 6th Ed. 2013. Wiley, Hoboken, New Jersey.

19. TAKING LEGAL ACTION

1. Gary Namie and Ruth Namie (2009), *The Bully at Work: What You Can Do to Stop the Hurt and Reclaim Your Dignity on the Job.* Source Books, Naperville, Illinois.
2. Janice Harper (2016), *Mobbed! What to do When They Really Are Out to Get You.* Backdoor Press, Tacoma, Washington.
3. Gary Namie and Ruth Namie (2019), *The Bully at Work: What You Can Do to Stop the Hurt and Reclaim Your Dignity on the Job.* Source Books, Naperville, Illinois.
4. Queensland Legal Services Commission, *'No-win-no-fee' costs agreements fact sheet.* (Accessed 2018 online.)
5. John Britton, Queensland Legal Services Commissioner, Ethical Considerations for the Personal Injury Law Practitioner. *Lexis Nexis Queensland Personal Injury Law Conference: Recent Developments and Current Trends.* 14 November 2008. (Accessed 2019 online.)
6. Gary Namie and Ruth Namie (2009), *The Bully at Work: What You Can Do to Stop the Hurt and Reclaim Your Dignity on the Job.* Source Books, Naperville, Illinois.
7. Michael Legg, Regulations needed for litigation funders who can't pay out when cases fail, *The Conversation*, 15 February 2017. (Accessed 2019 online.)
8. Queensland Legal Services Commission, *'No-win-no-fee' costs agreements fact sheet.* (Accessed 2018 online.)

9. Ashurst, *Class Actions in Australia*, Quickguides, 9 March 2017. (Accessed 2018 online.)
10. Vince Morabito, *An Empirical Study of Australia's Class Action Regimes. Fourth Report — Class Action Facts and Figures — 24 Years of Class Actions in Australia.* 2017. Department of Business Law and Taxation Monash Business School Ethical Regulation Research Group, Monash University. (Accessed 2018 online.)
11. Law Institute of Victoria website, *Find Your Lawyer.* (Accessed 2019 online.)
12. Law Institute of Victoria website, *Find Your Lawyer.* (Accessed 2019 online.)
13. Kathryn-Magnolia Feeley (2013), *Workplace Bullying Lawyers' Guide — How to get more compen$ation for your client.* Strategic Book Publishing and Rights Co., Houston.

20. TOUGHING IT OUT

1. Katherine Williams (2009), *Workplace Bullying: A Survival Guide.* Baico Publishing, Ontario.
2. Katherine Williams (2009), *Workplace Bullying: A Survival Guide.* Baico Publishing, Ontario.
3. Gary Namie and Ruth Namie (2009), *The Bully at Work: What You Can Do to Stop the Hurt and Reclaim Your Dignity on the Job.* Source Books, Naperville, Illinois.
4. Noa Davenport, Ruth D. Schwartz and Gail Pursell Elliott (2005), *Mobbing: Emotional Abuse in the American Workplace.* Civil Society Publications, Ames, Iowa.
5. John Clark (2005), *Working with Monsters*: *How to identify and protect yourself from the workplace psychopath.* Random House Australia, Sydney.
6. John Clark (2007), *The Pocket Psycho.* Random House Australia, Sydney.
7. Tim Field (2009), *The Bully in Sight — How to predict, resist, challenge and combat workplace bullying.* Success Unlimited, United Kingdom.
8. Janice Harper (2016), *Mobbed! What to do When They Really Are Out to Get You.* Backdoor Press, Tacoma, Washington.
9. Robert Sutton (2007), *The No Asshole Rule: Building a Civilized Workplace and Surviving One That Isn't.* Business Plus, New York.
10. Ronald Shapiro and Mark Jankowski (2005), *Bullies, Tyrants and Impossible People — How to Beat Them Without Joining Them.* Crown Business, New York.
11. Robert Sutton (2017), *The Asshole Survival Guide — How to Deal With People Who Treat You Like Dirt.* Penguin Random House, United Kingdom.

22. RESPECTFUL WORKPLACES

1. Attributed to Richard Branson.
2. World Health Organization, *Code of Ethics and Professional Conduct*, April 2011. (Accessed 2020 online.)

3. APS, Commonwealth of Australia, *Respect: Promoting a culture free from harassment and bullying*, 4th Ed., 2011. (Accessed 2020 online.)

4. Sharone Bar-David (2015), *Trust Your Canary — Every Leader's Guide to Taming Workplace Incivility*. Fairleigh Press, Toronto, Canada.

5. Christine Porath (2016), *Mastering Incivility — A Manifesto for the Workplace*. Grand Central Publishing, New York.

6. HR Central, *Maximising Productivity in the Workplace*, 26 June 2017. (Accessed 2020 online.)

7. HR Central, *Maximising Productivity in the Workplace*, 26 June 2017. (Accessed 2020 online.)

8. Robert Sutton, Why I Wrote the No Asshole Rule, *Harvard Business Review*. March 2007. (Accessed 2020 online.)

9. SAP SuccessFactors, Creating Resilient Cultures: Why Businesses Need to Invest in Employee Well-Being, *SAP White Paper*, 2018. (Accessed 2020 online.)

10. Kevin Kennemer, *Rules of Engagement Keeps Workplace Civil and Productive*, The People Group, 2017. (Accessed 2020 online.)

11. Carolyn Taylor (2014), *Walking the Talk — Building a Culture for Success*. Random House Business Books, London.

12. Carolyn Taylor (2015), *Walking the Talk — Building a Culture for Success*. Random House Business Books, London.

13. Richard Bayan (2006), *Words That Sell*. McGraw-Hill, New York.

14. Sharone Bar-David (2015), *Trust Your Canary — Every Leader's Guide to Taming Workplace Incivility*. Fairleigh Press, Toronto, Canada.

15. Christine Porath (2016), *Mastering Incivility — A Manifesto for the Workplace*. Grand Central Publishing, New York.

16. Sharone Bar-David (2015), *Trust Your Canary — Every Leader's Guide to Taming Workplace Incivility*. Fairleigh Press, Toronto, Canada.

17. Sharone Bar-David (2015), *Trust Your Canary — Every Leader's Guide to Taming Workplace Incivility*. Fairleigh Press, Toronto, Canada.

18. Christine Porath (2016), *Mastering Incivility — A Manifesto for the Workplace*. Grand Central Publishing, New York.

19. National Center for Organization Development, www.va.gov/ncod/crew.asp, *Civility, Respect, and Engagement in the Workplace*. (Accessed 2020 online.)

20. Tom Peters and Robert Waterman (2006), *In Search of Excellence: Lessons from America's Best-Run Companies*. HarperCollins Inc. Publishers, New York.

21. Tom Peters and Nancy Austin (1989), *A Passion for Excellence*. Grand Central Publishing, New York.

22. Anastasia Belyh, *Management by Walking Around (MBWA) — The Essential Guide*. (Accessed 2021 online.)

23. American Psychological Association, *Stress in America: Paying with our health*. 2015. (Accessed 2020 online.)

24. APS, Commonwealth of Australia, *Respect: Promoting a culture free from harassment and bullying*, 4th Ed., 2011. (Accessed 2020 online.)

25. Torben Rick (2014), *What is organizational culture?*, 2014. (Accessed 2019 online.)

26. Xanthé Mallett, Why men's aggression to women is so often expressed through sex. The Conversation, *abc.net.au/news*, 24 March 2021.

23. FINALLY...

1. Tarja Ketola, From CR-Psychopaths to Responsible Corporations: Waking Up the Inner Sleeping Beauty of Companies. *Corporate Social Responsibility and Environmental Management*. DOI: 10. 1002/csr.113. Volume 13, Issue 2, 2006. (Accessed 2020 online.)
2. Tessa Baily and Maureen Dollard, *Mental health at work and the corporate climate: implications for worker health and productivity.* Prepared for the Australian Government Productivity Commission. 2019. The Asia Pacific Centre for Work Health and Safety. University of South Australia. (Accessed 2020 online.)
3. Christopher Magee, Ross Gordon, Peter Caputi, Lindsay Oades, Samantha Reis, Laura Robinson (2014), *Workplace Bullying in Australia*. Macquarie University, Sydney, Australia. (Accessed 2019 online.)
4. Transcript Sex Discrimination Commissioner Kate Jenkins Interview. *Insiders*. *abc.net.au/insiders*, 7 March 2021.
5. Kate Jenkins, *Respect@Work: National Inquiry into Sexual Harassment at Work*. Australian Human Rights Commission 2020. (Accessed 2020 online.)
6. Kate Jenkins, *Respect@Work: National Inquiry into Sexual Harassment at Work*. Australian Human Rights Commission 2020. (Accessed 2021 online.)
7. Torben Rick (2014), *What is organizational culture?*, 2014. (Accessed 2019 online.)
8. Xanthé Mallett, Why men's aggression to women is so often expressed through sex. The Conversation, *abc.net.au/news*, 24 March 2021.
9. Simone Fox Koob, Suspected stroke before jail death. *Saturday Age*. 10 April 2021.
10. Katina Curtis, Government at risk of missing an opportunity with key sexual harassment changes: Sex Discrimination Commissioner. *Sydney Morning Herald*. 8 April 2021. (Accessed 2021 online.)
11. Laura Tingle, The government's credentials for dealing with COVID are turning to dust amid vaccine confusion. *www.abc.net.au/news*. 10 April 2021. (Accessed 2020 online.)
12. Kate Jenkins, *Respect@Work: National Inquiry into Sexual Harassment at Work*. Australian Human Rights Commission 2020. (Accessed 2021 online.)

HELPFUL READING

The references included in this section are for general readers. Not included are professional journals and other references whose main audience comprises academics, clinicians and other professionals. Many of the various organisations listed in the Who to Contact section include helpful information and guides about workplace bullying on their websites. There are many videos on the topic on YouTube.

Rather than provide a long list of further reading, I have provided a small selection which the general reader may find helpful. The list contains books that I found particularly useful. Most contain references to other readings.

Again, I caution readers that self-help books or advice on the Internet should not be the only sources of guidance for employees' problem-solving on workplace bullying. In some instances, the advice given may be totally unsuited to the employee's circumstances. Commonly, the authors have professional education, insights, experience, confidence and abilities that exceed those of many of us, so it can be misleading to believe that their advice can be put into practice readily by everyone.

Wherever possible, information and advice from books, including this one, and the Internet should always be combined with individual guidance from informed people personally familiar with a bullied employee's circumstances, such as a general practitioner, counsellor, State workplace health and safety regulator, trade union official or a lawyer.

REFERENCES

Andrea Adams with Neil Crawford (1992), *Bullying at Work: How to Confront and Overcome It*. Virago Press, London.

Paul Babiak and Robert Hare (2006), *Snakes in Suits: When Psychopaths Go to Work*. HarperCollins, New York.

Sharone Bar-David (2015), *Trust Your Canary — Every Leader's Guide to Taming Workplace Incivility*. Fairleigh Press, Toronto, Canada.

Carlo Caponecchia and Anne Wyatt (2011), *Preventing Workplace Bullying — An evidence-based guide for managers and employees*. Routledge, London.

John Clarke (2002), *Working with Monsters: How to Protect Yourself from the Workplace Psychopath*. Random House Australia, Sydney.

John Clarke (2009), *The Pocket Psycho*. Random House Australia, Sydney.

Mark Cross (2020), *Anxiety*. ABC Books under licence by HarperCollins Publishers Australia. Sydney.

Frank Darby and Andrew Scott-Howman (2016), *Workplace Bullying*. Thomson Reuters, Wellington, New Zealand.

Linnda Durré (2010), *Surviving the Toxic Workplace*. McGraw Hill, New York.

Kathryn-Magnolia Feeley (2013), *Workplace Bullying Lawyers' Guide — How to get more compen$ation for your client*. Strategic Book Publishing and Rights Co., Houston.

Evelyn Field (2011), *Strategies for Surviving Bullying at Work*. Australian Academic Press, Samford Valley, Queensland.

Tim Field (2009), *Bully in Sight: How to predict, resist, challenge and combat workplace bullying — Overcoming the silence and denial by which abuse survives*. Success Unlimited, Great Britain.

Janice Harper (2016), *Mobbed! What to Do When They Really Are Out to Get You*. Backdoor Press, Tacoma, Washington.

Moira Jenkins (2013), *Preventing and Managing Workplace Bullying and Harassment*. Australian Academic Press, Samford Valley, Queensland.

Margaret R. Kohut (2008), *The Complete Guide to Understanding, Controlling, and Stopping Bullies at Work*. Atlantic Publishing Group, Florida.

Roy H. Lubit (2008), *Coping with Toxic Managers, Subordinates...and other difficult people*. Pearson Education Inc., Upper Saddle River, New Jersey.

Gary Namie and Ruth Namie (2009), *The Bully at Work: What You Can Do to Stop the Hurt and Reclaim Your Dignity on the Job*. Source Books, Naperville, Illinois.

Gary Namie and Ruth Namie (2011), *The Bully-Free Workplace — Stop Jerks, Weasels and Snakes from Killing Your Organization*. Wiley, New Jersey.

Christine Porath (2016), *Mastering Incivility — A Manifesto for the Workplace*. Grand Central Publishing, New York.

Stephanie Sarkis (2019), *Gaslighting: How to recognise manipulative and emotionally abusive people...and break free*. Orion Spring, London.

Cynthia Shapiro (2005), *Corporate Confidential: 50 Secrets Your Company Doesn't Want You To Know — And What To Do About Them*. St Martin's Press, New York.

Robert Sutton (2007), *The No Asshole Rule: Building a Civilized Workplace and Surviving One That Isn't*. Business Plus, New York.

Robert Sutton (2017), *The Asshole Survival Guide — How to Deal With People Who Treat You Like Dirt*. Penguin Random House, United Kingdom.

Katherine Williams (2009), *Workplace Bullying: A Survival Guide*. Baico Publishing, Ontario.

Philip Zimbardo (2007), *The Lucifer Effect: Understanding How Good People Turn Evil*. Rider, London.

WHO TO CONTACT

Please note: While efforts were made at the time of preparing this publication to ensure the accuracy of the information provided in this section, the details may change.

EMPLOYMENT LAWYERS

Find a lawyer through the Law Society or Institute website relevant to each State and Territory. Employment lawyers advertise widely on the Internet. Try 'Employment Lawyers' (add your State).

TRADE UNION MEMBERSHIP

Trade union members have access to advice on wages, conditions and rights, assistance for workplace problems, access to union lawyers for workplace injuries, additional benefits such as low-cost banking and insurance. Unions can be particularly helpful for members who've been targeted for bullying and other mistreatment at work. Union fees are tax deductible. To find out more about union membership, visit the Australian Unions website: www.australianunions.org.au.

338 • WHO TO CONTACT

WORKPLACE HEALTH AND SAFETY AUTHORITIES

Each State and Territory has authorities whose role is to ensure the health, safety and welfare of workers. They provide a range of advice and information to employees and employers as well as monitoring and enforcing compliance with the relevant Act and regulations. This includes investigating reports of workplace bullying.

Australian Capital Territory
Email: worksafe@act.gov.au
Phone: 02 6207 3000
New South Wales
SafeWork NSW
Website: www.safework.nsw.gov.au
Email: contact@safework.nsw.gov.au
Phone: 13 10 50
Northern Territory
NT WorkSafe
Website: www.worksafe.nt.gov.au
Email: ntworksafe@nt.gov.au
Phone: 1800 019 115
Queensland
Workplace Health and Safety Queensland
Website: www.worksafe.qld.gov.au
Phone: 1300 362 128
South Australia
WorkSafe SA
Website: www.safework.sa.gov.au
Email: help.safework@sa.gov.au
Phone: 1300 365 255
Tasmania
WorkSafe Tasmania
Website: www.worksafe.tas.gov.au
Email: wstinfo@justice.tas.gov.au
Phone: 1300 366 322 (within Tasmania)

Victoria

WorkSafe Victoria

Website: www.worksafe.vic.gov.au

Email: info@worksafe.vic.gov.au

Phone: 1800 136 089 or 03 9641 1444

Western Australia

WorkSafe WA

Website: www.commerce.wa.gov.au/WorkSafe

Email: safety@commerce.wa.gov.au

Phone: 1300 307 877 (within Western Australia)

Information provided in the above section has been sourced from the Safe Work Australia website.

Fair Work Commission

The Fair Work Commission has powers to make anti-bullying orders when a worker has been bullied by an individual or group and there is a risk the worker will continue to be bullied at work. The Commission doesn't have the power to order any monetary compensation. Its aim is to get workers back in a bullying-free environment as soon as possible, while taking steps to remove future bullying risks.

National Helpline: 1300 799 675

Website: www.fwc.gov.au

HUMAN RIGHTS AND ANTI-DISCRIMINATION

Australian Human Rights Commission

The Commission is an independent statutory organisation established by an Act of Federal Parliament to protect and promote human rights in Australia and internationally.

It provides advice on or receives complaints about discrimination, harassment and bullying covered by anti-discrimination laws.

Website: www.humanrights.gov.au
Email: infoservice@humanrights.gov.au
Phone: (02) 9284 9600 or 1300 656 419 (National Information Service), TTY: 1800 620 241

States and Territories

Australian Capital Territory Human Rights Commission
Website: www.hrc.act.gov.au/
Email: human.rights@act.gov.au
Phone: (02) 6205 2222, SMS: 0466 169997, TTY: (02) 6205 1666
New South Wales Anti-Discrimination Board
Website: www.antidiscrimination.justice.nsw.gov.au
Email: adbcontact@agd.nsw.gov.au
Phone: (02) 9268 5555 or 1800 670 812, TTY: (02) 9268 5522
Queensland Anti-Discrimination Commission
Website: www.adcq.qld.gov.au/
Email: info@adcq.qld.gov.au
Phone: 1300 130 670, TTY: 1300 130 680
Northern Territory Anti-Discrimination Commission
Website: www.adc.nt.gov.au/
Email: antidiscrimination@nt.gov.au
Phone: (08) 8999 1444 or 1800 813 846
South Australia Equal Opportunity Commission
Website: www.eoc.sa.gov.au
Email: eoc@agd.sa.gov.au
Phone: (08) 8207 1977 or 1800 188 163, TTY: (08) 8207 1911
Tasmania Office of the Anti-Discrimination Commissioner
Website: www.antidiscrimination.tas.gov.au
Email: antidiscrimination@justice.tas.gov.au
Phone: (03) 6165 7515 or 1300 305 062, Web SMS: 0409 401 083
Victoria Equal Opportunity and Human Rights Commission
Website: www.humanrightscommission.vic.gov.au
Email: information@veohrc.vic.gov.au
Phone: 1300 891 848

Western Australia Equal Opportunity Commission
Website: www.eoc.wa.gov.au
Email: eoc@eoc.wa.gov.au
Phone: (08) 9216 3900

WORKERS' COMPENSATION

Workers' compensation is a form of insurance payment to employees if they are injured at work or become sick due to their work. It covers injuries, including psychological injury caused by bullying. Workers' compensation includes payments to employees to cover their wages while they're not fit for work, medical expenses and rehabilitation.

Employers in each State or Territory are required to take out workers' compensation insurance to cover themselves and their employees. Workers' compensation is governed by individual states and territories and each has their own regulator that administers and gives advice on workers' compensation. Contact details are as follows:

Australian Capital Territory
Access Canberra
Website:
www.accesscanberra.act.gov.au/app/home/workhealthandsafety
Phone: 13 32 11
New South Wales
State Insurance Regulatory Authority
Website:
www.sira.nsw.gov.au/claiming-compensation/workers-compensation-claims
Phone: 13 10 50
Northern Territory
WorkSafe
Website: www.worksafe.nt.gov.au/workers-compensation
Phone: 1800 250 713

Queensland
WorkCover Queensland
Website: www.worksafe.qld.gov.au/claims-and-return-to-work
Phone: 1300 362 128
South Australia
Return To Work SA
Website: www.rtwsa.com/claims
Phone: 13 18 55
Victoria
WorkSafe
Website: www.worksafe.vic.gov.au/make-claim
Phone: 1800 136 089
Tasmania
WorkSafe Tasmania
Website: worksafe.tas.gov.au/topics/compensation
Phone: 1300 366 322
Western Australia
WorkCoverWA
Website: www.workcover.wa.gov.au/contact-us/#Advice
Phone: 1300 794 744

Employees of Australian Government organisations and others which self-insure under the scheme:
Comcare
Website: www.comcare.gov.au/home
Phone: 1300 366 979

Contact details for workers' compensation have been sourced from the Fair Work Australia website.

Safe Work Australia

Safe Work Australia is an Australian government statutory body which develops national policy relating to worker health and safety and workers' compensation. It provides codes and guides, reports and case studies, videos, podcasts and seminars relating to workplace bullying.

See *Guide for Preventing and Responding to Workplace Bullying*, May 2016.

Website: www.safeworkaustralia.gov.au
Email: info@swa.gov.au

Fair Work Ombudsman

The Fair Work Ombudsman is an independent statutory agency of the Government of Australia that provides employers and employees with free information and advice on pay, conditions, workplace rights and obligations under the national workplace relations system. Complaints can be made to the FWO regarding underpayment of wages, conditions (such as annual leave), workplace rights and discrimination in the workplace.

The FWO does not help with tax or superannuation, bullying and harassment, workplace health and safety, unfair dismissal or employment separation certificates, but its website advises who to contact about these issues.

Website: www.fairwork.gov.au

VOLUNTEERING PEAK BODIES

Volunteering Australia
Website: www.volunteeringaustralia.org
Email: hello@volunteeringaustralia.org
Phone: 0408258723
Volunteering and Contact ACT
Website: www.volunteeringact.org.au
Email: info@volunteeringact.org.au
Phone: (02) 6248 7988 (Community Info Hub), (02) 6251 4060 (Office)

The Centre for Volunteering (NSW)
Website: www.volunteering.com.au
Email: info@volunteering.com.au
Phone: (02) 9261 3600
Volunteering QLD
Website: www.volunteeringqld.org.au
Email: reception@volunteeringqld.org.au
Phone: (07) 3002 7600
Volunteering SA-NT
Website: www.volunteeringsa.org.au
Email: reception@volunteeringsa-nt.org.au
Phone:
Adelaide (08) 8221 7177
Darwin (08) 8952 9630
Alice Springs (08) 8952 9630
Volunteering TAS
Website: www.volunteeringtas.org.au
Email: team@volunteeringtas.org.au
Phone: 1800 677 895, (03) 6231 5550 (Head office)
Volunteering VIC
Website: www.volunteeringvictoria.com.au
Email: info@volunteeringvictoria.org.au
Phone: (03) 8327 8500
Volunteering WA
Website: www.volunteeringwa.org.au
Email: info@volunteeringwa.org.au
Phone: (08) 9482 4333

ACKNOWLEDGMENTS

My partner, Corinne, provided me with unwavering support. As always, her encouragement kept my spirits and motivation high, especially when I became ill late in 2020 and my thinking about health, relationships and the meaning of life overshadowed the book's completion.

There are many other wonderful people who supported this project. Not all can be named because of the potential risks to their jobs, careers and privacy.

My friend Barrie Thomas funded the writing of this book, publishing costs, advised on content and commented on drafts. Barrie sponsored my work in the community sector for 25 years through the Triple A Foundation, The Body Shop Australia and New Zealand. I wrote most of this book while employed by the Triple A Foundation.

My friend Dr Max Liddell has mentored me for 30 years — during the seven years I worked with him at Monash University and then later when I returned to work in the community. He was involved with the project from the start and was always available for me to discuss ideas and read drafts. When I became ill, Max played a much bigger role with his help and encouraged me to keep going.

Stewart Harkness, John Goss, Terry Long, Neil Beaumont, Maurice Mitchell, Tony Lintermans, Dr 'Michael' and his wife 'Lisa', read drafts of the book and provided helpful suggestions.

Dr Les Fisher and Steve Christensen offered advice on publishing options, and Les gave me valuable advice on dietary supplements relevant to my illness.

I am grateful to the more than 50 people who shared with me their distressing and sometimes horrific experiences of being bullied at work. They include 'Jane', whose story features in this book's preface, and 'Lisa', the wife of a medical specialist who spoke candidly about the serious impact of her husband's bullying on his career and mental health, as well as the dreadful impact on her and their children's lives. The families of people who've been targeted for bullying can also suffer terribly, but with only a few exceptions, don't rate a mention in news media or the literature on this topic.

Catching up regularly with my old mates Steve, John, John and John, Greg, Ralph, Terry and Terry before and during my illness to reminisce and laugh has been a delight. My Irish Setters, Tully and Molly, are a source of joy (except for that one time they ran away for a night!).

Martin Taylor of Digital Strategies in Auckland, New Zealand provided valuable advice on the presentation of the book, publishing and marketing. Martin was very patient when 'chemo brain' overtook me every three weeks and my capacity to make sense faded.

Occasionally when cabin fever overtook me, I retreated with my laptop to my 'third place', Café Jett in Dromana, where I researched, wrote and drank too much coffee. The owners, Annie and Nick, and their staff were supportive and allowed me to hijack a table regularly.

I am grateful to the kind and capable medical staff who supported me during my treatment.

PROJECT TEAM

Dr John William Murphy (author) is a qualified social worker with 40 years' experience in the private, public and not-for-profit sectors. He taught social work at Monash University and worked in family and children's services, community development and volunteering. He has supported employees who have been bullied at work and advised employers.

www.bullyinginaustralianworkplaces.com

Barrie Thomas (advisor and funding) is a qualified social worker with a 42-year business career which included bringing The Body Shop cosmetics retail chain to Australia and New Zealand where he is currently managing director. He was an Adjunct Professor at Deakin University.

Dr Max Liddell (advisor and editing) has social work qualifications and has had a long career in family and children's services and private consulting. He was an Associate Professor and Head of the Social Work Department at Monash University and recently wrote a seminal history, *Child Welfare in Australia Since 1788.*

www.ingramcontent.com/pod-product-compliance
Lightning Source LLC
Chambersburg PA
CBHW031839200326
41597CB00012B/201